BARTON ROAD
BARTON STREET
School
Mission Hall
Orchard Court
Freemans Court
Parkers Ct
Watson Memorial Hall
Saffron Road
Allotments
Rails Meadow
Swilgate
Yarnalls Alley
Fish Alley
Hughes Alley
Fletchers Alley
Comptons Alley
Baptist chapel yd
Saving Bank Ct
High School
Almshouses
Bank Alley
Bull Court
Turners Alley
Mayalls Ct
Smiths Ct
CHURCH STREET
MILL BANK
Old Baptist Chapel Yard
Chandlers Court
MILL STREET
Abbey Mills
Aurora Passage
Abbey Almshouses
Abbey Girl Schools
St Mary's Abbey Ch
Abbey House
Grammar School
GLOUCESTER ROAD
VICTORIA GARDENS
CRICKET FIELD
PERRY HILL
PAGEANT MEADOW

The Book of Tewkesbury 1986
has been published as a
Limited Edition of which this is

Number 27

A list of original subscribers
is printed at the
back of the book

Best wishes

Kathleen Ross.

26. 3. 86.

THE BOOK OF TEWKESBURY

FRONT COVER: This beautiful old house was known as the Hat Shop from the beadle's hat, suspended until recently from the first floor window. It is now Ken's Carpets. Lithograph by Rowe, 1839. (CAGM)

Lithograph by Rowe of Key House, 9 High Street, which used to be a booking office for stage coaches, and is now a branch of the Halifax Building Society. On the ground floor ceiling the design incorporates mermaids; it is one of Tewkesbury's finest four-storey, jettied, 16th century houses — 1839. (CAGM)

THE BOOK OF TEWKESBURY

BY

KATHLEEN ROSS

BARRACUDA BOOKS LIMITED
BUCKINGHAM, ENGLAND
MCMLXXXVI

PUBLISHED BY BARRACUDA BOOKS LIMITED
BUCKINGHAM, ENGLAND
AND PRINTED BY BURGESS (ABINGDON) LIMITED
ABINGDON, ENGLAND

BOUND BY
STANDARD BOOKBINDERS LIMITED
LONDON, ENGLAND

JACKET PRINTED BY
CHENEY & SONS LIMITED
BANBURY, OXON

PHOTOLITHOGRAPHY BY
SOUTH MIDLANDS LITHOPLATES LIMITED
LUTON, ENGLAND

TYPE SET IN BASKERVILLE BY
ARMITAGE RAND LIMITED
BANBURY, ENGLAND

ISBN 0 86023 248 4

Contents

Acknowledgements

As a newcomer to Tewkesbury it may seem an impertinence for me to attempt this history, but I can only plead that a general, well-illustrated book was sorely needed, and that, having fallen in love with the town many years ago, I could at least promise to lavish upon it much thought and care. Very many people have helped me but I am particularly indebted to Jack Fletcher for guiding me through the maze of changes which have occurred in Tewkesbury since the end of World War I, and to E. F. Potter and Allen Moorhouse for their help with the chapters on the Manor and the Abbey. The generous townspeople who lent me photographs are listed below; without them it could not have been published.

The staff of the County Libraries, Museums and Record Office, and of the Tewkesbury Town Hall and Museums have been most helpful and efficient, and no praise is too high for them.

Above all, my thanks are due to my husband, Reg, who is not only responsible for the photographic reproductions, but who checked, corrected and criticised the book with unfailing patience over many months.

Key to caption credits

AS	Abbey School, Tewkesbury.
BGAS	Bristol and Gloucestershire Archaeological Society.
CAGM	Cheltenham Art Gallery and Museum.
CB	Clifford Burd.
CH	Charles Hilton.
CJS	C. J. Stephens.
DM	Dowty Mining Equipment.
DV	Dennis Vickeridge.
EJ	*Evesham Journal.*
EP	E. F. Potter MBE.
GCL	Gloucestershire County Library.
GDR	Gloucestershire Diocesan Records, by permission of the Bishop of Gloucester.
GE	*Gloucestershire Echo* incorporating *Cheltenham Chronicle.*
GL	*Gloucestershire and Avon Life.*
GRO	Gloucestershire Record Office.
HB	Photographs by the late Harry Butwell, lent by his wife, Joyce.
HS	Hilary Swan.
JB	James Bennett from his *History of Tewkesbury* and *Tewkesbury Register.*
JF	Jack Fletcher.
JMM	John Moore Countryside Museum.
KH	Kathleen Hall.
LP	Leslie Piers.
RFG	R. F. Green.
RR	Reginald Ross.
TBC	Tewkesbury Borough Council.
TL	Tewkesbury Library.
TM	Trustees of Tewkesbury Museum.
TR	*Tewkesbury Register.*
TTB	Tewkesbury Town Band.
TTC	Tewkesbury Town Council.
WAS	Worcestershire Archaeological Society

Foreword

by Rev Michael Moxon, Vicar of Tewkesbury

Tewkesbury — the very name oozes history! The great and famous have been here — FitzHamon, generations of de Clares, Despensers and Beauchamps, 'false fleeting, perjured Clarence', — all of them people who lived close to important events in the life of mediaeval England. Yet for centuries, long before Christian times, people have lived in this lush Severn Valley whose meadows are so prone to flooding. If the ghosts of the famous are here, so are those of countless numbers of abbots, monks and ordinary folk, whose lives were spent in this old town.

For many, Tewkesbury may only be known for its superb Norman Abbey, one of England's most beautiful churches. Yet even if there were no Abbey, a book about Tewkesbury would made fascinating reading. In few other places is there such a collection of half-timbered houses in such an unspoilt setting. We owe a great debt of thanks to Kathleen Ross for bringing Tewkesbury's historic past and busy present so attractively to our attention.

Dedication

For my daughter, Ruth Turnbull,
with love.

ENDPAPERS: FRONT — Map based on a 1902 guide map, with other features added, to aid the Special Constabulary during World War II, who needed to know the names of Tewkesbury's alleys and courts. Double Alley and adjacent alleys are shown opposite Tudor House, all of which featured in *Portrait of Elmbury*. The alleys were demolished to build the shopping centre. Rails Meadow carpark is shown as an orchard, and the Crescent (once the Bull Ring) had not yet been widened. (TBR). BACK LEFT — This early street map of Tewkesbury was published by Dyde in his *History of Tewkesbury*, 1798. The main structure of Tewkesbury, surrounded by its four rivers and water-meadows, has not changed since earliest times. The Oldbury estates had not been built when this map was drawn up, and the Mythe Bridge and Ledbury road were still to come. (TL) RIGHT — 1903 OS map of Tewkesbury 6" = 1 mile, 2nd edition shows the section around Barton Street: on the right, Oldfield not yet covered by the present estate, the cattle market next to Holy Trinity Church, the old Sun Street, the site of the Cross and the Eagle Factory in St Mary's Lane. (GCL)

Photograph by Alan Hannan of a skeleton of a Bronze Age woman at least 50 years of age c1800 BC found in the Oldbury. (TBC)

How It Began

As dusk fell on Christmas Eve 1204, a serf trudged home along the Tewkesbury Salt Way, most of which is today lost in the River Severn. On his back he carried a sack of firewood scavenged from the leavy floor of the Wood of Mutha (Mythe Wood), which stretched from the Severn for one and a half miles to the east and as far up the hill. Above him towered the newly built Manor House of Mythe. The scent of great log fires and the noise of music and laughter indicated that the Lord of the Manor, formerly Prince John, Duke of Cornwall, and now King John, was spending Christmas in Tewkesbury. Continuing down the hill towards Tewkesbury, the serf shuffled cautiously over the wooden logs which provided an inadequate causeway across the Ham, and over the two broken-down bridges, one of which spanned the Mill Avon cut out by the monks a few years earlier. Remembering how many had been swept to their deaths across this watery entry into Tewkesbury, the serf hoped that the news he had heard that day would prove true: that the King intended to build a bridge half a mile long across this treacherous ground. Thankfully our serf crept into his hovel in the shadow of the great Abbey as the voices of the monks chanting evensong rose in the chilly air.

This fanciful account depicts Tewkesbury at a time when it was of great national importance, but how and when did life begin there? It has flourished in the area since the Mesozoic Age (8000-6000 BC). This has been proved by the discovery of plesiosaurus and ichthyosaurus remains on Brockeridge Common near Twyning, and the horn of a wild elk at the Mythe brickworks on the banks of the Severn. Neolithic man (6000-3000 BC) settled on the fertile gravel soil at the Oldbury, where his pottery and flint arrow heads have been excavated. The Beaker People came next, ushering in the Bronze Age, and civilization had begun. Bronze Age people were buried in a flexed position, and the discovery of the skeleton of a woman buried in this way, with the remains of flint, stone and clay artefacts, tell us that there was a settlement in Tewkesbury about 1800 BC. Bronze was followed by iron. The Iron Age fort at Bredon was excavated 1935-1937 and revealed that a large community of the Dubonni tribe lived orderly, agricultural lives on the site. There were roads, drains, dwelling huts with hearths, and grain storage pits to keep the corn heads from rotting during the winter. Their artefacts included knives, axes, spears, slings, pots, drinking vessels, bill hooks, spindle whorls, hammers and ornaments. The Dubonni originally came from Cornwall, and they maintained roads to the south-west for tin, lead and copper, as well as north to Droitwich for salt.

For reasons not fully understood, most Iron Age hill forts were abandoned all over Britain about seventy years before the Romans arrived. Perhaps the climate grew colder, and the people moved to warmer and more fertile ground, such as Towbury, near Twyning, and, when the hill fort at Bredon suffered a massacre of all its inhabitants, it was never repopulated.

The Romans were the next to reach Tewkesbury. This mighty empire had at least two reasons for occupying a chilly, damp island off the coast of Europe: Gaulish refugees had fled to Britain, and Rome could not countenance a resistance movement. More important, she needed raw materials. Britain supplied her with slaves to maintain a labour-intensive empire, as well as coal, wood, silver, dogs and hides. By AD 49 the Romans had occupied south-eastern Britain, and were building their fort at Kingsholm, Gloucester. Among the twenty or so larger settlements of Roman origin in Gloucestershire, one was in the Oldbury. Where the Roses Theatre stands today, house foundations, post-holes for fences and roofs, hearths, corn querns, ovens, a well shaft and boundary ditches indicated a flourishing homestead. At Holme Hill, just east of Holm Hospital, excavations revealed a Romano-British cemetery from about 300-400, and evidence showing that corn, grapes and other fruit were grown nearby.

When the Romans withdrew after three hundred and fifty years, the Romanised Britons defended themselves time and again against the West Saxon invaders, but suffered a defeat at Dyrham in 577 when Cuthwine and Caewlin defeated and killed the British Kings Conmail, Condidan and Farinmail, and captured Gloucester, Cirencester and Bath. In their turn the West Saxons were defeated by the Mercians, and by 628 Gloucestershire, Worcestershire and south-east Warwickshire were ruled by the Hwicce tribe. In 775 Bredon was known as Breodun in Huie (Bredon among the Hwicce). The Hwicce became Christianised, and it was they who established a monastery at Deerhurst in 804. There have been few Saxon finds at Tewkesbury, but the many Saxon names such as Oldbury (an old fortified settlement) abounding in the area suggest a Saxon presence. Further evidence includes fragments of Saxon pottery found in an eighth century boundary ditch near Holm Hospital, a cemetery at Bishops Cleeve and the church at Deerhurst.

By the ninth century the pagan Danes had occupied much of England except for Wessex, where Alfred had established a Christian kingdom with emphasis on the arts of peace as well as the arts of war. In 893 Alfred beseiged the Danes at Boddington, six miles south of Tewkesbury, where many died of starvation before they fought their way out. Barrow, near Boddington, may have been named after a burial mound raised to cover the bodies of the dead after that battle. By 1012, however, the whole of England was virtually a Danish kingdom under King Swein.

After Swein's death in 1014 his son Cnut struggled with Edmund Ironside for the throne. Legend records that the two warriors met in single combat on an island called Olney at Deerhurst, two miles south of Tewkesbury, which has since been submerged. Edmund established his army on the west bank of the Severn and Cnut on the east. The battle being inconclusive, they agreed to divide the Kingdom between them, but Edmund died in 1014, leaving Cnut in an unchallengeable position. He was succeeded by his son Harthacnut, who died young, and then by the Saxon, Edward the Confessor, who was Cnut's stepson and had been designated by Harthacnut as his heir. In 1066 this peaceful return to Saxon rule came to an end when Edward died childless. The two rival claimants to the throne, Harold the Saxon and William of Normandy, fought at Hastings and, with the Norman victory, the most important era in the history of Tewkesbury had begun.

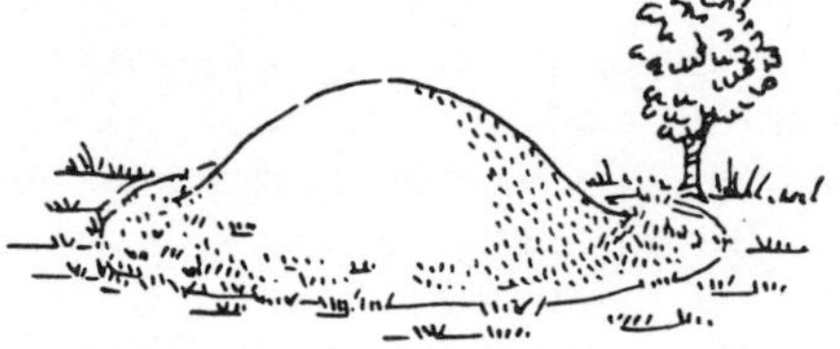

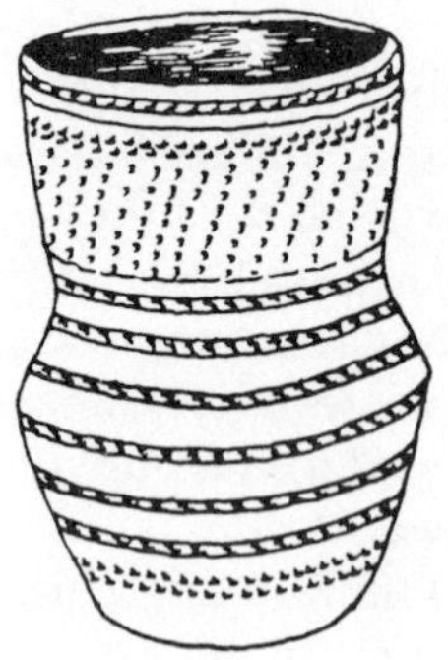

LEFT: Burial mound of the kind which may originally have covered the Bronze Age woman's grave. RIGHT: A Bronze Age beaker found at Leckhampton near Cheltenham, and now in Gloucester Museum. Both drawings by Audrey Hannan. (TBC)

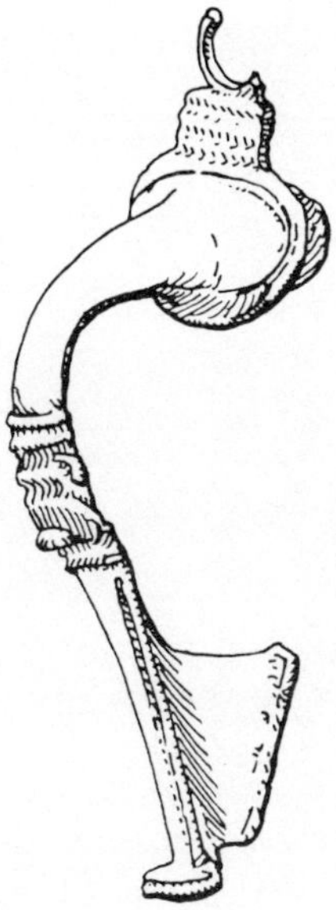

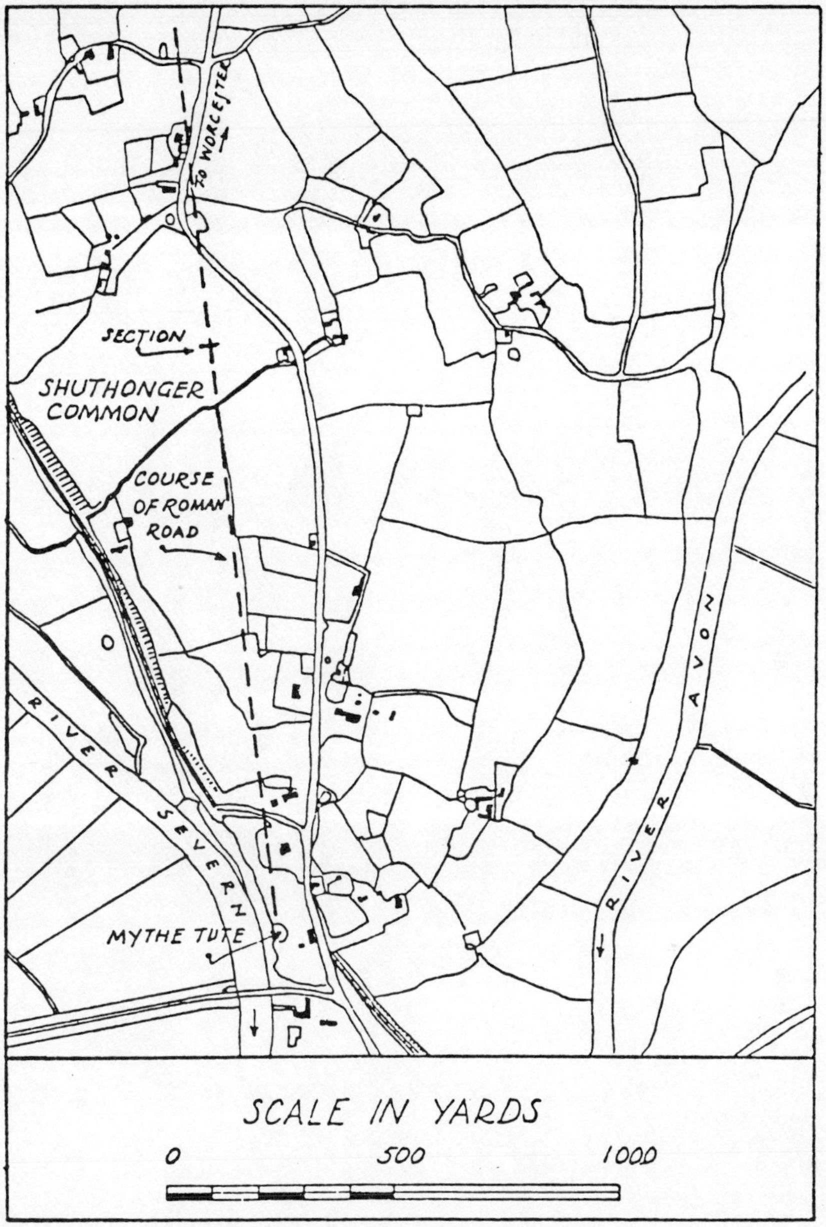

LEFT: A bronze brooch, typical of many found when excavating the Roses site, and worn during the Roman period. Drawing by Audrey Hannan. (TBC) RIGHT: Plan showing the Roman road north of Tewkesbury and the present A38, by Mrs M.G. Sanders and Graham Webster. (WAS) BELOW: Roman pottery also found on the Roses site. Drawing by Audrey Hannan. (TBC)

1798 Engraving of Edward le Despenser, who became Lord of the Manor of Tewkesbury in 1359, fought beside Edward III in France and was the tenth nobleman to be made a Knight of the Garter at its institution in 1350. (CAGM)

Manor of Tewkesbury

From the ninth century England was divided into parcels of land known as manors. Each manor was ruled by a lord; many lords owned several manors, often in different parts of the country. Provided the lord supplied his King with soldiers when required, he was left to administer his own territory much as he pleased.

The Saxon thane Britvic was the first lord of Tewkesbury Manor, and his estates included Hanley Castle, just north of Upton-upon-Severn, where he lived. He was the ambassador to Flanders for Edward the Confessor, and the story goes that his hand was sought in marriage by the Princess Maud, later the wife of William of Normandy, and he had the temerity to refuse. Deeply mortified, she later took a terrible revenge. When William had conquered England she asked for and received the Manor of Tewkesbury and put Britvic to death. Tewkesburians must forgive Maud, however, for she gave Tewkesbury its first charter and the right to hold markets.

In 1087 William II (William Rufus) gave the manor to a cousin, Robert FitzHamon. FitzHamon appeared to be what today we could call a typical Norman nobleman: fierce and ruthless in battle, but loyal to his King, and deeply pious. He defeated the last Welsh ruler, Iestyn ap Gwrgan, built Cardiff Castle, and seized much land in south Wales, which the grateful King left in his jurisdiction. When William was killed in the New Forest, FitzHamon fought on the side of his English-born son, Henry I, against the rival claimant to the throne, Henry's elder brother Robert, and died in a state of madness resulting from wounds he received. With the revenues from his estates FitzHamon founded Tewkesbury Abbey.

FitzHamon's eldest daughter, Mabel, married one of Henry I's many illegitimate sons, Robert FitzRoy, Earl of Gloucester, and owner of estates in Glamorgan, Kent and Normandy, and of a palace at Holme Hill, Tewkesbury. He completed the building of the Abbey, including the tower.

When Henry II died of a surfeit of lampreys in 1135, FitzRoy supported the claim of his half-sister Matilda to the throne, against that of Henry's nephew Stephen, and suffered imprisonment for her. He also sheltered her and her young son Prince Henry, but he seems to have been more scholar than soldier. Both Geoffrey of Monmouth and William of Malmesbury dedicated their chronicles to him, and he was patron of the Welsh poet, Caradoc of Llancarfin, and had a reputation as a just ruler. FitzRoy's heir had no son, so the manor reverted to the Crown, and was given by Richard I to John, Duke of Cornwall, who married FitzRoy's grand-daughter, Isabella. When John became King, he divorced Isabella, ostensibly on the grounds that they had a common grandfather in Henry I, but probably because she was barren and, on her second marriage to Geoffrey de Mandeville, Earl of Essex, John sold the Manor of Tewkesbury to him. There was still no heir, so the honour passed to Isabella's nephew, Gilbert de Clare, and so to his son Richard, Earl of Hertford and Pembroke. It has been estimated that Richard de Clare owned one tenth of England!

Richard's grandson, Gilbert de Clare II, known as the Red Earl because of his auburn hair, led the King's forces at the unsuccessful rebellion of Simon de Montfort against Henry III at Evesham, having previously plotted on the other side. Gilbert's wife was Maud, daughter of

Edward I, 'Hammer of the Scots'. On two occasions they entertained the King at Holme Castle 'with great splendour'. Their son, another Gilbert, was made Regent of England while the King was abroad, and fell at Bannockburn in 1314. Sadly, Gilbert's sister-in-law was married to the victorious Robert the Bruce; an example of the peculiar horror of civil war when families were divided in their allegiances.

Hugh le Despenser inherited the Manor of Tewkesbury through his marriage to Gilbert's sister Eleanor. He was a favourite of Edward II and, when Edward's cruel and traitorous Queen Isabella murdered the King in Berkeley Castle in 1327, she also disposed of his friends. Hugh was hanged, drawn and quartered. His son, another Hugh, married Elizabeth Montacute, daughter of the Earl of Salisbury, and succeeded his father. In 1359 the Honour of Tewkesbury passed to their nephew, Edward. He was the tenth nobleman to be made a knight of the Garter.

The male line of the Despensers came to an end in 1414, and the manor passed to Richard Beauchamp, Earl of Worcester, through his marriage to Isabella, grand-daugher of Edward de Despenser, but he was killed in the French wars in 1422 and, although Isabella married his cousin, Richard Beauchamp, Earl of Warwick, later Regent of France, they left no male heir.

The Manor of Tewkesbury then went to the powerful Earl of Warwick, Richard Neville, the 'King-maker', through his marriage to Isabella's daughter, Anne. After Warwick's defeat and death at the Battle of Barnet, Edward IV confiscated the Manor of Tewkesbury, eventually granting it to his brother George, Duke of Clarence, who was married to Warwick's daughter, another Isabella. Whether 'false, fleeting, perjur'd Clarence' met his end in a butt of Malmesley wine or not, he was certainly dispatched by Edward IV for his second attempt to seize the throne. His wife also died within the year, and their bones are interred behind the high altar. Clarence's son, Edward, Earl of Warwick and heir to the Manor of Tewkesbury, was beheaded in 1499 by Henry VII at the age of twenty four, and the Honour of Tewkesbury came to an end. The Manor was eventually sold to the Corporation of Tewkesbury by James I in 1609 for the sum of £2,453, the Crown retaining the right to appoint the Vicar of Tewkesbury, which it still exercises.

ABOVE: Four of the seven windows in the Abbey chancel were given by Eleanor de Clare, wife of the first Hugh le Despenser in the 14th century. Engraving by Lysons, 1802. (CAGM) LEFT: Tomb of Sir Guy de Brien. Engraving, early 19th century. (CAGM) RIGHT: Edward le Despenser kneeling in prayer on the roof of the Holy Trinity Chapel; he faces the altar — unusual for an effigy. (RR)

ABOVE: Tewkesbury Abbey from the Swilgate River showing the almshouses and Abbey House (the present Vicarage) in the foreground and the Abbot's Gateway beyond. Engraving by Hinchliffe, 1842. (CAGM) LEFT: Another view from the Swilgate of the east end of the Abbey Church, with the site of the former Lady Chapel, destroyed at the dissolution of the monasteries, indicated by the double line of arcading. Engraving by Roffe, 1804. (CAGM) RIGHT: West front of Abbey Church with grave diggers. Engraving by Higham, 1830. (CAGM)

Tewkesbury Abbey

Although there is no documentary evidence before the Middle Ages that a hermit named Theoc lived in a hut at the junctions of the Rivers Avon and Severn, it is traditionally believed that he was the founder of organised religion in Tewkesbury in the seventh century. A small monastery of Benedictine monks was founded in 715 by the Mercian dukes Oddo and Doddo. Again, the *Victoria County History* tells us that these claims are unsubstantiated. Tradition says the Priory was dedicated to the Blessed Virgin Mary, and consisted of a prior and four or five monks. Early in the ninth century, Hugh, a Mercian nobleman, became the patron and it seemed to flourish until Hugh's death in 812. In the next two hundred years the Monastery was looted and partially burned several times, and in 980 it became a cell of the newly founded monastery at Cranbourne, in Dorset.

In 1087 the fortunes of the monastery were transformed by FitzHamon, who rebuilt it on a much larger scale. He was aided by the Abbot of Cranbourne, Giraldus. In 1121, under the patronage of FitzRoy, the Monastery of Tewkesbury was consecrated as an abbey, with Giraldus as its first Abbot, and the Abbey of Cranbourne was subjected to it. During the twelfth century, the Abbey acquired many other churches and priories within its jurisdiction, notably in Bristol, but also in Cardiff, Wiltshire, Dorset and Gloucestershire, including Deerhurst. Even a great fire in 1178, the marks of which can still be seen in the triforium east of the south transept, seems not to have impoverished it, for in 1204 King John spent Christmas at Tewkesbury, and was on another occasion lavishly entertained by the Abbot.

Tewkesbury Abbey at the time of the Reformation must have been one of the wealthiest religious houses in England. It is believed that in 1215 one of the seven copies of Magna Carta was lodged there. It was situated on a main north to south route, and many travellers must have sheltered and fed themselves and their horses there. The large pension given to John Wakeman, the last Abbot, is another indication of its importance. He received £266 13s 4d annually, as well as the Manor of Forthampton but, when he became Bishop of Gloucester two years later, his pension stopped. The pension for the Prior was £16 and other pensions ranged from £6 to £13 6s 8d.

As friend and confessor to Henry VIII, John Wakeman must have known that resistance was useless, and he surrendered the Abbey without protest on 9 January 1540. The possessions of the Abbey, so extensive that it took 74 skins of parchment to record them all, were seized by the Crown, and the entire complex was condemned to demolition as 'superfluous'. But here the people of Tewkesbury rallied, and to their eternal credit demanded that the Abbey church and churchyard, already their parish church and burial ground since the completion of the nave, be left to them. Henry sold it to them for the large sum of £453, the estimated value of the lead on the roof and the bell metal. The King sold the land, which included 21 parsonages and 27 vicarages, to three speculators: Stroud, Erle and Paget, agents of the Earl of Essex. As the years passed, the estate was split among innumerable purchasers. In 1847 the 35 acre Abbey House estate was purchased by John Martin, one of the family who served Tewkesbury so long as

Members of Parliament, in 1883 by Hemming Robeson, Vicar of Tewkesbury, and by Thomas Collins, a local builder. Abbey House and the land around the Church was settled in a charitable trust and the rest was sold.

The Abbey Church interior suffered some damage during the Civil War, notably the destruction of the statues in the niches of the monuments, and bullet marks which can be seen in the nave.

In 1678 after the Restoration, the Vicar of Tewkesbury, Francis Wells, preached a sermon in which he accused Charles II of adultery, fornication and whoredom which, although obviously true, did not go down well with the King, and caused Wells to be deprived of his office.

Easter Sunday 1771 Rev Edward Evanson, Vicar of Tewkesbury, preached a sermon in the Abbey Church against the doctrine of the Holy Trinity, and also altered the Apostles' Creed. He followed this with a pamphlet putting the case for Unitarianism. The ecclesiastical court at Gloucester brought a case against him, and he might well have been ruined as the case dragged on for four years, had he not found a powerful ally in Mr Wedderburn, the Solicitor General, who not only fought his case free of charge, but eventually gave him a position as his private chaplain. Another Unitarian, George Williams, a footman, used to cause a disturbance in the Abbey Church during those parts of the service which he found doctrinally unacceptable. He published a pamphlet in 1765 which James Bennett, the local historian, found a 'foolish rhapsody', against the doctrine of the Holy Trinity.

From 1877 to 1892 the Abbey underwent a major restoration. The prime movers were the Vicar, Hemming Robeson, and the builder, Thomas Collins, of the building firm of Collins and Godfrey. Gilbert Scott was the architect. The original plans were extremely sweeping, including rebuilding the cloisters, but an outcry was raised by the Pre-Raphaelites, William Morris, Burne-Jones and Ruskin, and the restoration was modified. As a result of the controversy, Ruskin and his friends formed the Society for the Protection of Historic Buildings, to lay down guidelines for the future restoration of Britain's architectural heritage. Canon Robeson moved to Bristol as Archdeacon in 1891, but after his retirement he and his wife lived in Abbey Cottage, where he died in 1912. He gave Abbey House and other early monastic property to the Church. In 1939 Miss Woodhull, daughter of Mrs Victoria Cleflin Woodhull-Martin, gave the land at the east end of the precincts, together with Abbey Lawn House, which was demolished in 1964. The charming Queen Anne house, which is still standing, was also her gift.

In 1933 Rev Edward Pountney Gough founded the Friends of Tewkesbury Abbey, who raise a large proportion of the £60,000 needed annually to finance the great Church.

From the exterior, the most impressive feature of the Abbey Church is possibly the tower, which at one hundred and thirty-two feet high, is one of the tallest Norman towers in Europe. It used to bear a wooden spire, but this collapsed in 1559, whereupon the battlements and pinnacles were added instead. The inverted V shape on the tower indicates the original roof-line of the nave, which was lowered in the fourteenth century. The south wall, by the Swilgate river, shows clear traces of the cloisters, which were 80 feet square. At the east end of the choir the archway to the demolished Lady Chapel is blocked and contains a three-light 19th century window. John Wakeman, the last Abbot, was responsible for removing the chapel and rebuilding it at Forthampton Court. He also removed a stone effigy of William de la Zouch, second husband of Elizabeth le Despenser, which can be seen today by visitors to the Court gardens. Completing the circuit, the great west window, 62 feet high, and deeply recessed with six members, combines strength with grace.

Entering the building, the second largest parish church in England, one is at once struck by the strength and majesty of the nave. The seven pairs of Norman pillars support a beautiful lierne-vaulted roof which was added by Hugh le Despenser and Elizabeth Montacute about 1335, when they also vaulted the tower, reconstructed the choir and built the lovely chevret of chapels. The central roof bosses in the nave show scenes in the life of our Lord, from the nativity to His risen majesty. On each side are angels playing musical instruments, and symbols of the Evangelists. The sanctuary was restored and redecorated in 1984 and glows in its original colours of red, blue and gold. Originally the pillars were also painted, and the whole building must have been very colourful. Traces of the original decorations can be seen on the chancel arch.

Four of the seven windows in the chancel were given by Eleanor de Clare, wife of the first Hugh le Despenser. The glass links the sacred and the secular, the former being represented by our Lord, characters from the Bible, angels and the Last Judgement. The secular shows Eleanor and the principal lords of the Manor of Tewkesbury: FitzRoy, the Red Earl, Hugh le Despenser, FitzHamon, the other three Clares and Lord Zouch. The Despenser coat of arms is also shown.

Walking up the nave we come to the steps which mark the place where the stone screen divided the monks' choir from the people's church in monastic times. On the north aisle we see the Grove organ, presented by Rev Charles Grove to commemorate the Golden Jubilee of Queen Victoria in 1887. Some years ago it became unusable but, thanks to a fund raised by the Friends of Tewkesbury Abbey, restoration was completed in 1984 and a series of concerts have demonstrated it to be one of the finest instruments in the country. Grove was a wealthy clergyman who lived on Mythe Hill. He also erected four almshouses in the Oldbury which are still there, and in his will left an endowment for a public dispensary; a great blessing in those pre-national health service days. The window in the ambulatory with the inscription 'God be merciful to me a sinner' is said to contain a likeness of Grove in the person of the Publican.

The other organ owned by the Abbey Church is known as the Milton Organ, so called because it was at Hampton Court at the time when the young Milton was Cromwell's secretary, and as a fine organist he must presumably have played upon it when visiting Hampton Court on state business. At the Restoration it was returned to its first home in Magdalen College, Oxford, and in 1737 it was bought by the people of Tewkesbury for the Abbey Church. It has a remarkably fine case, dating from c1580, and is one of the oldest organs still in use.

The Chapel of St James in the north aisle, now the Abbey Shop, was the Free Grammar School from 1576 to 1862. Next to it is a chapel dedicated to St Margaret of Scotland. This unusual dedication is because St Margaret (daughter-in-law of the good King Duncan murdered in *Macbeth*) was an ancestress of the Clares. At the entrance to this chapel lies the tomb of Sir Guy de Brien, standard bearer to Edward III at the Battle of Crecy, Knight of the Garter and third husband of Elizabeth Montacute. Next is the chapel dedicated to St Edmund and St Dunstan, the latter being the patron saint of bell-ringers. The Abbey Church now has a peal of eight bells, which was housed in a separate bell-tower where the National School (Abbey Hall) now stands. The bell-tower was used for many years as a town gaol. Nearby stands the Wakeman Cenotaph, said to have been chosen by Abbot Wakeman as his memorial, but it remains empty, and he lies beneath the altar stone in Forthampton Church. The cadaver shows a decaying corpse being consumed by a frog, mouse, snake and snail. On the right of this monument stood the Lady Chapel, before its destruction at the dissolution.

The Clarence vault behind the high altar was disturbed in 1709 at the instigation of one Sam Hawlings, who paid £1 6s 6d for the privilege of sharing a Royal tomb, the Clarence bones being unceremoniously swept away to make room for him! Sam was later re-buried in the churchyard, leaving the ducal bones to rest in peace.

The Lady Chapel in the south transept was dedicated as recently as 1939, its previous dedication probably being to St John the Baptist. It contains a beautiful Venetian mosaic over the altar, showing Christ enthroned in glory.

Opposite the sacristy is the chantry chapel built in 1378 by Elizabeth le Despenser in memory of her husband Edward. It is called Trinity Chapel, because the fresco on the east wall represents the Holy Trinity, with Elizabeth and Edward kneeling behind angels. An effigy of Edward kneels in prayer on the roof facing the altar.

Perhaps the most magnificent chantry in the Abbey Church is the Beauchamp or Warwick Chantry. This was erected by Isabella in memory of her first husband, Richard Beauchamp, Earl of Worcester, about 1430. It has two storeys: the first was probably intended to contain an effigy of Worcester, and the second of Isabella and her second husband, Richard of Warwick. The remaining chantry is the Founder's Chantry, built in 1397 in memory of FitzHamon.

There are many other interesting memorials. That to Abbot Alan commemorates the scholarly abbot who served in Canterbury as a young monk under Thomas à Becket, and to him we owe most of what we know about the murdered saint, because Alan was commissioned to edit his letters and write his biography. When Alan first came to Tewkesbury he was homesick, but later he came to love this 'garden of delights'. He was an able administrator; his letters show him to be merciful and kind; he was liked and respected by King John, not himself a religious man. Alan of Tewkesbury died in 1202.

A plate in the centre of the chancel floor marks the spot where Prince Edward, son of Henry VI and Margaret of Anjou, is reputed to be buried. All his short life of eighteen years was spent in war and intrigue. The original brass plate to his memory is in the south wall of the Lady Chapel, and in translation reads 'Here lies Edward Prince of Wales cruelly slain while still a youth, on May 4th 1471. Alas, the savagery of men. Thou art the sole light of thy mother and the last hope of the flock'. It was put there in 1796 by Robert Knight, then Vicar of Tewkesbury, when the church was newly pewed. Other earlier brasses were destroyed by the Cromwellians.

A wall tablet commemorating a happier life is that to Dinah Maria Mulock who, under the name of Mrs Henry Craik, wrote numerous and popular Victorian novels. *John Halifax, Gentleman* is set in Tewkesbury, was published in 1857, and became a best-seller. The book has some merit as a novel, and the first half is fascinating reading for anyone interested in Tewkesbury's history. The second part has fewer Tewkesbury connections. It has recently been re-printed in paper-back.

Examples of fine carving occur in the roof bosses and tombs and it is interesting to pick out masons' marks on the nave pillars, and the consecration cross on the north porch, made nearly nine hundred years ago.

The altar stone was consecrated in 1239. At the dissolution the monks feared it would be desecrated, so they buried it. About a hundred years later it was dug up and used as a communion table in the middle of the choir. About 1720 it was taken down, cut into two from end to end and used as seats in the porch. In 1879 it was re-dedicated and restored to the place it first occupied seven hundred years before. It is made of Purbeck marble and is thirteen feet four inches long — probably the longest mensa stone in England.

The Abbey Church was closed for burials in 1855 and this is commemorated in an angry inscription in the nave to the Banaster family. George and Elizabeth Banaster had three children who pre-deceased them: William , aged two, Mary Ann, aged 11, and Sarah, aged twenty. Their mother died in 1850, but George survived to be 83 and died in 1858. The inscription reads: 'His earnest wish to be laid in this Grave besides the remains of his beloved Wife and Children was frustrated by an act of the Government prohibiting interment within the Walls of this Church. His mortal remains lie in his Father's Vault in the Church yard.'

The digging of new graves in the churchyard ceased in 1857, but there are interesting old graves to look for. James Bennett, whose *History of Tewkesbury* and *Tewkesbury Register,* published between 1830 and 1849, are obligatory reading for the local historian, is buried there. So is John Hart, a sixth descendant of Shakespeare's sister Joan. He moved from Stratford-on-Avon and started a chair-making business which did not thrive. He died in 1800, leaving a widow and three children. William, the eldest, had five daughters and a son and, though his wife earned three or four shillings a week as a stocking maker, William's income of about fifteen shillings a week making chairs barely kept them alive. He sold a jug said to have belonged to the dramatist to Bennett in 1841, and there was also a cane belonging to Shakespeare which he likewise sold, saying dolefully that it was the only good thing his illustrious forebear had ever done for him. Both jug and cane were bought in 1844 by Elizabeth Fletcher, the Tewkesbury gunsmith, who also claimed, probably erroneously, to be descended from

Shakespeare. William Hart died in 1834 and is buried in the graveyard behind the old Baptist Chapel. His grandson, George Hart, moved to Birmingham and then emigrated to Australia, so ending the Shakespeare connection in Tewkesbury.

Near the Calvary to the Cartland family is the pulpit stone at which the hermit Theoc is reputed to have preached. The splendid pair of iron gates nearby originally hung in the porch entrance, and were presented in 1734 by Lord Gage, one of the two members of Parliament for Tewkesbury, and were probably made by William Edney of Bristol. The arms, motto and initials of Lord Gage appear on them. The other member of Parliament, William Dowdeswell, also gave a pair of gates, which have not survived.

Close to Abbey House stands the Abbot's Gateway; the main gateway to the Abbey would have been where the Crescent lies today in Church Street. One has to picture the former Abbey as occupying the whole area from the River Avon to the Swilgate. The main road to Gloucester is a comparatively modern structure; when the Abbey was founded this road followed the Severn, and even today traces of the Abbey's outer wall can be seen in the Victoria Pleasure Gardens, and the Abbey Mill stood where the mill now called Abel Fletcher's Mill stands today.

The gold and silver once owned by the Abbey were seized by Henry VIII, but the Church does possess some treasures. Among them is a splendid Florentine cope made in 1600, and another cope given by Sir John Evetts, Commander of the British forces in India in the Second World War. There are a fine modern silver cross and two silver processional lights made from staves of office once carried before the Governors of Madras.

View of the Abbey Church from the Severn: left, Abbey Mill, then the campanile, later used as a town gaol and right, the Abbot's Gateway; in the foreground, a Severn trow. Engraving, 1816. (GCL)

LEFT: The garden front of Abbey House c1900; now the Vicarage, this was once the Abbot's lodging or guest house, modernised in 1825 and again in this century though still with its interior timber-framing. The churchyard front has a lovely early Tudor oriel window in Cotswold oolite stone. (CH) RIGHT: the Abbot's Gateway. Engraving from Bennett's *History of Tewkesbury,* 1830. (TL) BELOW: Abbey Church choir and chancel showing the old pulpit and pews. Engraving by Rowe, the famous Cheltenham engraver, 1837. (CAGM)

ABOVE LEFT: Remains of the cloisters of Tewkesbury Abbey, pulled down at the dissolution. Engraving by Lysons, 1802. (CAGM) BELOW: Nave of the Abbey Church, one of the finest Norman buildings in the country. Engraving by Coney, 1820. (CAGM) ABOVE RIGHT: Early 16th century tomb of Abbot Cheltenham. Engraving by Lysons, 1802. (CAGM) BELOW: Chancel roof, with its beautiful 14th century lierne vaulting. (RR)

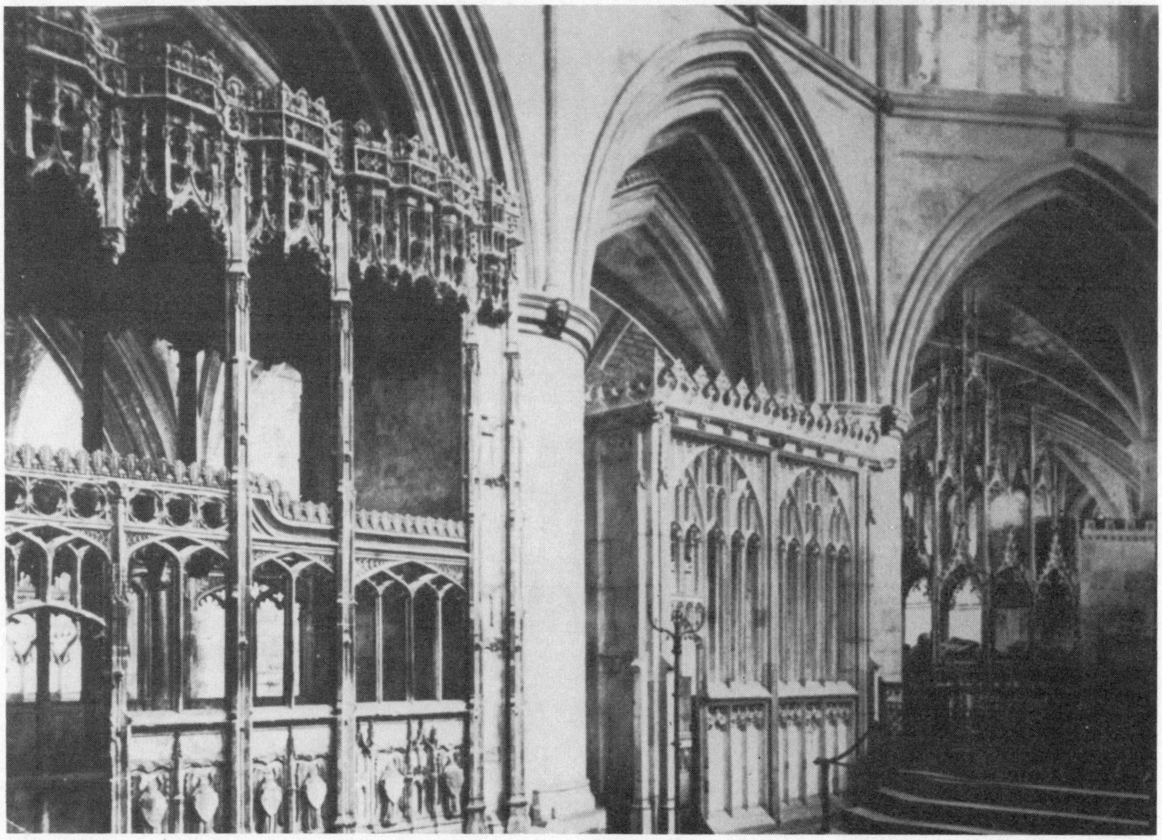

LEFT: Wakeman cenotaph. Abbot Wakeman, the last Abbot of Tewkesbury, intended this as his memorial, but it remained empty and the Abbot was buried at Forthampton. The cadaver shows a decaying corpse being consumed by a frog, mouse, snake and snail. (RR) CENTRE: Tomb of Abbot Robert Forthington, who was noted in the 14th century for many healing miracles. Engraving by Lysons, 1802. (CAGM) RIGHT: Interior of the sacristy door, covered with iron plates, believed to have been made from the armour of the men who fell in the Battle of Tewkesbury, 1471: marks made by gunfire are clearly visible. (RR) BELOW: Warwick Chapel, erected by Isabella le Despenser in memory of her first husband, Richard Beauchamp, Earl of Worcester, about 1430. Photograph, c1900. (CH)

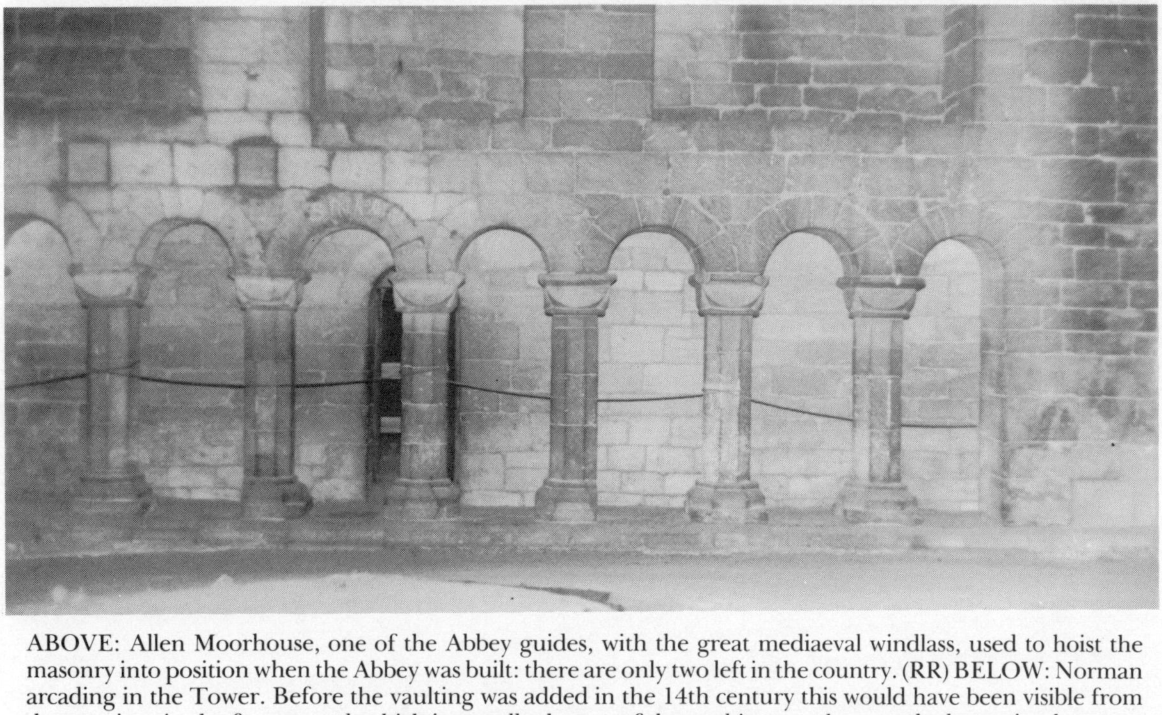

ABOVE: Allen Moorhouse, one of the Abbey guides, with the great mediaeval windlass, used to hoist the masonry into position when the Abbey was built: there are only two left in the country. (RR) BELOW: Norman arcading in the Tower. Before the vaulting was added in the 14th century this would have been visible from the crossing; in the foreground, which is actually the top of the vaulting, can be seen the large circular cover which is removed when the bells are lifted or lowered. (RR)

7 vii . uitti 7 v . bord cū . vi . car . Ibi . v . serui . 7 ii . molini
de . xx . solid . Ibi pbr . T.R.E. ualb . xii . lib . Modo . vi . lib.
In *CIRECESTRE* hd habuit Elmar *HVNLAFESED*.
in quo erant . iii . hidæ 7 dim . Eps baiocsis tenuit . M est
in manu regis . In dnio . ē . i . car . 7 iiii . uitti 7 iiii . bord
cū . iii . car. Valuit . iiii . lib . m . L . sot.
In *TEODECHESBERIE* fuer T.R.E. quat xx . 7 xv . hidæ.
Ex his sunt in dnio . XLV . 7 erant quiete ab omi ser
uitio regali 7 geldo . p̄ter seruitiū ipsius dni cuj erat M̄.
In capite M̄ erant in dnio . xii . car . 7 L . int seruos
7 ancillas . 7 xvi . bord circa aulā manebant . 7 ii . mo
lini de . xx . solid . 7 una piscaria . 7 una salina ap Wichā
ptin ad M̄.
Ap Sudwichā . iii . hid . In Trotintune . vi . hidæ . In Fiten
tone . vi . hide . In Pamintonie . viii . hidæ . In Natone . iii . hidæ . 7 dim.
In Waltone . iii . hidæ. In Estone . vi . hidæ.
Ibi erant uitti . xxi . 7 ix . Radchenist . hntes . xxvi . car.
7 v . colibti 7 un bord cū . v . car . Hi Radchenist
arabant 7 herciabant ad curiā dni.
In Glouuecestre erant . viii . burgses . reddtes . v . solid
7 iiii . den 7 seruientes ad curiā.
In tota Teodechesberie sunt . cxx . ac p̄ti . 7 silua . una
leuga 7 dimid long . 7 tantd lat.

163 c

Ap Teodekesberie sunt m . xiii . burgses reddtes . xx . sol
ꝑ ann . Mercatū qd regina cstituit ibi . redd . xi . solid
7 viii . denar . Ibi . ē una car plus . 7 xxii . int seruos
7 ancillas . Vna piscaria 7 una salina ap Wichā
Ibi . iii . Radchenist . T.R.E. ptineb . Vn eoz tenebat
jn Estone . vi . hid . Modo ten Girard . Alt tenebat
jn Waltone . iii . hid . Modo ten Radulf . Terci teneb
jn Fitentone . ii . hid . Modo ten Bernard.

Entry in the Domesday Book for Tewkesbury.

Poor, Nasty, Brutish and Short?

'In Tewkesbury before 1066 there were 95 hides. 45 of them are in lordship; they were exempt from all royal service, apart from the service of the lord himself whose manor it was. In the head of the manor there were in lordship 12 ploughs; 50 slaves, male and female. 16 small holders lived round the hall. 2 mills at 20s; a fishery; a salt-house at Droitwich which belongs to this manor . . . In the whole of Tewkesbury, meadow, 120 acres; woodland 1½ leagues long and as wide.'

This is how the Domesday Book described Tewkesbury in 1086. Society was complex. A serf or bondman was a slave belonging to the lord of the manor. He was unable to own property and was subjected to his lord's command, protected by the common law only against rape and murder. A bordar held a cottage with land, though he had to supply the lord with produce such as poultry. A villein was a sort of high class bordar, and these two groups merged later and became known as yeomen. In every sphere the peasant (Saxon) had to do forced labour for the lord (Norman); as the lord owned the mill, even the use of that had to be paid for in flour. About 20% of the population of Gloucestershire were serfs.

By the early 14th century there were 19 free tenants of Tewkesbury Manor and 56 customary (bound) tenants. Of the latter, 41 had one yardland (about 30 acres) each and 15 had half a yardland. For each yardland the tenant paid in 221 winter works, 59 summer works as well as ploughing, harrowing, sowing, carrying, threshing and malting. He also had to provide four hens at Christmas, pay 1d for salt and buy his own grain seed. Nicholas the Smith held one yardland, which in 1307 he paid for by making the ironwork of nine ploughs for the lord, who provided Nicholas with 4s for the coal. It can be seen that the peasant had little time to work on his own land.

The lord's power over life and death is shown in the gruesome story of the Jew of Tewkesbury, who fell into a sewer on a Saturday and refused to be pulled out because it was the Jewish Sabbath. Richard de Clare refused to have him pulled out on a Sunday because it was the Christian Sabbath, and by Monday the poor wretch was dead.

The three field system whereby each year one field grew winter corn, one spring corn (that is, oats, barley, peas, beans and vetches) and the third field lay fallow, ensured that the land was kept in good heart. The woodlands provided pannage to fatten the pigs in autumn and cover for game as well as timber for building houses, fences, implements, artifacts and for firewood. The Ham provided common grazing land for cattle, sheep and geese. The fields were owned in strips, each strip being about as much as one plough could turn up in a day: around an acre in area and a furlong (that is: long furrow) in length. The characteristic ridge and furrow marks can still be seen in many places around Tewkesbury where the land has not been too much disturbed by modern tractors, such as the Severn banks at the Mythe, and in the old orchards at Twyning. The six or eight oxen used to draw the heavy plough would be owned by several peasants, so ploughing would be a communal activity, and all the more important events of the agricultural year would be attended by jollification, such as the harvest feast, and the Church also held many feast days. So although Hobbes was right in describing human life as poor, nasty, brutish and short, Tewkesburians in Norman times must have had their happy days as well.

Tewkesbury Abbey would have been extremely important in Tewkesbury life. As well as teaching the faith, the monks were educators, doctors, nurses, and teachers of every craft, including agriculture. Merchants, soldiers, Royalty and every other traveller found hospitality within those walls and in the chapels-of-ease such as that at Stoke Orchard and the early inns for pilgrims. The only man-made beauty in the little town would have been in the colourful carvings and later glass in the huge Church. One could say that they gave good value for the tithe exacted from each man, especially when such an Abbot as Alan of Tewkesbury was in charge, to ensure that charity was dispensed where needed.

Later abuses sprang up, and William Langland of Malvern, writing in about 1379, claimed that the clergy would do anything for money. As a result of the Black Death the income of the Church dropped dramatically, and the use of pardons to absolve sins, and the failure to help the poor became a scandal in some places. 'The beggars sup without bread even in mid-summer, and the winter is far more terrible for them; for then they trudge about with wet feet, famished and parched with thirst, and so foully abused that it is pitiful to hear how the rich folk spurn them and kick them out of their way'. Against this, however, we must set Chaucer's portrait of the Poor Parson: 'Christ's lore and his Apostles twelve, he taught, but first he followed it himself'.

Cross House, one of Tewkesbury's finest early 16th century buildings, on the corner of Tolsey Lane, here called Guest Lane, was restored c1860 by the builder, Thomas Collins, then owner-occupier. This engraving by Rowe shows it before restoration, 1839. (CAGM)

ABOVE: Abbey Cottages, in Church Street, a row of mediaeval merchants' homes, timber framed with clay and wattle walls; the house with the shutters has been reconstructed to its original plan; the shutters dropped down to form a counter and the room behind was shop and living room. (RR) BELOW: The earliest map of Gloucestershire was by Christopher Saxton in 1557. (BGAS GCL)

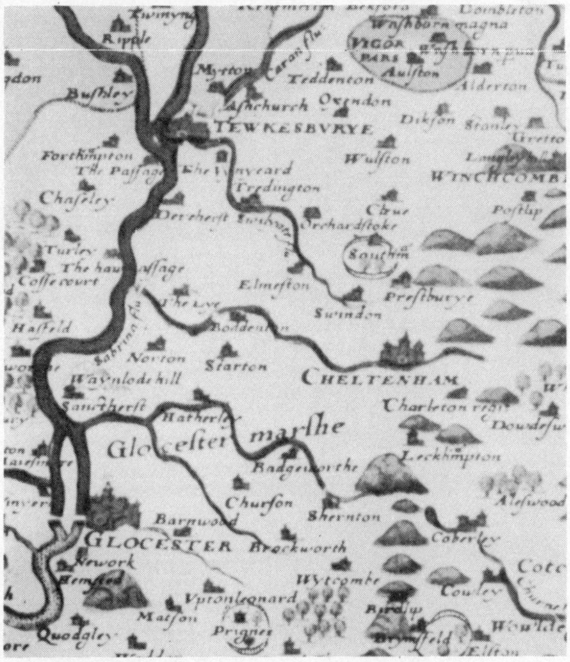

ABOVE: Actors gathering for a mock Battle of Tewkesbury as part of the town festival, 1985. (RR) BELOW: Gupshill Manor, 1958, where Queen Margaret is reputed to have slept the night before the battle. (TR TL)

Brazen Throat of War

As the fifteenth century progressed, the terrible slaughter between the Royal houses of York and Lancaster, which we call the Wars of the Roses, reached a climax. Edward IV became King in 1461 at the age of nineteen; he was tall, handsome, well-mannered, an excellent soldier, and possessed a remarkable personal magnetism, but he was also crafty and licentious. He unwisely married Elizabeth Woodville, an unpopular choice. Many nobles, including his brothers, Richard, Duke of Gloucester and George, Duke of Clarence, disliked her and Richard Neville, 'Warwick the Kingmaker', was angry enough to transfer his allegiance to the deposed Henry VI and his queen, Margaret of Anjou. In 1470 Warwick rose against Edward and succeeded in placing Henry VI upon the throne once more, but the following year Warwick was defeated and killed at the Battle of Barnet. Edward sent Henry back to the Tower, but Margaret, with the young Prince Edward, escaped to France but returned the next year and assembled an army at Exeter. She marched through the west country to Bristol, gathering the support of Lord Wenlock of Somerset, John Langstruther (Lord Prior of Jerusalem), Edmond and John Beaufort and the Earl of Devonshire as she came. She intended to press on to Gloucester and Berkeley to join up with Lord Pembroke, who was mustering an army in Wales, but she was prevented from entering Gloucester by Richard Beauchamp, so she marched on to Tewkesbury to await Pembroke there. Too exhausted to cross the Severn, her army camped on the low ridge of land on which Gupshill Manor now stands. Tradition says she slept there. 'The town and the Abbey were at their backs, afore them and upon every hand of them, foul lanes and deep dikes and many hedges, with hills and valleys, a right evil place to approach as could well have been devised'. At this time the road from Tewkesbury to Gloucester ran further west through the Lower Lode, by the Severn.

Edward had rested at Cheltenham on the night of 3 May 1471 and early next morning marched on to the Tredington area. He was supported on his left flank by his loyal and devoted brother, Richard of Gloucester, and on his right by the Marquis of Dorset and Lord Hastings. His other brother, Clarence, he wisely kept with him, for Clarence had already changed sides once. Troops at the rear were commanded by Lord Hastings.

Margaret's right wing was commanded by Edmund Beaufort, Duke of Somerset, and the left wing by John Courtenay, Earl of Devonshire. The centre was commanded by Prince Edward, with the support of John Lord Wenlock and Sir John Langstrother, Prior of St John's. Tradition has it that the Queen watched the battle from the Abbey tower.

Edward made his stand where Stonehouse Farm stands today. Before the battle he sent two hundred of his cavalry to the hill at Tewkesbury Park in case Margaret had laid an ambush there. He then attacked Somerset with a hail of arrows. Somerset tried to advance, but was driven back. Some accounts say Somerset then turned on Wenlock in a fury for not supporting him and slew him. Gloucester advanced, and then made as if to retreat, drawing Somerset and Devonshire after him. Simultaneously the cavalry appeared suddenly from Tewkesbury Park. The Lancastrians were caught in a pincer movement and fled. They were cut down at Lincoln Green in what has since been called Bloody Meadow. More were slain on Severn Ham and while crossing the Swilgate, which must have been wider and deeper than it is today. The nobles took refuge in the Abbey Church but, although the Prior saved them from immediate death, on Monday, 6 May, twenty-one Lancastrian nobles were executed in the market place, where the Methodist Church now stands. Prince Edward may have been murdered after the battle, as described by Shakespeare but, as half-a-dozen contemporary sources say he was killed in battle, this is more likely. About three thousand Lancastrians died that day, which was about equal to the population of Tewkesbury. Some blood must also have been shed in the Abbey Church, for it had to be re-consecrated.

Margaret of Anjou was captured, imprisoned for five years and finally ransomed by her father, Rene King of Anjou, but Henry VI was murdered in prison three weeks after the battle. Lord Pembroke and his nephew Henry escaped to France. In 1485, when Richard of Gloucester had become Richard III, Richmond raised an army, defeated the King at the Battle of Boswell, and became Henry VII, the first of the Tudors.

The battle was interesting in that cannon were used on both sides; an early example of guns in war. The Yorkists had 3,436 archers on their payroll, and used about 1,500 cavalry.

During the 17th century Civil War Tewkesbury tried to stay neutral. Stationed on the road between Gloucester, held by Colonel Massey for Parliament, and Worcester, held by Sir William Russell for the King, Tewkesbury changed hands four times in 1643 alone. The bridge at Upton-on-Severn was the only one across the Severn between Worcester and Gloucester, and the battle for its possession was won by Massey. From 1646 Tewkesbury remained in Parliament's hands.

The ordinarily peaceful Englishman suffered considerable financial loss during the Civil War. John Weaver, of Boddington Mill, records in 1643 how he forfeited £9 12s 0d and £10 0s 0d 'lost by the King's army' in money, corn and goods. Also 'plundered by Captain Scryven, governor of Boddington: £3 10s 0d'. All this amounted to nearly four years' rent: a grevious loss. The Royalist commander, Sir Henry Bard, addressed a letter to the 'constable, tithingmen and parishoners of Twyning' demanding his monthly contributions, which ran: 'Unlesse you bring into mee to Worcester . . . the monthly contribution of six months past, on Thursday next, being the 6th day of this present month, you are to expect an unsanctified partie of horse amongst you, from whom if you hide yourselves (as I believe each of you hath his hiding hole), they shall fire your houses without mercy, hang up your bodies wherever they finde them, and scare your ghosts into dribling garrisons to make new Committee Men; from whom neither the 21 troopes of Teuxbury nor 17 of Stensham shall defend you'.

As well as the destruction of so many statues in the Abbey Church, the cannon marks on the pillars of the nave bear witness to how narrowly Tewkesbury escaped major disaster at the time.

In 1806 Tewkesburians were again expecting war on their own soil. The Government believed that a Napoleonic invasion was imminent. It shrank from the prospect of paying for a greatly enlarged army, and instead encouraged the formation of voluntary companies under the control of the War Office. Two companies were formed in Tewkesbury: the Yeomanry under Captain James Martin and the Infantry under Major James Pitt Nind. The Yeomanry was 45 strong and each man provided his own horse, while the Infantry consisted of 220 men and officers.

Fortunately the invasion did not take place and, after England's victory, the Government was appalled to find itself with companies of armed men around the country, who were usually poor and often unemployed. It hastily disbanded them, and in 1814 the Tewkesbury Infantry generously donated its funds of over £200 to charity and celebrated its own demise with a dinner given by Major Nind. The faded colours of the company hang at the west end of the Abbey Church.

In 1852, however, a Tewkesbury company of the Gloucestershire Volunteers was formed under Captain James Primate Sargeaunt and Sergeant Raynsford. When one remembers that a working man's week was about 70 hours, to attend two or more parades a week showed great keenness. Furthermore, in 1885 a volunteer company of riflemen was formed which, in 1888, became the 'D' Co, Second Battalion, Gloucester Regiment, the Volunteer Rifle Corps. Weapons issued were rifle, pistol, sword and bayonet. By 1902 a bugle band had been formed, and also a drum and fife band.

The South African War broke out in 1899. Men from Tewkesbury volunteered and were sent in 1900 and 1902, and in May 1902 six newly returned soldiers were given gold medals issued by the Borough at a banquet. After the war the grateful townspeople subscribed to buy and convert a disused malthouse in Red Lane into a small drill hall and gymnasium, with armoury, clubroom, stores and offices. It is now a drill hall for army and sea cadets. The Company added to the sporting and social life of the town by arranging competitions for field craft, shooting and drill. The annual presentation of prizes was a grand affair, usually held in the Bell or the Swan for higher ranks, and for privates in the Berkeley or the Wheatsheaf. There was an annual ball in the Town Hall. In 1902 the Russian gun, purchased after the Crimean War for a total sum of £76 17s 0d, and set up first at the Cross, later in the Abbey churchyard, then left to lie derelict, was finally dragged to the Victoria Pleasure Gardens by the Volunteers, where it remained until taken for scrap metal in 1941. It was about 10 feet long and five feet high at the muzzle.

When war broke out in August 1914, 40 of the Company were sent to France with Lt Harold Moore and his brother, 2nd Lt Lionel Moore, in command. All the officers and most of the men were killed. A new company was formed under Mr Brierly of Southwick Park and incorporated into the 3rd Battalion the Gloucestershire Volunteer Regiment in 1915. Tewkesbury suffered 152 dead and many injured in World War I and the effects of shell-shock and poison gas could never be estimated. The Company was disbanded in 1919.

Between the wars the 12th Platoon, 'C' Company, the 5th Battalion of the Gloucestershire Regiment drilled in the hall and was sent overseas in 1939. A Civil Defence unit was formed, but fortunately not needed. Using the Shakespeare Inn in Smith's Lane (demolished in 1971) as their headquarters, the 'E' Co of the Home Guard consisted of 100 men equipped with Lewis guns, grenade launchers, and Molotov cocktails, as well as rifles, pistols and grenades. Their commander was Major J. W. Healing. Their last muster was in December 1945 in the Vineyards. The blackout descended; rationing arrived and stayed for 15 years; waste paper was collected; iron railings were gathered in for scrap metal, with the Abbey Church gates having a narrow escape; Anderson shelters were put up and about 400 school-children were evacuated to Tewkesbury from Birmingham. A big army depôt was built at Ashchurch. After Dunkirk, ditches were dug on the Ham to prevent the landing of enemy gliders, and road blocks set up to foil Hitler's tanks. A British Restaurant was open in Abbey Hall and run by the WVS (later the WRVS). A good, hot, three-course meal was served for 6d. A maintenance and repair organisation for RAF marine craft was set up at Lower Lode. In 1943 the RASC left Ashchurch and was replaced by the American 3025, 3026 and 3043 Ordnance Coys. From 1943 small numbers of Italian and German prisoners of war were held in a camp at Newtown.

Tewkesbury suffered no enemy damage in the Second World War, and thankfully her dead were far less than in the Great War. They are commemorated by a Cross at the junction of the three main roads. There was a Cross in Tewkesbury in early times which was believed to have been erected to the memory of Somerset and the other Lancastrians, who were executed at this site. It was pulled down in 1650 and the materials used to assist in the repair of the Long Bridge, the upkeep of which was always a financial drain upon the town.

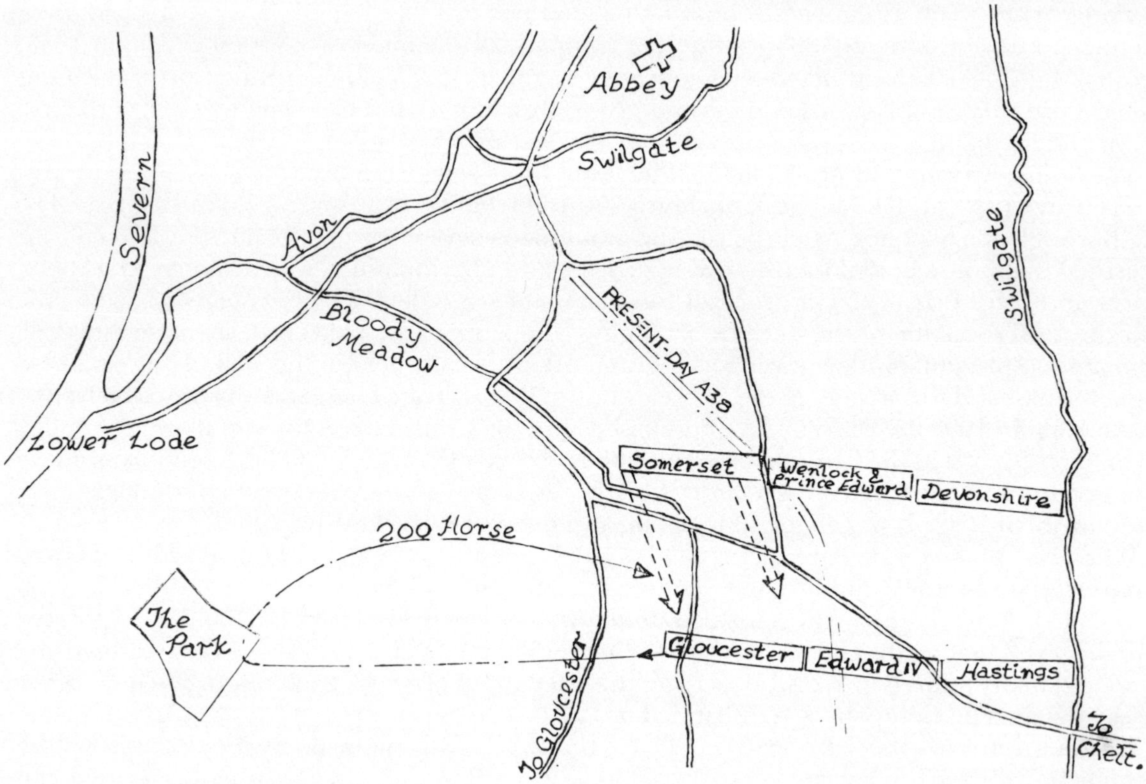
Abbey
Swilgate
Severn
Avon
Bloody Meadow
PRESENT-DAY A38
Swilgate
Lower Lode
Somerset
Wenlock & Prince Edward
Devonshire
200 Horse
The Park
Gloucester
Edward IV
Hastings
To Gloucester
To Chelt.

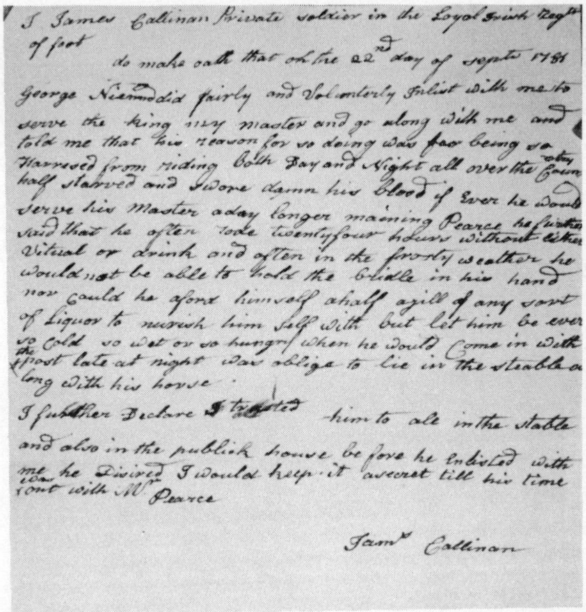

I James Callinan Private soldier in the Loyal Irish Regt of foot
do make oath that on the 22d day of septr 1781
George Nienand did fairly and Volontarly Inlist with me to
serve the king my master and go along with me and
told me that his reason for so doing was for being so
Harrased from riding both Day and Night all over the country
half starved and swore damn his blood if ever he would
serve his Master a day longer maining Pearce he further
said that he often rode twentyfour hours without either
Vitical or drink and often in the frosty weather he
would not be able to hold the bridle in his hand
nor could he afore himself a half a gill of any sort
of Liquor to nurish him self with but let him be ever
so cold so wet or so hungry when he would come in with
the post late at night was obliga to lie in the steable a
long with his horse.
I further Declare I trusted him to ale in the stable
and also in the publick house be fore he enlisted with
me he Disired I would keep it a secret till his time
was out with Mr Pearce

Jams Callinan

OPPOSITE ABOVE: Battle of Tewkesbury, 1471: the scanty records available do not enable us to be sure of the battle position, but the map depicts the most likely. (RR) LEFT: The Battle of Tewkesbury. (TL) RIGHT: Execution of the Duke of Somerset, while John Langstrother, Prior of the Hospital of St John of Jerusalem, wearing the order of Jerusalem, awaits his turn on the block. Both engraved by Lysons from the Ghent Mss. (TL) ABOVE LEFT: A 1781 affidavit written by James Callinan, saying that his fellow private George Nienand had enlisted with him because he was badly treated by his master, Postmaster Pearce. Pearce had taken action against the boy's officer, Yeend, maintaining he had encouraged Nienand to run away from his position as post-boy. Yeend came from an old Aston-on-Carrant family. (GRO) RIGHT: Tewkesbury soldiers in the Gloucestershire Regiment in World War I: Ted Woodward on the left of the back row, and Charles Hawlings on the right. Seated in front: Fred Underwood on the left, and Fred Green on the right. (RFG) BELOW: Mitton Manor, an attractive late 17th century building, during World War I a Red Cross hospital, now flats. (CB)

ABOVE: YMCA club in the former Methodist Chapel, Tolsey Lane, during World War I, decorated for Christmas. (CB) BELOW: United States troops were stationed in Tewkesbury in World War II: band leader, 'Rusty', and Eddy Neilson in the centre. (KH)

ABOVE: Auction of the Red Cross charity donkey, given by Bob Perry, in December 1940, for the war effort. Front row, left to right: Fred Green, Bob Perry, Sam Loveridge, Tom Woodward. On stand: Leonard Hone (auctioneer) behind the lady. Others include Ted Warner, Gerald Hone, Mrs Dot Booth. (RFG) BELOW: The opening of the 'Hot Pot', Tewkesbury's British Restaurant, (where a good hot meal could be bought for 6d), by Ald. R. A. Gaze (Mayor of Tewkesbury) in May, 1941: run by the WVS, later WRVS, with manageress Mrs Sharpe and voluntary labour. Left to right: Ald H. G. Brown, A. M. Sharp, Coun. S. C. J. Moulder (Deputy Mayor), Mrs Colchester-Wemyss, the Mayor, Mrs L. M. Faithful and the Mayoress. (GE GCL)

LEFT: The Cartland Calvary. Popular novelist Barbara Cartland lived in Church Street when a child; her father, Major Bertram Cartland, of the Worcester Regiment, was killed in May 1918. In May 1940, within 24 hours of each other, Miss Cartland's two brothers Ronald and Anthony were killed at Dunkirk. Their memorial stands near the Gage gates. (RR) RIGHT: Silver processional cross, made by Birmingham art students, presented to the Abbey Church to acknowledge kindness shown to Birmingham evacuees during World War II. (RR) BELOW: 'Dig for Victory': harvesting oats on G. Smith's farm at Walton Hill, 1941. (GE GCL)

Worthy of his Hire

'The Warwickshire Avon Falls into the Severn here, and on the sides of both, for many miles back, there are the finest meadows that were ever seen. In looking over them, and beholding the endless flocks and herds, one wonders what can become of all the meat!'

So Cobbett wrote c1820, and every writer, from William of Malmesbury in the twelfth century to John Moore in the twentieth, has praised the fertility of Tewkesbury soil. The monks grew grapes in what are still known as the Vineyards, and they owned two mills, which by 1594 had increased to four. One was probably on the Swilgate near Gander Lane bridge, and the other on the Mill Avon was always known as Abbey Mill until the fame of *John Halifax, Gentleman* caused it to be re-named Abel Fletcher's Mill, after the Quaker tanner in the story. The Mill Avon was probably cut by the monks in the twelfth century to power their mill. In 1793 the mill was rebuilt with eight pairs of stones and four wheels. It went out of use in the mid-nineteenth century, but was working again by 1883 and still in use in 1921. The Abbey also owned a windmill around 1291, and in the eighteenth century there were two windmills in use around Holme Bridge.

There has been a mill on the Avon where Healing's stands today since the 13th century. Healing's Mill, first called the Borough Mill, was built in 1865 by Samuel Healing, and was steam-powered. It was extended in 1889 and 1935 and changed from steam to electricity in the fifties. In 1976 it was rebuilt, keeping the attractive 19th century exterior, and made into one of the most up-to-date mills in Europe, and one of the largest inland flour mills in the country. Its huge lorries are a familiar sight in Tewkesbury's High Street. Since 1961 it has been owned by Allied Mills.

From the mid-14th century the boom in sheep farming caused great misery to peasants, as the landowners enclosed the open fields, turning out the peasant owners and often burning their houses. The displaced peasants either worked for the farmers on the new big farms, or became tradesmen or craftsmen in towns. The open fields system was dead. The introduction of the turnip in 1577, which provided food for sheep and cattle during the winter months, not only enabled people to eat fresh meat all the winter, but the extra manure produced by the cattle increased the fertility of the land enormously.

Gaston Field between Southwick Park and Gupshill, and the Mythe, were both enclosed in the sixteenth century, and Southwick Field south of the Park by 1686. The Oldbury was an open field in the twelfth century and in 1314 it measured nearly 17 acres, all owned by burgesses (freemen). It consisted of pasture plus four furlongs of land: Upper, Middle, Nether (lower) and Hollam (from the old English world hol = hollow). About 94 acres of the Severn Ham was included in the Manor of Tewkesbury when it was granted to Thomas Seymour, Lord Sudeley, in 1547. In 1610 the freehold was granted to Tewkesbury Borough Corporation, which conveyed it, except the aftermath, to William Ferrars for 20,000 years in 1615. In 1640 the title was sold to Richard Dowdeswell of Pull Court, Bushley. From 31 July to 2 February burgesses could pasture their beasts there. By the late seventeenth century every freeman could pasture three horses, six cows or ten of his own sheep. 100 years later the right was for resident freeholders and occupiers and applied only to cattle. In 1811, under an Act passed in 1808, the Borough Corporation enclosed the Ham and the Oldbury and adjoining meadows. The latter was quickly built on, using bricks from the Mythe brickworks, now the Red Pools. The Ham then comprised 106 acres owned by Thomas Dowdeswell, 41 acres owned by the Earl of Essex and 40 acres divided among small owners. In 1933, to the great benefit of Tewkesburians, Rev George Berens-Dowdeswell sold his estate to the Borough Council. Since the late twenties the hay from the Ham has been sold by auction and divided among the owners; the aftermath (second reaping) was also sold and distributed among the commoners. The latter are now the householder-occupiers of the three main streets: Church Street from the Cross to the Bell; the High Street, and Barton Street from the Cross to number 48 on the north side, and the Cross to number 51 on the south side. Shops and business premises do not qualify unless the owner lives in the house and occupies the whole of it.

William Camden referred to Tewkesbury mustard as early as 1586, and Shakespeare uses it as a proverb in *Henry IV:* 'his wit is as thick as Tewkesbury mustard'. Thomas Fuller, writing in 1662, recommends it highly: 'The best in England . . . It is very wholesome for the clearing of the head, moderately taken'. James Bennett lamented that it was no longer made: 'The good housewives here . . . uniformily pounded the mustard seed in an iron morter, with a large cannon ball, or other hard substance of a similar shape and size; and after the flour had been carefully sifted from the bran, it was mixed in a cold infusion of horse-radish and well beaten or stirred up for the space of an hour. It was considered that the horse-radish imparted great additional pungency to the mustard, and that the continued beating gave it that consistency and strength which was deemed essential to its good preservation'.

The population engaged in agriculture was cut by a half between 1831 and 1841. The 13 farms in 1850 were mostly small: one farm of 400 acres, six between 50 and 100 acres, and the rest 10 to 50 acres, with about 50 acres of market gardening. The 13 owner-occupiers provided work for about 90 men between them. In 1907 the area was mainly permanent pasture for Hereford cattle; fruit growing and cider and perry making were also important. The chief cheeses were Double Gloucester, Single Gloucester, Stilton and Cheddar. The principal timber was elm. The Corn Laws introduced in 1815 to maintain the price of wheat by regulating its importation, together with poor harvests, caused famines in 1816 and the eighteen-forties. A petition was organised in Tewkesbury for its repeal, and in 1847 a 'food scarcity' meeting was held, at which Tewkesburians were urged to cut down their consumption of grain, eat wholemeal bread and to try bread substitutes. The Corn Laws were repealed in 1849.

Since the fourteenth century Tewkesbury has been connected with the clothing industries. Dyers, tailors, hosiers, mercers (textile merchants), are mentioned in Corporation records. Robert Atkyns wrote in 1712: 'The chief Trade in this Town is knitting of Stockings, and working of Cotton, and other woollen Manufactures. It hath also a great Trade in making of Malt'.

By Tudor times life for the ordinary Tewkesburian must have been easier than for his Norman forebears. Houses were larger and more comfortable, and there were more furniture and artifacts, requiring a great variety of trades. In 1575 Tewkesbury Borough Corporation set up guilds to regulate trades; they also provided apprenticeships and protected the consumer against poor workmanship and the members against competition. Between 1488 and 1686 these guilds are recorded in Tewkesbury: tailors, cordwainers (shoe makers), haberdashers and mercers, weavers, whittawers (saddlers), glovers, pointmakers (lacemakers), pursers, pouchmakers, coopers and joiners, butchers and bakers. By 1699 they were used more for ceremonial occasions than as true guilds, though a guild for smiths was recorded as late as 1705 and one for brewers in 1743.

The preamble to the grant from the Borough to the Company of Tailors in 1574 begins: 'Tyme out of mynde there hath ben a fellowshipp or brotherhoodd of the misterie of taylors' in

Tewkesbury. It went on to allow them to re-unite with the drapers' and dyers' companies. Members had to serve a seven year apprenticeship and pay a fee varying from 3s 4d for a local apprentice to £4 for a stranger. The Cordwainers Society also had apprentices for seven years. In 1562 their retail charges were 21d for one dozen double-soled adult shoes, and 16d for childrens'. This guild continued in Tewkesbury until 1941, when its remaining four members dissolved it. By 1730 it was a prestige social club; women were barred and dignitaries such as Edward Popham of Tewkesbury Park and other local members of Parliament were made Master. Sumptuous dinners were held, at the Swan from 1872-1909 and the Bell from 1909-1913. From 1873 it was regarded as an unofficial Conservative club.

After stocking knitting, malting was Tewkesbury's chief trade in the early 18th century, and by 1781 there were 45 malt houses in the town, but by 1842 only 26 were left and in 1919 there was one survivor in Station Street. After it ceased to produce malt it housed a small Dowty electronics factory, which has now gone, and there are plans to convert the building into flats. The former FitzHamon Art Centre, now the property of the Bell Hotel, was known as the Maltings, and was the site of the Abbey malthouse. The upper storey of the Maltings was a slipper baths and the lower a fire station between the World Wars. In 1540 a horse-driven brewery mill was recorded in Quay Lane, and this is probably the works owned by David Jones, who is said to have built a brewery in his garden at 39-40 High Street. This was taken over by Blizard and Colman about 1863, when there was also a distillery in Tewkesbury. Blizard and Colman's name can still be seen on the old wall today.

In 1843 Edmund Rudge, a famous Tewkesbury miser, died at the age of 84 worth £140,000; a millionaire by modern standards. He made his fortune as a tanner. He lived in a 'mean and filthy habitation and neighbourhood in St. Mary's Lane'. He was scrupulously honest and attended the Baptist Church. By walking everywhere on business, pushing his hides in a wheelbarrow to Gloucester and back, and living chiefly on fat mutton, bread, milk and beer, he kept his expenses down to just over £30 a year. His tannery was probably on the Avon behind St Mary's Lane, which in 1921 housed the Electricity Works, and was by 1952 the boat builders, Durrant and Vickeridge. Rudge would not have made a fortune in the later nineteenth century when the industry declined. In 1910 there were two saddlers and 13 boot and shoe makers, but attempts to establish shoe factories failed. The Tewkesbury Marina now stands on the site of an old tannery.

From being known for its stout hand-knitted stockings in the time of Daniel Defoe, Tewkesbury became a great centre for stocking framework knitting. In Henson's history of the industry he states there were 40 frames in Tewkesbury in 1714, but this seems rather early and perhaps 1740 was the date meant. The number continued to increase until it reached its probable maximum in 1810 with 800 frames. Bennett estimated that in 1830, 700 people (one quarter of the population) were engaged in the industry, and Tewkesbury was a larger centre than either of her two closest rivals, London and Northampton. Bennett reckoned that 600 frames would employ about 720 people, who would be mainly women. The wages in 1810 were 12s a week, but by 1826 this had dropped to 7s. A quarter of a pound of beef and a pint of soup cost about 1½d. It must have been difficult to feed, clothe and keep a family warm on that wage, and the beef must often have been absent.

In addition to manning the looms, workers would be employed in ancillary processes such as seaming, scouring, bleaching, sewing on calico bands and buttons and embroidering, and also needed would be needle makers, and framesmiths to repair the looms.

By 1857 the power loom was coming into use, but they cost £700, and the Tewkesbury hosiers said they could not afford to install them. In order to compete, they cut their prices and consequently their already low wages. In 1842, 220 frames stopped work for six weeks, and the wretched workers were left to the mercies of the Board of Governors of the Poor. 'Shortly afterwards', says Bennett, 'the prospects of trade having a little improved, the manufacturers took their workmen back into full employment; and although the wages they obtained were extremely low, the operatives, who had conducted themselves with much propriety in the season of adversity, thankfully accepted work on such terms as were offered'. By 1891 only 216 were employed in the industry in Tewkesbury, and before the First World War the industry had died.

Some of the stocking frame knitters' cottages can still be seen in Tewkesbury, distinguishable by wide, curved-top windows on the first floor to light the frames. 28-32 St Mary's Lane are three late eighteenth century cottages which have been restored and are now owned by the Landmark Trust. One of the largest factories, off East Street, has been converted into private dwellings. Another stocking factory on the corner of the High Street and Smiths Lane, with a chimney stack 135 feet high, built in 1861, later became first a brewery and then a garage.

A cotton thread lace factory was established in the Oldbury in 1825 but, although the machinery was of the 'most costly and perfect kind' and it employed 150 women and children, by 1835 the machinery was obsolete, and it closed soon after 1850. A silk factory started in the Oldbury in 1847, employing 200 people, but moved to Coventry in 1870. A silk finishing factory was built about 1840 on the Avon, north of St Mary's Lane. Later it became the Halifax shoe factory, closed, and re-opened in 1883 as the Tewkesbury Manufactory Co, employing about 300 people making collars, shirt-fronts, wrist bands and cardboard boxes. Production had ceased by 1921. It was known as the Eagle Factory, and in 1964 the building was largely in ruins except for one part which was a dress factory, and another part which was in use as a St John Ambulance Brigade Headquarters.

Metal workers have plied their trade in Tewkesbury. 14th century records name smiths, cutlers, lorimers (makers of the metal parts of harnesses), ironmongers and goldsmiths. In the following century Tewkesbury had two bell founders, and Brasier's Lane was named before 1666 and meant 'the lane of the brass workers'. This may have become the modern Smith's Lane. A successful pin factory was established in 1849 by James Savory and John Purnell and sold to Kerby Beard and Co from Gloucester, who carried on the business in the original premises 'near the bottom end of the High Street', but it did not last long. Braziers, cutlers, gunsmiths, millwrights, blacksmiths and whitesmiths were also established about that time.

In 1805 nails were made 'in great quantity' in Nailers Square, which lay approximately between today's Post Office Lane, Tolsey Lane and the Avon, but the industry lapsed, was revived again around 1830 and employed 50 people in 1835. In 1842 there were four nail shops off Barton Street, but by 1870 only one nailer was left. A number of minor trades continued to engage between one and five people in Victoria's reign: chairmaking, coopering, clockmaking, ropemaking, and hat-making (especially straw hats). The Mythe brickworks were established in 1634 but they were worked out by the second half of the 19th century. Two brickmakers flourished about 1850: John Jeffries, and Sam Fryzer after whom the court is named.

The book trade has done well in Tewkesbury. 1608 records mention a parchment-maker, three paper-makers and a stationer, and there was also a book-maker about that time. From 1760-1780 Samuel Harward published some chap-books, and about 1780 Richard Dyde moved into Harward's premises and wrote and published his famous history of Tewkesbury.

The first effort at a news sheet of which we have a record in Tewkesbury is in 1633, when a scribe was paid £5 for six months by the Tewkesbury Borough Council to send news from London to Tewkesbury. In 1843 the *Tewkesbury Magazine and Literary Journal* was launched, but as it was high-brow, monthly and at 6d an issue very expensive, it is not surprising that it only survived three issues. Ten years later the Liberal *Tewkesbury Monthly Record and General Advertiser* began publication, changing its title in 1855 to *Tewkesbury Weekly Record*. This ceased publication in 1922. John Garrison, printer, was responsible for it in 1863 and by 1903 W. J. Gardner was editor. He was an influential figure in the town, being Superintendent of the Baptist Sunday School 1889-90 and again 1894-1907. In 1858 William North, a printer and local historian who functioned at 139

High Street, launched the *Tewkesbury Register and Gazette*, with Frederick Moore as its first editor, and the paper ran triumphantly for 106 years. It was Conservative in tone, and its editorial pontifications on the news of the day make amusing or outrageous reading a century later. At first there was little local news, but a great deal of humour, home hints, fashion articles, nature articles, serials by such well-known writers as Philip Gibbs and lengthy reports on the words and actions of the local MP. A leader in 1858 stated that, although the stocking trade had collapsed in Tewkesbury, the silk mills needed 200 operatives. It goes on 'Until this gap is filled up, we do not clearly see how parents possessing, as most of our poor folk do, a quiver full of children, are entitled to complain of destitution . . . On previous occasions of depressions in other trades, we have known families rescued from actual want by the wages earned by *industrious* children in Tewkesbury Silk Mills'. Fortunately, the passing of the Education Act of 1870, by enforcing school attendance up to the age of ten, made it much easier to prevent small children carrying out the role of family bread-winner so blandly advocated by the *Register*. In 1930 it was sold to W. H. Smith and became politically independent. In 1961 the *News of the World* endeavoured to make it viable, but the effort failed, and it ceased publication at the end of 1964. Now the free *Admag* gives the best news coverage for Tewkesbury.

Attempts to establish circulating libraries in Tewkesbury in 1802, 1814 and 1828 were unsuccessful. In 1833 the Tewkesbury Reading Society was formed, becoming the Tewkesbury Literary, Scientific and Mechanic's Institution. It lasted only 10 years, probably because, after a working day of up to 10 hours, the mechanics found it a formidable task to sit through lectures on such subjects as the trial of Mary, Queen of Scots; infusorial animacules; education in Germany, and the anatomy of insects. In 1926 the first public library collection arrived in the form of a box of 100 books deposited in the Abbey Boys' School and available for loan from 7pm to 8pm every Wednesday evening. Not surprisingly, all but two of them were lent the very first evening. From the school the Library moved to the YMCA and later the council offices in Oldbury Road. Since 1957 the Library has been housed in the ground floor of the old grammar school. It is over-crowded and it is to be hoped that, with 7,750 registered readers, the long awaited new building will materialise in the near future. The Friends of Tewkesbury Library was started in 1982 to provide a support for and interest in the service.

The writer and broadcaster, John Moore, came from a long line of Tewkesburians. In 1610 mention is made of a Thomas Moore, cordwainer, who may have been of the same line. In 1741 the auctioneering firm which was to remain in Tewkesbury for two centuries was established, and members of the family are recorded as wine merchants, charity administrators and Borough Councillors. In the late 19th century the auctioneering firm was Weaver and Moore. John Moore was apprenticed to his uncle, Thomas Weaver Moore, who died in 1938. The firm still functioned under the name of Moore and Sons until the nineteen sixties.

John Moore was born in 1907. He spent his boyhood until the death of his father, a former Mayor, when he was 11, in Tudor House, formerly the Academy, and now Tudor House Hotel, and attended Malvern College. After his first book was published when he was 23, he left for London, but he continued to write of country matters. His best-known books are the trilogy: *Portrait of Embury; Brensham Village* and *The Blue Field*, which are set in Tewkesbury, Bredon and the surrounding villages, and were published 1945-1948. He was in the Fleet Air Arm during the war. He loved the English countryside, country life, Shakespeare and flying, and was a writer in the romantic tradition. He organised the Tewkesbury Festival 1934-1939 and was the first Artistic Director of the Cheltenham Literary Festival. He married an Australian, Lucile Stephens, in 1944. Romantic writing is not fashionable at present, but John Moore's work has always been enjoyed by lovers of the country scene and of clear prose spiced with humour, and there are signs already of a wider revival of interest. His early death in 1967 after a short illness was a shock to the townspeople, and he was sorely missed.

Other professions were represented in Tewkesbury. There was a notary in 1469, Thomas Vaughan practised law there in the early 17th century; there were five attorneys in 1784 and nine in 1820. In 1818 Lechmere and Hartland's Provident Bank was established in Tewkesbury. The word 'bank' can still be seen in the stonework above the first floor window of the takeaway restaurant, 99 Church Street. Surprisingly, there were 32 insurance agents in Tewkesbury in 1863.

The first mention of boat building in Tewkesbury is in 1401, when the town was ordered to provide a boat for Henry IV's navy, but it almost certainly had been an industry since pre-historic times for, until the great rail and road building programmes of the early nineteenth century, water was the normal way of transporting goods. Henry VI declared the Severn a free river at Tewkesbury, and it remained so until 1842. In 1558 Tewkesbury was ordered to make a 25 ton pinnace, which was locally supplied and manned. Severn trows were being built in the early seventeenth century in Tewkesbury. John Seymour describes them as 'strange, heavy, beamy, mediaeval-looking boats, some setting square sails on two masts, some fore-and-aft in rig, with high after-castles. They worked the fierce tidal reaches of the Severn estuary, riding out the famous Severn Bore . . . It is said that the hauliers were rough men, and that men would lock up the chickens — and their daughters — when they heard the sound of the hauliers' voicers singing as they hove on the ropes!'

There is no record of boat building in the eighteenth century, but a boat builder was recorded in 1844 and 1863, and in 1909 Tewkesbury's best known boat builder, Bathurst, was advertising his docks and boat building yard adjoining King John's Bridge. In 1926 Bathurst owned four steam boats, a motor boat, 50 pleasure boats and four rafts. The firm closed for a while just before the Second World War, and was bought by a boat builder named L. A. Robinson, who made small boats for the Admiralty during the war. The yard returned to the production of pleasure craft after 1945.

Bill Shakespeare's International Marina was bought by Peter Richards when the owner, who had won many trophies racing his own craft, died on Lake Windermere in 1972. Later David Cottrell bought the firm and expanded it in 1974, but it failed to prosper and closed down after a few years. The yard at the end of Smith's Lane is now being demolished.

Jim Beecham ran Beechams (Marine) Ltd on the north side of King John's Bridge, the site of a former tannery, and made large, diesel-powered yachts. The Tewkesbury Marina is there now.

In 1952 the boat building firm of Durrant and Vickeridge started up Back of Avon. Lieut-Commander Vickeridge had served his apprenticeship with Bathurst, and his war-time naval experience helped with their work of repairing and overhauling Admiralty boats. They also made self-drive launches and ran pleasure launches. The partners retired in 1978, when fibreglass was introduced for boat construction. The firm of Telestar Pleasure Cruises now occupy the site, but boat building in Tewkesbury is dead.

One of the most interesting of Tewkesbury's factories was that of Thomas Walker & Sons. The original site was a theatre that backed on to the Wheatsheaf, later a silk factory and possibly a pin factory. The firm was established in 1871 and made fairground equipment. In 1909 a fire destroyed their premises and 5,000 casting patterns as well as 100 roundabouts. At that time they were employing 60 hands. The firm recovered and flourished in a new site at the back of Trinity Church until about 1928, soon after which it became an agricultural machinery depot.

Finally, a note about the strangest industry of all in Tewkesbury: in 1636 tobacco was being grown in Tewkesbury 'in great store', but in 1627 and again in 1644 the crops were destroyed, as the Government was already committed to the revenues they received from a tax on the importation of what James I called 'this stinking smoke'.

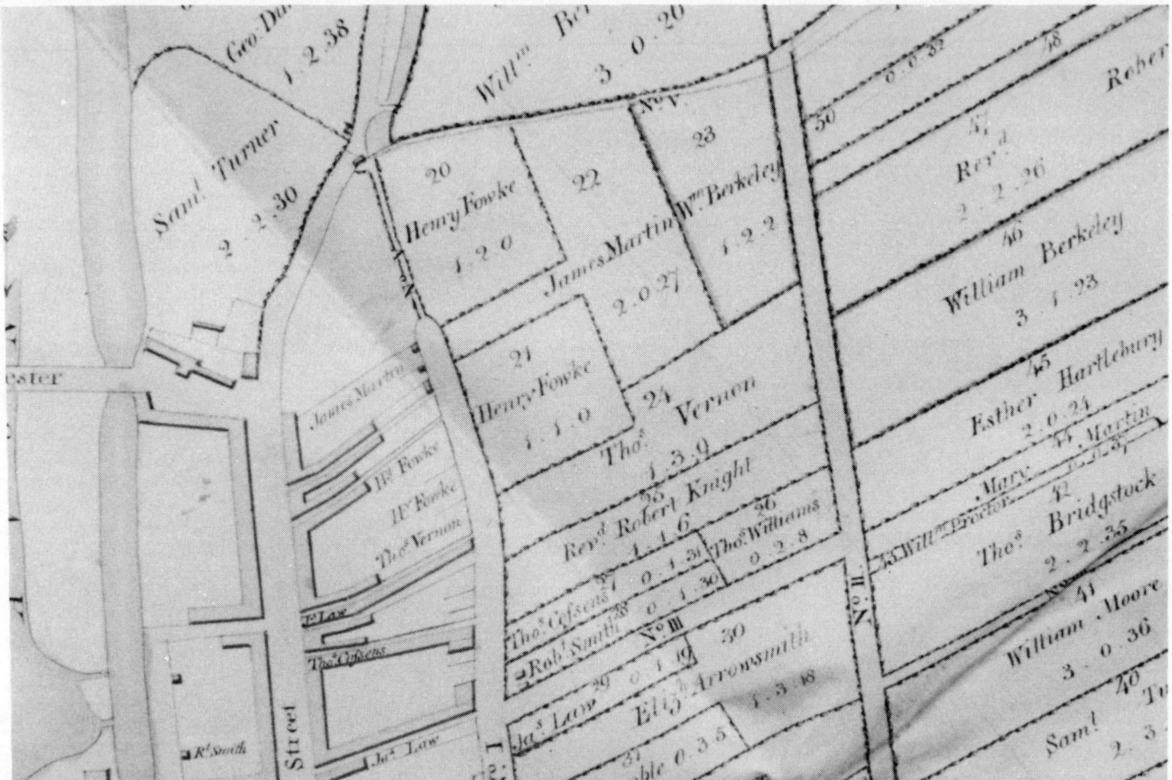

When the Enclosure Act was passed in 1811, a map was drawn up to show who owned property on the Oldbury and the Ham prior to building houses on them. The fields are numbered and the area of each plot is given in rods, poles and perches. (A rod equalled 30¼ square yards). All the well-known Tewkesbury names are there: Turner, Dumble, Moore, Fowke the Town Clerk, Hartland the Quaker, Robert Knight the Vicar, Garner, Elizabeth Arrowsmith, etc. (GRO)

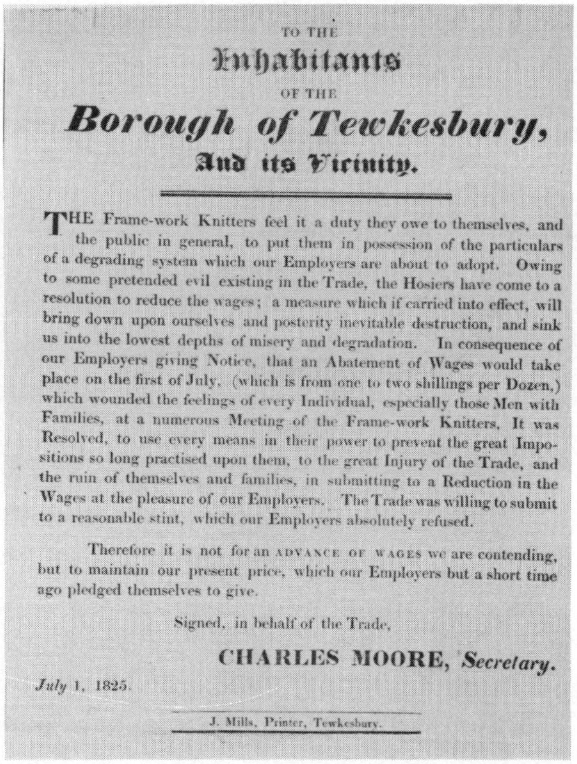

TO THE

Inhabitants

OF THE

Borough of Tewkesbury,

And its Vicinity.

THE Frame-work Knitters feel it a duty they owe to themselves, and the public in general, to put them in possession of the particulars of a degrading system which our Employers are about to adopt. Owing to some pretended evil existing in the Trade, the Hosiers have come to a resolution to reduce the wages; a measure which if carried into effect, will bring down upon ourselves and posterity inevitable destruction, and sink us into the lowest depths of misery and degradation. In consequence of our Employers giving Notice, that an Abatement of Wages would take place on the first of July, (which is from one to two shillings per Dozen,) which wounded the feelings of every Individual, especially those Men with Families, at a numerous Meeting of the Frame-work Knitters, It was Resolved, to use every means in their power to prevent the great Impositions so long practised upon them, to the great Injury of the Trade, and the ruin of themselves and families, in submitting to a Reduction in the Wages at the pleasure of our Employers. The Trade was willing to submit to a reasonable stint, which our Employers absolutely refused.

Therefore it is not for an ADVANCE OF WAGES we are contending, but to maintain our present price, which our Employers but a short time ago pledged themselves to give.

Signed, in behalf of the Trade,

CHARLES MOORE, ***Secretary.***

July 1, 1825.

J. Mills, Printer, Tewkesbury.

LEFT: Brewing is one of Tewkesbury's oldest industries: Bayliss and Merrill stood on the site now occupied by the Black Bear garden. Photograph, c1909. (GLC) BELOW: Abbey Brewery in the High Street, later the Tewkesbury Garage. Advertisement, c1903. (GCL) RIGHT: Protest by stocking workers about the cut in wages which the depression in the trade had forced upon employers. Poster, 1825. (GCL)

ABOVE: Interior of the Patent Renewable Stocking Factory, from the *Illustrated Times*, 24 November 1860. (GLC) LEFT: Stocking frame knitters' cottages, 28-32 St Mary's Lane, before recent restoration by the Landmark Trust; built in the late 18th century, the wide, curved-top windows on the first floor were to light the frames. (TM) RIGHT: This factory started life as a silk finishing workshop about 1840, on the Avon, north of St Mary's Lane. Later it became the Halifax Shoe Co, and later still the Tewkesbury Manufacturing Co, employing about 300 making collars, shirts, wristbands and cardboard boxes: production ceased about 1920. Advertisement. (GCL)

ABOVE: Thomas Walker and Son, established 1871 on a site behind the Wheatsheaf, made fairground equipment. These premises were destroyed by fire in 1909, and Walkers moved behind Trinity Church until about 1928, when they closed and the building became an agricultural machinery depot. A carpark now occupies the site. Water colour by A. Phipson, 1902. (GCL) BELOW: One of Walker's products: the Jolly Cake Walk, in 1908 and still in use at Nottingham Goose Fair, Stratford Mop Fair, etc. (CJS and TM)

ABOVE: Healing's Mill, showing Quay Bridge and wagons waiting on the rails, on the right Rice's Mill. Oil painting by W. A. Rixon of Turkdean Manor, 1929. (GER GCL) BELOW: Abel Fletcher's Mill, previously called Abbey Mill, and now Abbey Mill Restaurant, with delivery by boat on the Mill Avon. Engraving by R. Ackerman, 1801 (TTC)

ABOVE: Records of boat building in Tewkesbury date back to 1401, but boats were made here long before that. At the turn of this century Bathurst's boat building yard adjoined King John's Bridge, where the Winking Frog is now. During World War II the firm made small boats for the Admiralty. (GRO) BELOW: Early 18th century view from the quay, showing (left to right) Mythe Tute, Mythe House, three men in a rowing boat pulling a barge with lowered mast, Long Bridge, fishing boats, Bredon Hill, 40 ton barge, 99 ton trow (unusually large), granary and malt houses. Engraving. (GRO)

ABOVE LEFT: Bill Shakespeare's International Marina at the end of Smith's Lane; Shakespeare, world speed record holder, here with one of his own boats equipped with two 100hp Mercury engines, in 1965; he tragically died racing his own craft on Lake Windermere in 1972. (GL) RIGHT: Sheep shearing at Hillend, Twyning, using a hand-cranked shearer, Tom Goodall assisted by Frank Roberts and his two sons in 1939. (RFG) BELOW LEFT: Frank and Dennis Roberts outside the family shop, Hillend, Twyning in 1936: the three carthorses and attendants were hired out to Gloucestershire County Council for road works. (RFG) RIGHT: In the early 19th century Isaac Jenner, printer, bookseller, stationer and bookbinder, occupied 139 High Street next door to Clarence House, ran a circulating library and dealt in musical instruments and patent medicines! In 1858 the shop was bought by William North. From 1858 North published the *Tewkesbury Register* guides and books on local history. On his death in 1901 he was succeeded by his son, another William, author of such books as *Historic Houses of Tewkesbury*. (TR TL)

LEFT: E. Reddell ran a printing office, book shop and circulating library from 7 High Street from 1816 until at least the late eighteen-twenties. Engraving. (CAGM) RIGHT: Frederick Moore, founder and first editor of the *Tewkesbury Register* and member of the family of auctioneers from which writer John Moore was descended. Photograph, c1880. (TR TL) BELOW: Dowty Mining Equipment Ltd was established in Ashchurch in 1948 and invented the Roofmaster hydraulic roof support for mines. (DM)

Come to the Fair

Tewkesbury was recorded in the Domesday Book as having a market, and the Manor of Tewkesbury included a fair as far back as 1199. In 1324 Hugh le Despenser granted an annual ten-day fair from 19 June, and in 1441 this was replaced by two eight day fairs at St Matthias (24 February) and St Bartholomew (24 August). When the Manor was granted to the Corporation in 1610, the right to hold fairs and markets went with it. Additional fairs on 3 May, 11 June and 29 September (Barton Fair) were established, and in the early 19th century another two were added on the second Wednesday in April and the first Wednesday in December. In 1827 the June and December fairs were replaced by two great markets on the same days and one on the second Wednesday in August. Hiring (mop) fairs were held on the Wednesdays before and after Barton Fair, which was moved to 10 October. After further revision in 1870, fairs were held only on the second Monday in each month, except in October when Barton Fair and the two hiring fairs took place. The three great markets were also retained. Now Barton Fair is the only one left, and there are markets on Wednesdays and Saturdays.

Markets were held in the old Town Hall until it was demolished in 1789, when a Market House was erected by 20 speculators where the Methodist Church now stands. The prime movers were auctioneer Philip Thomas and his son, Edward. In 1870 a descendent, George Hone, a farmer with over 1,000 acres, became sole owner. He moved the cattle market to the Oldbury, where the present swimming pool lies, and the sheep and pigs to the old Sun Street, near Hawkes' smithy. G. L. Hone built a new market which was opened in 1927.

Markets create some difficulties. In 1612 the town bailiffs found that the nuisance from horses standing in the market place was so objectionable, that they ordered that they should be stabled at a fee of ½d per horse with food, or 1d per three horses without food. When a circus was camped on Swilgate Meadow in 1841, an elephant escaped and wandered round after dark causing great consternation. He was finally caught while trying to squeeze into a brewery. In our own century the cattle were driven through the streets of Tewkesbury and the local butchers slaughtered the cattle they bought in their own slaughter houses. Jack Fletcher writes 'One local butcher — Healey — had the pigs killed by Wednesday evening and the products: roast pork, chitterling, trotters, brawn, lard, etc . . ., all spread invitingly in the shop window the following day. This was also the heyday of the cooked meat shops . . . when it was easy to get cooked faggots and peas, tripe, pork pies, black pudding, nearly all from locally bred animals and all tasty and nutritious'.

Market standings or stalls gradually evolved into permanent buildings, and the shop as we know it developed.

Tewkesbury is 'large and populous, and consists of three handsome high built streets, besides many lanes.' So wrote Atkyns, the Gloucestershire historian in 1712. We know that in early times one of these streets contained shops because in Church Street we have the Abbey Cottages, a row of mediaeval merchants' homes, one of which was returned to its original state in 1967, when the row was restored. The house is timber-framed with clay and wattle walls. Heavy wooden shutters let down to form the counter when the shop was open. Behind is a general living room with a fire in the centre, the smoke from which found its way up the stairs towards a vent in the roof, warming the building as it did so. The stairs lead into the bed-chamber, with its huge four-poster bed, truckle bed and cradle. The other furniture consists of a chest for clothing, some forms, a cooking pot and a spit for the occasional joint. This is how the merchants lived; the hovels of the peasants must have been much more primitive.

In Edwardian times the shops in Tewkesbury reflected the town's agricultural interests. T. Durrant at 115 High Street (now part of the new shopping complex) specialised in working men's boots, and Haywards at 125 and 126 High Street were forward-looking in providing the latest equipment, whether in gas, electricity or above all, agriculture. A Mr Hayward was mentioned in Tewkesbury as far back as 1806, when he sold property in the High Street, and a Miss Hayward sold the Wheatsheaf in 1815. Haywards (Tewkesbury) Ltd was founded in 1820 by George Hayward, master cutter. His son married the daughter of an ironmonger named Brydges. The firm still trades at 126. C. E. Hopkins, the drapers, occupied Clarence House, 140 High Street from Edwardian times onward. It was recently sold and is at present a fancy goods shop. Bayliss and Merrill, where the Black Bear garden now stands, was a major warehouse for home brewed ales as well as for wines and spirits.

Gloucestershire Agricultural Show on the banks of the Severn, lasted several days and included flower-shows, a regatta and 'athletic sports'. Engraving from the *Illustrated London News,* July 1865. (GCL)

LEFT: The Market House at the Cross was erected chiefly by the auctioneer Philip Thomas and his son Edward, later owned by George Hone and demolished in 1878 when the Methodist Church was built on the site. Engraving, 1830. (JB) RIGHT: Ray Bloxham, after winning third prize at Bredon Show. His father was a butcher in Church Street, and Ray used to drive his little gray pony and box cart for many miles delivering meat. He had a distinguished World War I record, serving in Palestine, and was awarded the MC for bravery. His niece, Kathleen Hall, lives in Tewkesbury. Photograph. 1911. (KH) BELOW: Fairs were held in Tewkesbury as far back as 1199, and the first Barton Fair was inaugurated around 1610, continuing to the present day, as Tewkesbury Fair here in Barton Street, 1910. (CB)

ABOVE: The new cattle market adjacent to Holy Trinity Church the day before it was opened in May 1927: it was owned by G. L. Hone. (GE GCL) BELOW: Drawing by John Sowden looking up Mythe Road, c1890. (TL)

ABOVE: Upper High Street, not yet tar macadamised in 1920, showing the Black Bear next to a timber-framed building, the top two storeys of which have been demolished; the Tewkesbury FC now occupy the ground floor. The tree has gone, and also the house and gas-lamp on the right. (KH) LEFT: Papps' drapers occupied four shops at the Cross end of the High Street around the turn of the century: 144 is now Curry's. Advertisement, 1903. (GCL) RIGHT: Smith's, milliner and drapers, with a fine display of hats and ladies' knickers: known as Victoria House, it is now occupied by Cut Price and is outwardly unchanged. Photograph, 1925. (GRO)

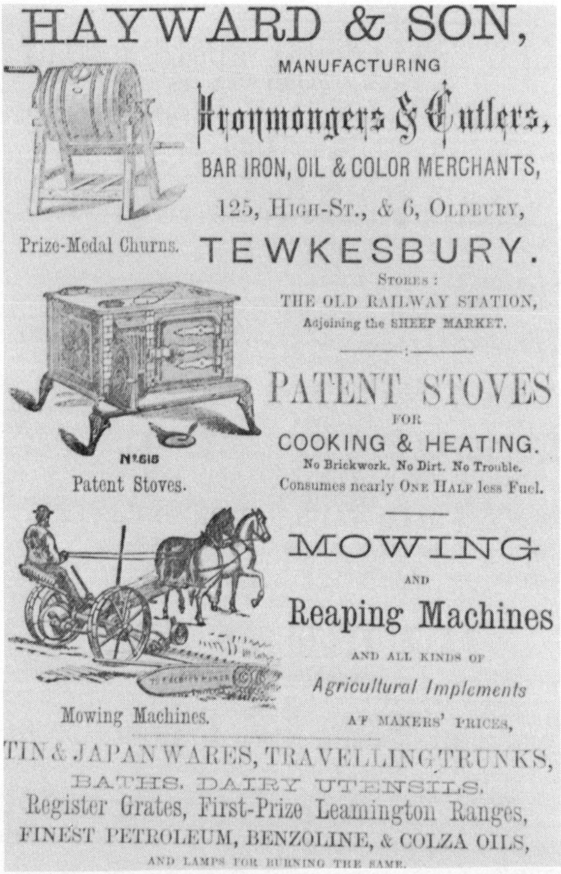

LEFT: Hayward's occupied 125 High Street for over a century and are still at 126. Advertisement for milk churns, stoves and mowing machines, 1878. (GCL) RIGHT: Albion House later known as Clarence House, one of Tewkesbury's finest buildings, and possesing a magnificent mid-17th century plaster ceiling on the first floor, though the house dates from the early 16th century. Lithograph by Rowe, 1839. (CAGM) BELOW: C. Mellor's furniture, pottery and second-hand shop at 26 Barton Street, with baby carriages outside c1900: the Police Station now occupies the site. (CB)

ABOVE LEFT: Hopkins the drapers occupied Clarence House from the end of the 19th century until 1982: next door are the offices of North the printer. Photograph, c1920. (EP) CENTRE: 12-13 High Street were once the Fleece Inn, and among the carved wooden corbels restored by Thomas Collins is the fleece sign and the date 1591. Dobell's, the Tewkesbury brewers and publicans, ran the Britannia Inn at 30 High Street from 1866 until the late nineteen sixties and also owned the shop here, now the Victoria Wine Shop. 1933. (EP) RIGHT: 22 Barton Street is a typical 16th century Tewkesbury House. The two windows on the first floor were replaced not long ago. It was occupied by members of the Howell and Coutts families from 1872-1939, except for two years as a temperance café and reading room. From 1963 it has been the Joan Marian dress shop: c1933. (EP) BELOW LEFT: Willow Café, 61 High Street was a well-known and popular cafe until the Co-op developed the site in the 1970s. It had also been a coffee shop and c1836-1865 the Ship and Castle beer house. Photograph, c1933. (EP) RIGHT: Bloxham the butcher at 18 Church Street, now flats: A Bloxham, proprietor on the right and his son Alan on the left. Their grand-daughter, Kathleen Hall, lives in Tewkesbury. Photograph, 1912. (KH)

LEFT: Berkeley Arms in Church Street may have originated as a mediaeval inn. It has a 16th century shop front on a 15th century tavern with an unusual stone-walled cellar, and was probably previously called the 'Queen's Arms'. (RR) RIGHT: Wheatsheaf Inn at 132 High Street was built about 1500, and has a beautiful four-storey jettied front. There was a skittle alley at the rear, and in the 18th and early 19th centuries a fives court. Lithograph by Rowe, 1839. (CAGM)

Home from Home

Tewkesbury's inns are numerous, architecturally fascinating and hospitable. Perhaps the most photographed is the Bell in Church Street, opposite the Gage Abbey gates. It was at one time known as the Angel, a name frequently given to inns established by the Church for travellers and especially pilgrims. The sign over the door says 1696, and this could be a good date for the whole building, though some people believe it contains some mediaeval portions, and some of the panelling could have come from the old Abbey Church pews removed in 1796. There was a bowling green, where a terrace of town houses now stands, dating from monastic times, and the hotel was at one time called the Bell and Bowling Green.

Another picturesque, timber-framed inn is the Berkeley Arms. It has three storeys and at the rear the house appears to incorporate a sixteenth century barn or warehouse. Entrance to the top floors was once by a stair ladder. The Berkeley was famous for its faggots and peas, and it is still a favourite lunch-time resort for workers in the town.

The Duke of York in Barton Street is outwardly a brick, eighteenth century house which, like so many Tewkesbury houses, conceals an early sixteenth century interior. It used to be called the Duke of Yorke, and this may have been in deference to the Forthampton Court family. The United Friendly Society had its headquarters and bank here, and a treasurer, William Hale, was convicted in 1832 of stealing £39 from their funds and was transported for life.

The Black Bear, claimed to be the oldest inn in Gloucestershire, is mainly early sixteenth century, though tradition dates it to 1308. A lot of the exterior work facing on to the High Street was done by Thomas Collins, of Collins and Godfrey, who was responsible for the Abbey Church restoration at the end of the last century. The garden, which extends down to the river, occupies the site of the Bayliss and Merrill warehouse and the stables and outhouses of the Gaze dairy. In the public bar is a leather ceiling, decorated with astronomical signs.

The Britannia opened in the High Street in 1785 as a wine and spirit merchant, and later on became a beer house. The Dobell family, who also owned what is now the Victoria Wine shop at 12 High Street, ran the Britannia from 1866 for nearly a century. It is an impressive, solid-looking eighteenth century building. Another fine building of the same period is the Riverside Hotel, 66 High Street. It has beautiful matching fanlights on its two doors, though it has lost its glazing lights on the ground floor. At the rear is a splendid circular bay window overlooking the garden and river, which is striking when approaching the town from Worcester. An attempt to turn it into a night-club failed, and the house was closed for several years, but happily it is now flourishing again.

The Swan was an inn in the thirteenth century, and some of the original building may have been retained when two adjoining inns were combined about 1784, and a courtyard was built under a Venetian window into which the stagecoaches drove. The railways killed the service for the long distance traveller, but the Swan remained a posting house for local stagecoaches, until the Tewkesbury to Malvern line was opened in 1864. Its sash-framed windows are unusual in that they retain their original blown glass (now unobtainable) and glazing bars. The Hop-Pole in Church Street was the other great posting house for coaches. Built in the late eighteenth century, it was called the New Inn and later incorporated the adjoining Bull and another Riverside Hotel. A visit from Queen Mary in the twenties justified the addition of the word Royal to the inn's name. A more famous visit was from Mr Pickwick, who took refreshment there, thus enabling the Pickwick Bar and Dickens Room to be so named. There was a Dickens Fellowship in Tewkesbury from 1919 to 1977.

The Wheatsheaf was once an important inn, but is now a restaurant specialising in old English cookery. It was built about 1500 and has a four-storey jettied front. Some of the original wattle filling can be seen preserved under glass. The initials J.V. in the panel over the door lintel may stand for John Underwood, who died there in 1719. The mullioned windows are beautiful, and there is also some attractive modern engraved glass. There was a skittle alley at the rear for many years, and before that, going back to the early nineteenth century, a fives court. Many organisations' festive dinners were held here, including those of the Primrose League, the Independent Englishman's Society, the Cordwainers' Society and the Tewkesbury Volunteers. Another restaurant of outstanding architectural interest is the Ancient Grudge, whose name probably derives from the Wars of the Roses. The front is late mediaeval with herring bone framing, and the restaurant has moulded sixteenth century ceiling beams, a magnificent fireplace arch and so much linenfold panelling that it even extends to the ladies' toilet.

It is impossible to list all Teskesbury's interesting buildings, since almost every building has some point of interest, either historically or architecturally, but one can make suggestions as to what to look for. Because Tewkesbury's growth was limited by the flooding of her four rivers, and because householders who had a frontage on the three main streets had to pay tax, the Tudor builders built upwards and back from the streets. That is why Tewkesbury is so rich in three and four storey houses, jettied to provide extra room on the upper floors, and why at one time it contained a warren of alleys, of which in most cases only passage ways remain today. Another point to look for are the moulded terracotta keyblocks over the windows, of which Tewkesbury has many fine examples. Because Tewkesbury failed to prosper from the mid-nineteenth century, householders could not afford to rebuild their dwellings, though they often encased them in a 'modern' facade, as with the apparently nineteenth century houses in the Crescent. From the back and inside the early structure is clearly visible. Until the old Sun Street and Double Alley were pulled down, and the shopping centre locally known as the 'Kremlin' was built in their place in the late seventies, Tewkesbury had remained basically a Tudor town with later additions.

One of the finest buildings is now endangered. This is Cross House, also called Corner House and at one time the Manor Court House and also referred to as Tolsey House, at 107-8 Church Street, at the Cross. Thomas Collins, of the building firm Collins and Godfrey lived there and restored it c1860, and later it was the home of Frank Godfrey. Its beautiful mullioned windows went when it was converted into two shops, but the fine spacious Tudor staircase restored by Collins can still be seen. Its third storey and attics were added on to its original 16th century structure 100 years later (attics were not built before c1600). Key House, 9 High Street, which used to be a booking office for coaches, is another 16th century house with beautiful moulded beams and mermaids disporting themselves on the ground floor ceiling. It is now a branch of the Halifax Building Society. Until recently a feature of 100 Church Street near the Cross was a large beadle's hat suspended over the door, where a gentleman's outfitter named Williams flourished in Edwardian times. It has the date 1664 on the doorhead, but its foundations are earlier. Jessop House, also in Church Street, is currently being saved from disrepair by conversion into flats. The Grammar School was housed there 1862-1899. Another house with a previous owner of local fame is Kingsbury House, named after James Kingsbury, stocking manufacturer and magistrate. In 1814 he was threatened with murder unless he raised the wages of his wretchedly paid workers.

It is a fine 18th century brick house which retains its original glazing bars in the Venetian window, and is now occupied by Messrs Lear.

One of Tewkesbury's few Victorian houses is the dignified Trafalgar House in the High Street, which was erected on the site of the Woolpack Inn c1865. It is unfortunate that the sole example of Victorian domestic gothic in the town, North House, home of Dr Devereux, was pulled down in the late nineteen-thirties and a pleasant row of semi-detached houses built in its place in Bredon Road. North House had a garden and orchard which extended from Moore, Brown and Dixon's office at 69 High Street to the Police Station and back to the Oldbury.

A separate book could be written on Tewkesbury's alleys, which were often named after the owners of the cottages in them. A typical example is Fletcher's Alley, so called from the Fletcher family of gunsmiths who resided at 75 Barton Street and also owned some cottages in the alley 1800-1875. The first Tewkesbury Fletcher was a whitesmith and cutler named Thomas, born c1720. The last gunsmith, George, died in 1878 of the effect of burns received in a fire at Turner and Yorke, ironmongers, when he was captain of the volunteer fire brigade. His widow, Sarah, was a remarkable lady, who died in November 1924 intellectually alert, although aged 102, and her obituary in the *Tewkesbury Register* of 29 November, referring to her own memories dating back over ninety years, makes fascinating reading. I am greatly indebted to Sarah's great-grandson, Jack, for much of the information in this book which concerns this century.

Bell Inn in Church Street opposite the Abbey, was originally the Angel, a name frequently given to inns for pilgrims, sketched here for a book published in 1894 by J. Hissey. (GCL)

ABOVE: The Swan Hotel in the High Street, looking towards the Cross, goes back in name to the 13th century, and in 1783 two mediaeval buildings were converted into a posting tavern. The horse-drawn 'bus standing outside was used to convey guests to and from the station. Photograph, c1890. (CH) BELOW: The Black Bear c1900, claims to be the oldest inn in Gloucestershire, but the bulk of the timber-framing is 16th century and in the late 19th century Thomas Collins supervised the renovation of the ground floor facing onto the High Street. (CH)

ABOVE: Tudor House Hotel today. John Moore describes playing as a small boy in the garden which then stretched as far as the river and the drill hall. Photograph. 1985. (RR) BELOW: 88 Church Street is a late 15th century house with a side entry and jettying at the back. These drawings by Hilary Swan of the kitchen and parlour show what cosy homes these cottages make. (LP)

ABOVE: Tewkesbury Grammar School was founded in 1576, and 1899 merged with Abbey House School c1900 under J. E. Priestley, Headmaster. In 1904 a new grammar school was built in the school garden shown here, and now houses the public library, health clinic, and registrar's office. Also shown is the Abbey malt house, later the FitzHamon Art Centre, and now the property of the Bell. Abbey House School was pulled down in the 1970s for the Bell carpark. (JF) BELOW: Tewkesbury High School for Girls was founded by Archdeacon Robeson, Vicar of Tewkesbury, in 1882 at Avonbrook House, Church Street: on the bank, Olive Day, Minnie Edwards, on the steps, H. Muirhead; seated, N. Woodward, Winnie Fisher; playing tennis, Christobel Thomas, Marjorie Mercier, Marjorie Westfield, Marjorie Badham; umpire, Helen Thornton. The photograph is signed Dorothy Dark, 1909. (AS)

Unwillingly to School

'The saide Towne of Tewkesburye is a very grete Markett Towne, where is kept Markett twyse everye Weeke, whereunto is contynuall accesse of a grete numbre of people, besydes those (which are no small numbre) that been inhabyted within the same Towne, havinge many Children likely and apt through good instruction to atteigne to Learninge, whiche the premysses tenderly consydered, the Inhabytaunts of the same Town are moste humble Suters, that it maye please the Kinges Majestie . . . to give and appoynt some coveyent Stypend for the mayntenance of a free Scole, there for ever to be kept and establyshed, for the better education and bringynge up of the saide youthe in knowledge of vertue and good learninge.'

This appeal to Edward VI in 1547 led to the establishment of a free grammar school in 1576, made by walling up the two chapels of St James and Nicholas on the north side of the Abbey Church, where the Abbey shop is now located. There were 16 pupils. In 1609 Sir Dudley Digges, Tewkesbury's first Member of Parliament, gave £160 to be invested in land to help support the school, and left money for a schoolmaster's salary. 12 boys were to come from Tewkesbury, and four from Ashchurch. In 1698 William III granted Tewkesbury its final charter, and in it was a clause stating that the 'free grammar school of William Ferrers, Citizen and Mercer of London' should exist 'forever', and consist of a master and an usher with an income of £30. The boys were aged between five and 15 and were taught Latin, Greek, English, reading, writing, geography and arithmetic. In the 1830s a scandal broke: the discipline was too strict, and the brutal flogging of the two sons of William Thomas caused an investigation to be held and the number of pupils dropped to one. However, the next year, William Moore, who had first protested against the floggings, was applying to have his own son, Francis, admitted under the same Headmaster, William Prosser! In 1849 the school closed for a while. In 1862 it moved to Jessop House in Church Street, the home of the Headmaster, John Morgan.

Meanwhile a similar establishment known as Abbey House School had been set up in 1853 in a house adjacent to the Bell. The Headmaster was Joseph Priestley, and under him the school expanded with many boarders, some sleeping at 40 Church Street and some at 5 Abbey Terrace. Priestley died when the school was only 23 years old, and his son, J. E. Priestley, took his place. The boarding part of the school began to decline, and in 1899 Abbey House School and the Grammar School were united under Mr Priestley as Head. In 1906 the 'new' grammar school was built in what had been the garden of the Abbey School, and in 1910 the school was recognised by the Board of Education as a public secondary school. Priestley's son, Raymond, was in Shackleton's expedition to Antarctica in 1907 to 1909, and later presented the school with a sledge used by Scott on his fatal 1911 expedition. The building was too small from the start, and there was a great lack of sports facilities, so in 1952 it moved to Southwick Park, where it stayed until the comprehensive school came into being in 1972. This was formed by amalgamating the Grammar School, Tewkesbury High School, Tewkesbury Secondary Boys' School and Elmbury Secondary Girls' School, and is known as Tewkesbury School. Abbey School was pulled down soon afterwards to make the Bell car park.

A more famous, but short-lived school was the Academy, a non-conformist school run by Samuel Jones, who moved his school from Gloucester to Tudor House in Tewkesbury's High Street in 1712. He seems to have been an earnest and scholarly man and several of his pupils had distinguished careers, notably Thomas Secker, Archbishop of Canterbury, and Samuel Butler, later Bishop of Durham. Unfortunately, dissenting schools were disapproved of by Queen Anne, a narrow and bigoted Anglican, and opinion in the country was inflamed against dissenters by Henry Sacheverell, a High Churchman and Tory favourite of the Queen. He wished non-conformists to be treated to the 'wholesome severities of hanging, burning, confiscation, imprisonment, loss of estate, liberty, and life'. As a prelude to this charitable programme he proposed closing down dissenting schools, but fortunately the Queen died before the Schism Bill could become law, and it lapsed. On the night of the coronation of George I in 1714 a rabble attacked the Academy, and injured the High Bailiff, who was trying to turn back the mob. Jones died in 1719 at the early age of 38, and the school moved to Nailsworth. A fascinating account of the curriculum is given in a letter written by Thomas Secker at the age of 18 to his patron, Isaac Watts, the hymn writer. At this time the Academy was still at Gloucester.

'Mr Jones then I take to be a man of real piety, great learning, and an agreeable temper; one who is very diligent in instructing all under his care, very well qualified to give instructions, and whose well-managed familiarity will always make him respected. He is very strict in keeping good order, and will effectively preserve his pupils from negligence and immorality . . . Our Logic, which we have read once over, is so contrived as to include all Heereboord, and the far greater part of Mr Locke's Essay, and the Art of Thinking. What Mr Jones dictated to us was but short, containing a clear and brief account of the matter, references to the places where it was more fully treated of, and remarks on, or explications of the authors cited, when need required. At our next lecture we gave an account both of what the author quoted and our tutor said, who commonly then gave us a larger explanation of it, and so proceeded to the next thing in order . . . I began to read Hebrew as soon as I came hither, and find myself able now to construe, and give some grammatical account of about twenty verses in the easier parts of the Bible after less than an hour's preparation. We read every day two verses a-piece in the Hebrew Bible which we turn into Greek . . . and this with Logic is our morning's work. Mr Jones also began, about three months ago, some critical lectures . . .The principal things contained in them are about the Antiquity of the Hebrew Language, Letters, Vowels, the Incorruption of the Scriptures, ancient Divisions of the Bible, an account of the Talmud, Masora, and Cabala . . . This is what we set about in the afternoon; which being finished we read a chapter in the Greek Testament, and after that Mathematics . . . We are obliged to rise at five of the clock every morning, and to speak Latin always, except when below stairs amongst the family. [Mr Jones] manifests so great an affection and tenderness for his pupils, as cannot but command love and respect.'

A Poor or Quaker School, later known as the British School, was opened on a plot of land at the upper end of Barton Street. The land was given by Nathaniel Hartland, a Quaker from Notcliffe House, Deerhurst; Charles Hanbury Tracy MP gave £300 and the school was opened in 1813. Twenty years later it had 190 pupils. In 1889 a separate infants' school was opened on the opposite side of Barton Street. In 1907 it was conveyed to the County Council and in 1964, as the Tewkesbury Junior County Primary School, it had 116 pupils. In 1906 a mixed Senior School was opened in Chance Street. In 1961 the girls moved to Elmbury County Secondary School in Ashchurch Road, and the boys stayed in Chance Street. Now the latter school is known as the Tewkesbury Church of England School, and is once more a primary school. The original British School is now a youth centre, and the building opposite houses a luncheon club for the elderly.

The National School was opened in 1817 on the site of the former Abbey bell tower, which had been used as a gaol. Trinity Church opened its Infant School in 1839, now a Masonic Hall. In 1911 the Abbey National School, as it was then called, opened a new building for boys in Oldbury Road behind North House, while the girls stayed on in the old building, which is now the Family Centre. Later the old National School was closed and is now a church hall for the Abbey Church; the junior girls joined the boys in the Oldbury Road building and the infants attended Trinity School.

Among a number of forward-looking actions performed by Archdeacon Hemming Robeson, Vicar of Tewkesbury, was the foundation in 1882 of the Tewkesbury High School for Girls, in Avonbrook House in Church Street. Originally a boarding school, by 1953 it was entirely a day school with 170 pupils. The building has great charm, with a garden that runs down to the Swilgate River, and an old mulberry tree, which nourished many generations of school silkworms, is still there. Perhaps it is related to the one which struggled to survive the activities in the Grammar School yard and those in the Abbey churchyard. In 1972 the school closed and the pupils went to Tewkesbury School, but happily the following year a preparatory school for boys was opened in the same building, with five pupils. The venture flourished, and in 1986 occupies four large houses in Church Street which have been restored and renovated. Girls are also admitted now, and there are places for 20 boarders, most weekly. There is a choir which sings Choral Evensong in the Abbey Church on weekdays during term time.

Choir of Abbey School, founded 1973, in Avonbrook and adjoining houses in Church Street (previously the High School for Girls), practising for evensong in the Abbey, 1984. (AS)

LEFT: Tewkesbury Presbyterian Academy, founded in Tudor House (now Tudor House Hotel) in 1712, became the home of John Moore. This c1840 engraving shows the Tudor gateway (still there), and facade, before Victorian additions. (JB) RIGHT: National School was opened in Church Street in 1817 on the site of the former Abbey bell tower, once a gaol. (RR) BELOW: The British School was built in Barton Street in 1813. In 1907 it was conveyed to the County, became the Junior County Primary School, and is now a youth centre. Drawing, 1891. (GRO)

ABOVE: A Senior Council School was opened in 1906 in Chance Street and is still in use as Tewkesbury Church of England School: a class c1930, with Head Teacher Mr Leatham. (KH) BELOW: Barton Street Infants School, opened opposite the British School in 1889: a class in 1920 with Head Teacher Miss Haffner in cap and gown, and assistant teacher, Miss Bedford. Jack Fletcher, the owner of the photograph is second to right in the second row. (JF)

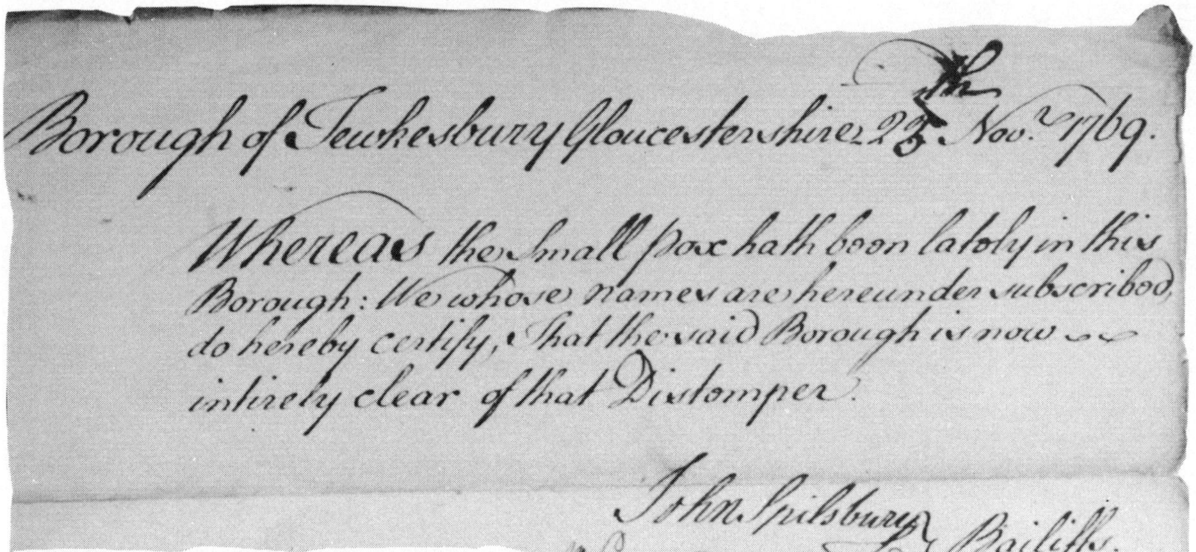

Borough of Tewkesbury Gloucestershire 23th Nov.r 1769.

Whereas the Small pox hath been lately in this Borough: We whose names are hereunder subscribed, do hereby certify, That the said Borough is now intirely clear of that Distemper.

John Spilsbury } Bailiffs.
Walter Dewynard }
John Pitt

Geo. Turberville } Justices.

~~Minister~~

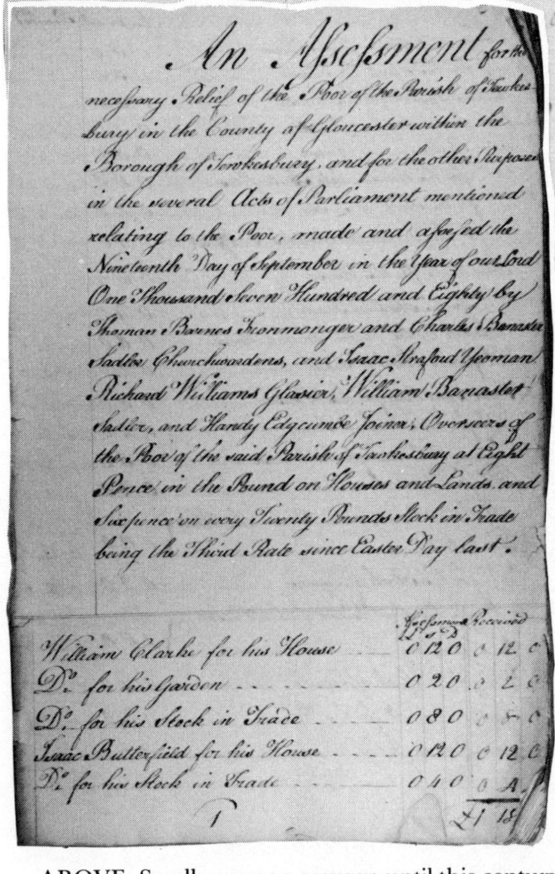

An Assessment for the necessary Relief of the Poor of the Parish of Tewkesbury in the County of Gloucester within the Borough of Tewkesbury, and for the other Purposes in the several Acts of Parliament mentioned relating to the Poor, made and assessed the Nineteenth Day of September in the Year of our Lord One Thousand Seven Hundred and Eighty by Thomas Barnes Ironmonger and Charles Banaster Sadler Churchwardens, and Isaac Strafford Yeoman Richard Williams Glasier, William Banaster Sadler, and Handy Edgcumbe Joiner, Overseers of the Poor of the said Parish of Tewkesbury at Eight Pence in the Pound on Houses and Lands and Sixpence on every Twenty Pounds Stock in Trade being the Third Rate since Easter Day last.

	Assessed	Received
William Clarke for his House	0 12 0	0 12 0
Do. for his Garden	0 2 0	0 2 0
Do. for his Stock in Trade	0 8 0	0 8 0
Isaac Butterfield for his House	0 12 0	0 12 0
Do. for his Stock in Trade	0 4 0	0 4
		£1 18

ABOVE: Smallpox was a scourge until this century. This certificate, signed by three bailiffs and a magistrate, affirms that Tewkesbury was free from infection. Mss, 1769. (GRO) LEFT: Assessment for Poor Law rate: featuring separate assessments for dwelling-house, garden and business, so William Clarke paid 12s on his house, 2s on his garden and 8s on his stock in trade. Mss, 1780. (GRO) RIGHT: Walton Spa pump room was built in 1835, but never fully used, through lack of funds. Demolished in 1961, Wellfield and Springfield Gardens were built around the site. (CB)

Second Blessing

'Look to your health; and if you have it, praise God, and value it next to a good conscience; for health is the second blessing we mortals are capable of.' (Izaak Walton)

The Black Death swept across England in 1348, killing a third of the population. There were 200 villages in Gloucestershire alone left deserted, such as the Ditchfords between Blockley and Todenham. The peasants grew more powerful because of the shortage of labour, and the average daily wage rose to 4d a day for a tiler and a carpenter, and ½d a day for an agricultural labourer.

The plague was endemic in Europe in the 16th century, and Tewkesbury suffered several outbreaks. From September 1591 for nearly two years it must have been like a ghost town. It started in Barton Street, infecting 150 houses and causing 560 deaths. Markets and fairs ceased, and no Tewkesburian was allowed to visit another market. The townspeople were kept alive mainly on gifts sent in from neighbouring estates. In another outbreak in 1598 40 died; there were more casualties in 1604 and 1609, and in 1624 a pesthouse was erected in Oldbury Field, where 20 died. Diptheria affected the town in 1729 when many died of 'sore throats and a fever'. Smallpox was the next scourge. In 1744 Elizabeth Martin of Overbury Court wrote to her uncle Nicholas Jackson that she was staying in London being prepared to be 'innocalated for the small pox', which in fact visited Tewkesbury in 1741 and 1758, and Bennett records that a considerable number died of smallpox and measles in the autumn of 1832.

In the 18th and early 19th centuries 'taking the waters' became a fashionable form of medication. The first Montpelier pump room was opened in Chelthenham in 1809 and attracted such patrons as Katherine Martin of Overbury, who made the journey there and back in a day once a week and put her good health down to this treatment. Therefore it must have seemed an opportunity for Tewkesbury townspeople to attract more wealth to the town when Nicholas Smithsend of Walton House discovered that the water in his well was similar to that of Cheltenham. William Dyde, the Tewkesbury printer and historian, in 1790 published the second edition of his *History and Antiquities of Tewkesbury*, and included with it a treatise entitled *Some Account of the Medicinal Water, near Tewkesbury; with Thoughts on the Use and Diseases of the Lymphatic Glands*, by James Johnstone MD. He states: 'Its resemblance in taste, and other appearances to the Cheltenham Water, strikes everyone who makes the comparison. Its operation on the Body, also, is exactly the same, a Pint or more, acts as a gentle Laxative and Diuretic: And it occasions a slight giddiness in some persons, in others a sort of heavy pain in the head'. Johnstone then described how he analysed the water and found it much the same as Cheltenham's. He also details the effects on the body with medical frankness! Walton Spa failed to develop, however. It was too near Cheltenham, and a lot of money was essential if the assembly rooms and ballroom needed, to supplement medical treatment with fashionable social intercourse, were to be built. Not only was the money not forthcoming, but later the owners of Cheltenham Spa bought the property to prevent its development. A little pumproom, built about 1835 on the north side of the Tewkesbury road on the site of an earlier spa, was never fully used, and was demolished in 1961 to make room for Springfield and Wellfield Gardens.

Alarmed by news that cholera was devastating London, the townspeople of Tewkesbury held a meeting in the Town Hall on 3 March 1882, and decided to divide the town into sections under 32 superintendents, with a view to visiting every alley and court to see that all slaughterhouse refuse was cleared out and the cottages whitewashed. Seven medical men were appointed, each one in charge of a district. On 24 July the pestilence struck. The first case was in Barton Street, and from there it spread. Every night fires were lit in the alleys, barrels of pitch were burned, and chloride of lime given to house occupiers to wash down their cottages. All bedding and clothes belonging to the victims and their families were burned. Vagrants were allowed to stay only one night in Tewkesbury. Part of the Workhouse garden was used as a burial ground. The Government gave £20 a week towards helping the afflicted families. £200 was collected locally for soup and beef for the destitute. 2,300 people received one pint of soup and ¼lb of beef at least twice weekly. This cost £28 a week, so each meal appears to have amounted to 1½d per head. A house in the Oldbury was made into a hospital, and five tenements in Mount Pleasant between Barton and Chance Streets were made into a refuge for the families of cholera victims. 13 October was held as thanksgiving day for the termination of the visitation. 76 had died and 82 recovered. But in 1848 the disease returned, killing 54 victims, but this time the illness was mostly in the St Mary's Lane and Wilkes Alley areas, and in the Workhouse. The treatment appeared to be external heat, opium and stimulants.

The Poor Board Union claimed that the dead in 1832 were chiefly from the 'destitute, filthy and the dissolute', and analysed them as follows: 27 stocking makers; 14 labourers; four washerwomen and watermen; three hay trussers and nurses; two tailors, nailers, shoebinders, prostitutes and bricklayers; and one seamstress, hatter, chimney sweep, fortune-teller, ropemaker, hostler, carpenter, carrier, sawyer, fruit seller and a 'female cottager'. This hardly bears out the Poor Board's claim.

Following the second epidemic, Thomas Webster Rammell was sent to Tewkesbury in 1850 by the Board of Health at the town's invitation, to enquire into its sewerage, drainage, water supply and sanitary conditions. The report makes horrifying reading. The drains which had been built from 1824 to 1845 had to receive most of the slops of the town, since there were few water closets and only two public privies. Five drains discharged into the Avon and three into the Swilgate. In summer the Swilgate was a 'mass of foetid and putrifying matter which could be smelt 100 yards away'. Privy soil was received in brick vaults which leaked and were left untouched for as long as seven years. The poor used the Avon for cleaning, washing and cooking. Witnesses described how sewage would float into kettles and pots used for cooking. Only the better houses had wells. Most lanes and alleys had a pump, but these were often out of order for as long as seven years. Rammell estimated that there were 38 lanes, courts and alleys off the High Street, 37 off Barton Street, the same number off Church Street and 12 off the Oldbury: 124 in all and mostly without privies and drains!

Lodging houses emptied their slops into the two rivers or threw them into the lanes. Overcrowding was appalling. A three roomed house in St Mary's Lane belonging to Ragman Jack housed ten, plus his donkey in the kitchen. A lodging house in Smith's Lane, with four rooms including the kitchen, housed a family of nine and about seven lodgers. The family slept in one room: the parents and the eldest daughter in one bed, five small children in another bed and the eldest son on the floor.

The Abbey Church burial ground was full and the others unsuitable, being in crowded areas. Rammell found the death rate in Tewkesbury high: one death to every 35.5 inhabitants. The rate for Gloucestershire was 45.8. He concluded that what was needed was proper drainage, better privy accommodation, a supply of pure water, improved dwelling house ventilation and a proper burial ground.

Dr Frederick J. Prior, Medical Officer to the Poor Board Union from 1842 to 1850, disagreed. 'I attribute this excess of fever . . . to the inferior diet, to the diet of poorer classes. I have expressed the opinion before, and I repeat it now, that measures insuring better drainage and water-supply will not much alter the character of the diseases of the town'. He added, however, that privies would 'tend to the greater decency and morality of the poor'.

It is understandable that Dr Prior should be on the defensive because, under his administration, the typical pauper lodging was quite incredibly overcrowded. A house in Wilkes Alley, off the High Street, housed up to 30 people of both sexes for the night, in an attic with a roof sloping from six feet to four feet high, 12 feet wide and 15 feet long. No wonder the young John Halifax preferred to sleep under the stars. The homeless received 3d a night: 2d for their lodging and 1d for their food. In 1848 between 300 and 350 were receiving aid at any one time, and about 80 vagrants passed through Tewkesbury every week.

In a County Council survey published about 1940, the sewage situation was still not satisfactory in Tewkesbury. In times of flood, sewage works were completely submerged, and crude sewage passed into the Severn, about 1,660 yards from the Gloucester and Cheltenham Water Board's intake for water. After the war, new sewage works were built off Lower Lode Lane. The present graveyard south of the town was opened in 1856.

Amusing light is thrown on domestic medical remedies in use a century before Rammell in a letter from Charles Hancock, MP for Tewkesbury, to his aunt, Mrs Dowdeswell, in 1714. 'Dear Aunt, The good effect of ye snail water you were pleased to send me had on my servant Dirk emboldend me to become your petitioner for Mr Bishop's wife who is a very weak and languishing condition of a consumption'.

Lack of housing plagued Tewkesbury until about 20 years ago. In John Moore's time an effort was being made to move people from the crowded alleys into a council estate at Priors Park, but many landlords resisted the pressure, and some tenants did not want to leave their homes. The account in *Portrait of Elmbury* of Old Sal and Double Alley differs little from Bennett's account of two old women in Double Alley written 100 years earlier. The women hated each other, yet shared not only their one-room lodging but their bed. The alleys were gradually cleared and are now chiefly passages between buildings, except where cottages have been converted into attractive housing with modern amenities.

Tewkesbury Voluntary Hospital was opened in 1865 in the Oldbury. A prospective patient had to be recommended by a subscriber who, for one guinea a year, could nominate two patients, although only one could be admitted at a time. The would-be patient then reported to the hospital between 11am and 12 noon on a Thursday. Provided the patient was not three months or more pregnant, suffering from an incurable or infectious disease, or from chronic insanity, he or she would be allowed to stay. There was a matron in charge, and a nurse who was paid 8s a week. By 1910 it had 26 beds and the Hospital was placed under a joint hospital board of Tewkesbury Borough and Tewkesbury Rural District Councils. The hospital in Barton Street was opened in 1934 with 22 beds, largely through money raised by a town lottery, and the Oldbury Road building became the Borough Council Offices. Holm Hospital, built as a workhouse in 1796, became first an isolation hospital and later a hospital for the chronic sick. It was closed in 1979 and is at present awaiting conversion into old people's homes. Since 1948 Tredington Hospital has been used firstly for infectious cases and latterly for geriatric patients. The old building in the Oldbury was used by the Borough Council staff until about 1974, when they moved into their new offices in Tewkesbury Park.

Private charities and public measures to deal with the poor have gone hand in hand in Tewkesbury. In 1616 a Beadle of Beggars was appointed to keep vagrants out of the town. In 1630 it was estimated that there were about 500 poor in Tewkesbury. The population was not known, but there were about 2,000 communicants. Lord Coventry gave £200 to set the poor to work. In 1756 a workhouse was set up at Millbank in a house given by Sir William Strachan, and in 1792 an Act of Parliament enabled Tewkesbury to establish Guardians of the Poor with nine directors, and a new workhouse was established in 1796 on the site of Holme Castle. This was later Holm Hospital, a grim looking building, now shortly to be redeveloped. The inmates of the Workhouse worked at knitting stockings and at shoemaking in the early 19th century, but their earnings were only £119 in 1803 compared with expenses of £2,000. In that year there were 83 residents, 93 received regular relief, and 302 occasional relief. In 1833, 76 of the relief recipients died of cholera. In 1835 Tewkesbury Poor Law Union was formed, which covered 23 parishes, and they became responsible for the workhouse.

Charities in Tewkesbury date back to at least mediaeval times, because the Abbot was obliged to maintain 13 almsmen in the town and parish and these were known as the founder's almsmen, and later as Queen Mary's almsmen because of her patronage. Giles Geast, who was a wealthy mercer, gave houses and gardens to trustees, who were to distribute the rents to the poor and be accountable to the town bailiffs. His will was dated 1558, and in 1564 John Bartlett bought an account book from London (price 1s 6d) in which are entered all the accounts of the charity from 1564 to 1891. Bound in red calf with a strap and buckle, it is known as the Feoffee Book. In the margins are entered national and local events, and the town's historians have used it as a source book. It records when the 'great armada of Spain' was 'by the great mercy of God overthrown', and that in 1634 many died in an exceptionally heavy snow fall in Tewkesbury. The first record of the High Street having been paved was noted in 1736, and 1776 saw the 'greatest crop of cider and perry that has been known for years'. The distribution of the money took the form of a distribution of sixpennies, which became known as 'the battle of the running sixpences'. On the appointed day, the poor of Tewkesbury gathered to receive a sixpence, but villagers from outside Tewkesbury also flocked in, and those who had already received a sixpence pushed back into the crowd to get another. In the 18th century lists were drawn up by the bailiffs, magistrates and trustees and the money was distributed in an orderly manner. Later still, meat, blankets, coal or groceries were substituted for money. At the end of the 19th century the 32 principal charities were gathered together and are known as Tewkesbury Consolidated Charities. Many date from the early 19th century. Between 1812 and 1826 the SPCK, the Church Missionary Society, the Bible Society and the Religious Tract Society were all set up to educate Tewkesburians and others in the Christian faith. In 1832, under the terms of the Lying-In Charity, 100 women received food, clothes and blankets from a fund of £60 7s 6d. Blankets for the Poor and a District Visiting Society were also established. In 1835 a Reward Bank 'to encourage the industrious poor of Tewkesbury in the habit of saving part of their weekly earnings' was established by 'patriotic and influential ladies' of Tewkesbury. To every 1s saved, not less than 3d was added at the end of the year from a subscription fund, the money to be spent on clothes, bedding, furniture and so on. In 1835 deposits equalled £39 7s 0d and subscriptions £44 13s 6d. In 1815 a Public Dispensary was established and, under the will of Charles William Grove, a trust was left for the sick poor which lasted up to the formation of the National Health Service. The Baptist Church also had numerous charities, including cottages for the poor of the congregation and money for the Sunday School.

During 1840, and for a number of years into this century, coal charities were formed. In a typical year coal was bought in bulk and sold at half price to those whose wages were below 14s a week. Each family received one hundred weight weekly from December to March, which was enough to maintain one fire if carefully husbanded, and in the case of illness an extra half hundred weight was supplied. 825 poor families were helped in this way. In some years, sixpenny tickets for meat, bread and potatoes were given out as well.

In 1651 Edward Richardson left £60 to the Corporation for the poor, and with this seven houses were purchased in Gander Lane. These were repaired by the town in 1739, and in 1965 demolished and replaced by four modern almshouses, attractively designed. In 1674 Francis Russell gave a range of buildings north of the Abbey Church, with land, for the use of 10 poor widows aged 50 or over. They were rebuilt in 1831 with a gothic, ashlar front, and gables over the porches, and in 1957 improved internally and the number of occupants reduced to six. In 1880 Samuel Barnes erected some almshouses in the Oldbury Field. 'The inmates are subject to proper regulations, and are to attend divine service at the parish chuch twice every Sunday', wrote Bennett approvingly. By 1955 the houses were delapidated and were pulled down. In 1890 Charles William Grove built and endowed four almshouses in Cotteswold Road which are still in use.

DIETARY LIST
of the
TEWKESBURY RURAL HOSPITAL

ORDINARY WEEKLY ALLOWANCE, ADULT

Meat — Male 3lb; Female 2lb.

Sugar, ½lb; Butter, 4 to 6 ounces.

Milk, Rice Pudding, Cocoa, Bread, and Potatoes, at discretion of the Nurse. Extra diet, with Wine, Beer, and Spirits, only allowed by special order of the Medical Attendant.

TIMES OF MEALS

Breakfast at 8, Dinner at 12, Tea at 5, Supper at 8.30.

The Patients' Friends will only be admitted between 3 and 5 in the afternoon, unless they have special permission.

LEFT: Although surrounded by water, Tewkesbury suffered from a shortage of piped supplies until after World War II: the pump by Abel Fletcher's Mill and the cottages overlooking Mill Avon, c1935. (CB) RIGHT: An ambulance carriage presented to Tewkesbury Rural Hospital, now Graham Court, by Mrs Devereux on behalf of the Hospital Ball Committee: acting honorary surgeon was Dr W. C. Devereux of North House. Photograph, 1908. (GE GCL)

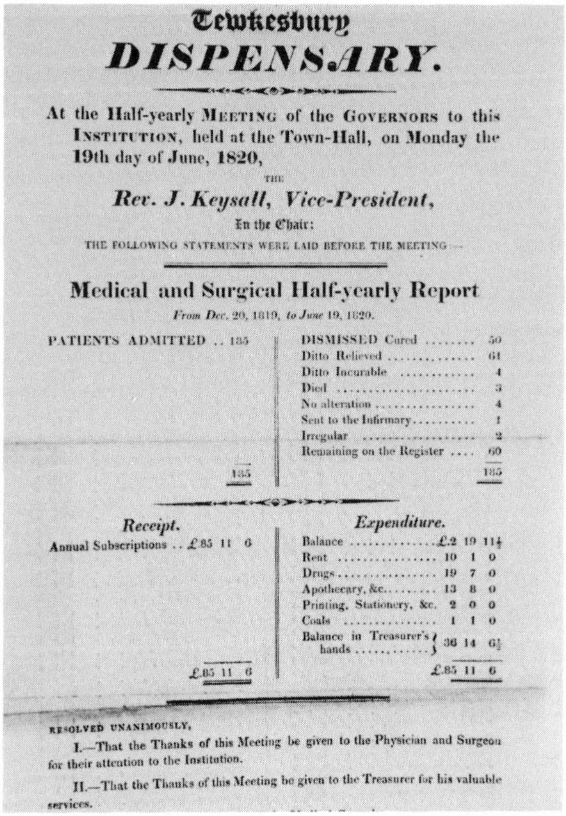

Tewkesbury

DISPENSARY.

At the Half-yearly Meeting of the Governors to this Institution, held at the Town-Hall, on Monday the 19th day of June, 1820,

THE

Rev. J. Keysall, Vice-President,

In the Chair:

THE FOLLOWING STATEMENTS WERE LAID BEFORE THE MEETING:—

Medical and Surgical Half-yearly Report

From Dec. 20, 1819, to June 19, 1820.

PATIENTS ADMITTED ..	185	DISMISSED Cured	50
		Ditto Relieved	61
		Ditto Incurable	4
		Died	3
		No alteration	4
		Sent to the Infirmary..........	1
		Irregular	2
		Remaining on the Register	60
	185		185

Receipt.		Expenditure.	
Annual Subscriptions ..	£85 11 6	Balance	£2 19 11½
		Rent	10 1 0
		Drugs	19 7 0
		Apothecary, &c.........	13 8 0
		Printing, Stationery, &c.	2 0 0
		Coals	1 1 0
		Balance in Treasurer's hands	36 14 6½
	£85 11 6		£85 11 6

RESOLVED UNANIMOUSLY,

I.—That the Thanks of this Meeting be given to the Physician and Surgeon for their attention to the Institution.

II.—That the Thanks of this Meeting be given to the Treasurer for his valuable services.

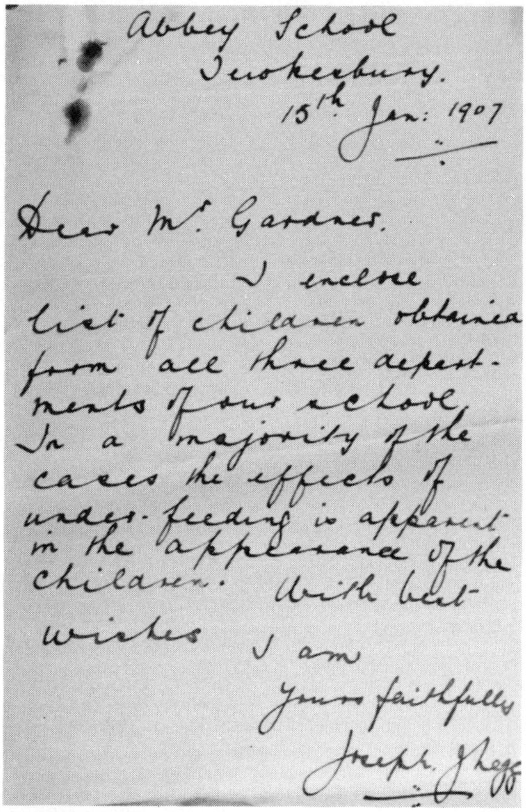

Abbey School
Tewkesbury.
15th Jan: 1907

Dear Mr. Gardner.

I enclose list of children obtained from all three departments of our school. In a majority of the cases the effects of under-feeding is apparent in the appearance of the children. With best wishes

I am
Yours faithfully
Joseph J. Legge

LEFT: Half yearly report of a Public Dispensary established in 1815 for the relief of the sick poor and maintained by charity. Mss, 1820. (GCL) RIGHT: Letters from head teachers asking for free breakfasts for the children include this one from Joseph Legge, Headmaster of Abbey School. Mss, 1907. (GRO) BELOW: 17th century almshouses in Gander Lane, left by Edward Richardson for the poor, were demolished in 1965 and replaced by four modern almshouses. Photograph, c1960. (GRO)

The Lord's Power Came Over Them

Tewkesbury had a large number of Dissenters in 1676 — about 75% of the population. After that it dropped dramatically to 7% in 1735, probably as a result of two pieces of cruel and oppressive legislation. The first was the Act of Uniformity of 1662, which insisted that all churches should use the revised church liturgy, and the second was the Conventicle Act, which imposed fines, imprisonment or transportation on those attending non-conformist services. It took great courage to be a Baptist or a Quaker in those days, and it is believed that members of the Baptist Church received their baptism secretly at night in the Mill Avon. Quakers were punished by JPs for refusing to pay their church tithes and army tax. In 1689 an Act of Toleration was passed and Dissenters could register their own house of worship.

In 1655 George Fox, the founder of the Religious Society of Friends, visited Tewkesbury. 'And at night', he wrote in his journal, 'I had a great meeting and there came in their priest [probably Robert Eaton] with a great deal of rabble and rude people, and the priest boasted he would see whether he or I should have the victory. And I turned the people to the divine Light . . . And the priest began to rage against the Light and denied it, and so went away . . . and . . . left his rude company amongst us. But the Lord's power came over them, though mischief was in their hearts.'

In 1670 three houses in St Mary's Lane were used as a Friends' Meeting House, with an adjacent burial ground, and in 1750 there were 50 Quakers in Tewkesbury. In 1804 they built a Meeting House in Barton Street with a burial ground, part of which can still be seen from Orchard Court. The old burial ground was made into a little garden by the Girl Guides of Tewkesbury to celebrate the Jubilee in 1977. But Quakerism declined. In 1853 the Meeting House was let as a school; in 1861 it was sold and became a 'music hall', that is, a concert hall, and today it is incorporated into the George Watson Memorial Hall.

The Old Baptist Chapel, off Church Street, is one of the most famous non-conformist places of worship in the country. The registers of Baptists in Tewkesbury date from 1623, only 20 years after the Baptist movement first spread into England. In 1690 a chapel was formed by converting three mediaeval cottages, which in turn had originally been a large timber-framed hall-house. It had a double-storey centre bay and a gallery at either end. In 1720 a minister's room was provided in the west gallery, which was then cut off from the rest of the building. Graffiti on the wall reads 'R. Yarnell 1795'. William and Richard Yarnall, chairmakers, later gave their name to the alley off Barton Street. The communion table was made in the 17th century and the baptistry and pulpit 100 years later. In 1805 the Baptist Church off Barton Street was opened; in 1985 it was closed for the area to be reconstructed. The Tewkesbury Baptists have always been mindful of the poor, and most of the original Chapel was converted back to two cottages and the rents given to the needy of the congregation. In 1976 Tewkesbury Borough Council acquired the whole of the Court, apart from the burial ground, where the first minister, Eleazer Herring lies, and it has been restored to what it is believed to have looked like in 1720.

When George Whitefield, one of the great founders of Methodism, preached in Tewkesbury in 1739, the bailiffs tried to stop him but, finding they had no warrants, he sent them away and preached to a congregation of 3,000 in a field. Next day he returned again with a company of 120 horsemen and preached to 6,000. Five years later, and many times between 1744 and 1790, John Wesley also preached in Tewkesbury, and in 1777 a Methodist meeting house was opened in Tolsey Lane. This proved too small, and a new one was opened in 1814. By 1851 this too had been out-grown, and in 1878 a new Wesleyan Church with a gothic stone front was built at the Cross on the site of the old Market Hall — it is still in use. The old Chapel was used as the headquarters of the YMCA in 1909, and later by the local scouts, and in 1964 it was being used as a Masonic temple. Now it is the Tewkesbury Auction Sales.

Three houses in Tewkesbury were licensed for Congregational worship in 1672; an Independent Chapel was founded about 1690, a Presbyterian Meeting in 1707 and, fifty years later, there were said to be about 100 Presbyterians and Independents in the town. Philip Doddridge, author of many hymns including *Hark the glad sound* and *Ye servants of the Lord* married Mercy Maris from Upton-on-Severn and, after her husband's death in 1751, Mercy and her family moved to Tewkesbury and were buried in the Independent Chapel at the upper end of Barton Street. In 1964 it was known as the Congregational Church. It now belongs to the Jehovah's Witness Church.

There seem to have been few Roman Catholics in Tewkesbury until the last 120 years or so. One or two were recorded in 1676, 1715 and 1723. Although in the early 19th century the townspeople of Tewkesbury twice petitioned against the lifting of the remaining restrictions on Roman Catholics, such as the right to stand for Parliament and to hold civil office, the passing of the Catholic Relief Act in 1829 took place without local disturbance. The Chapel of St Joseph was built at the Mythe in 1870 by the Marquis de Lys of Mythe House. It is a low red brick building incorporating a priest's house, and is in part a conversion of a coach house. The present Church was opened in Chance Street in 1978 and was converted from a telephone exchange built in 1938.

It is interesting to see what 'going to Sunday School' entailed in the early 19th century. The Baptist Church published a centenary history of their Sunday School in 1909, which shows great devotion to education on the part of both children and teachers. From 9am to 10.30am reading and writing were taught, with a break for hymn singing. 10.30am to noon was devoted to divine worship. After an hour's break, school re-assembled until 5pm to repeat texts, learn and repeat the catechism and listen to addresses on religion. Teachers were fined 1s for non-attendance and 6d for unpunctuality. Children were fined from 1d to 3d for absence, unpunctuality, lying, swearing or being dirty. Daniel Trotman was minister for 40 years from 1803; his son Ebenezer designed Holy Trinity.

Holy Trinity was built in 1837 and a new parish was formed in 1893. It is a good example of the Victorian gothic style, with a two-tiered gallery. It was designed to provide extra seating accommodation for Anglican Tewkesburians, when the population of the town had risen to 5,780 and the Abbey Church could seat only 1,200, mostly in rented pews. It was agreed that Holy Trinity should retain at least half its seating accommodation as free sittings.

OPPOSITE ABOVE: An indictment by the Magistrates of Tewkesbury against Francis Wells, Vicar of Tewkesbury, in 1678, when Wells accused Charles II in a sermon of 'Adultery fornication and whoredom . . . to ye contempt and disgrace of yr kings most excellent Majexty wch hath given great offence to ye magistrates of Tewkesbury and is much discussed of in ye Country who wondered at the folly of you Mr Wells Vicar of Tewkesbury'. (Signed). Henry Dobbins. Joseph Smith. ???? Knight. (GDR) BELOW: Centenary celebrations for Holy Trinity: clergy, choir and helpers. Left to right, back row: E. L. Green, J. J. Whiteley, L. J. Wright, C. Mew, A. Mew, W. Cromey (verger). Second row: B. Spencer, W. Aldridge, Miss Portmen, C. Sweet, Mrs Copner, N. Statham, L. L. Green, L. T. Coop, Miss Holbrook, L. Newbury. Third row: Choristers W. Long, H. Moore, E. Moore, E. Cudmore (Organist), Rev C. Cooper (Vicar), Choristers Chambers, Vosper, K. Parsons. In front: Choristers Heath, Hale, C. Langley, W. Pearson. Photograph, 1937. (TR TL)

Henry Dobbins
Joseph Smith
Joseph Knight

LEFT: Moses Goodere was a Tewkesbury Quaker warmly in favour of building a workhouse for 'the better relief and employment of the poor' but the poor felt they were being exploited and his windows were broken by an angry mob more than once. He died in 1838, aged 86. (JB) RIGHT: A small Ebenezer Methodist Chapel at Isabel's Elm, Aston Cross, built in 1846, and now empty. (RR) BELOW LEFT: Thomas Collins JP, five times Mayor of Tewkesbury. (GRO) RIGHT: Interior of the Old Baptist Chapel 1920. In 1976 Tewkesbury Borough Council restored the chapel. (GRO)

The Punishment and the Crime

One of the earliest records we have of any crime connected with Tewkesbury is in the reign of Henry VI, when the inhabitants of Tewkesbury complained that foresters from the Forest of Dean were pillaging their boats on the way to Bristol, and even murdering their sailors. Under an Act of Parliament the Tewkesburians brought an action of debt against the Commonality of the Forest of Dean and the Hundreds of Bledisloe and Westbury, for 'robberies, oppressions and wrongs', demanding compensation.

Tewkesbury had its own gaol as far back as 1547, in a manor barn in Barton Street, which was previously a stable and a grange for the King's horses. In 1582 the Abbey belltower was turned into a prison, and it remained the town gaol until the National School was built on the site in 1817. A new gaol was opened in Bredon Road and a treadmill introduced there in 1828. Sarah Fletcher, who died in 1904, remembered that it was always the same coach which conveyed prisoners for transportation: 'Paul Pry', a four-in-hand. The prisoners were removed from the gaol and chained to the coach before driving off. In 1832 there were 82 people committed, but in 1841 there were only 11 inmates, so the Tewkesbury Corporation asked that Tewkesbury malefactors should be incarcerated in Gloucester gaol. A prolonged argument developed with Gloucester Sessions about the fee for maintaining Tewkesbury prisoners, Gloucester asking 2s 6d a day and Tewkesbury claiming that the cost was only 1s 6d. Gloucester countered with an offer to settle at 2s and a deal was finally struck in 1854. The old gaol was used as a police station and enlarged in 1882. The new police station in Barton Street was opened in 1966 and the old one is now a dental surgery.

Under the Municipal Corporation Act of 1835, Tewkesbury was obliged to maintain a police force, which in 1839 was established in the Town Hall. By 1850 it consisted of one inspector and four constables. In 1869 it merged with the county constabulary and moved to the prison in Bredon Road. The 'Instructions' current in 1840 state that the constables must arrest these offenders: prostitutes soliciting in public, beggars, tramps, fraudulent charity collectors, anyone betting in public and vandals damaging street lamps. One assumes that the more serious crimes incurred arrest as a matter of course.

Distress obviously led to crime, and there was plenty of distress. In 1800 there was a poor harvest, and bread was 3s a loaf (about three days' wages for an agricultural worker). In *John Halifax, Gentleman*, the author describes the fury of the rioting workers when the mill owner, Abel Fletcher, throws a bag of wheat into the Avon rather than yield to their demand for cheaper flour. When finally given food 'they fell to it like wild beasts'. Fletcher has no protection from the constabulary because he is a Quaker and even as late as that 'the law don't help Quakers'. Similar riots had been organised by women in 1795. In 1825 financial speculations at the end of the Napoleonic Wars led to bankruptcy and poverty, and many of the desperate unemployed became highwaymen.

In 1805 effigies of James Hawkins, tax-inspector, and William Holland, surveyor, were drawn through the streets. William Martin, wine merchant, and three labourers were summoned and, while the labourers received sentences ranging from nine to 12 months in gaol, Martin, defended by no less a lawyer than Thomas Erskine, later Lord Chancellor, got off completely. Farm wages were reduced from an already low 9s a week to 6s, causing a riot of 300 people in Overbury. In 1814 James Kingsbury, a hosier, received a letter threatening him with murder if he did not raise the wages of his stocking-makers. His unfortunate employees were blackmailed into giving £10, to increase a reward for apprehending the writer of the letter to £60, but no more was heard of the matter. In 1831 a 'vast concourse of the lowest order of society' pelted the members of the Borough Council with mud, and burst into the Swan Hotel, laid for a municipal dinner, and stole some silver. The 14th Light Dragoons were sent for from Gloucester, but the riots appeared to be merely an expression of anger against the anti-reformers, and no one seems to have been hurt.

Punishments were apparently more severe for those who stole property than for those who murdered unless, presumably, the victim was a member of the upper classes. On the same day in 1834 that Thomas Hawkley was sentenced to seven years' transportation for stealing a bushel of flour and a tin can, Samuel Meadows, for 'feloniously slaying' James Thomas, received merely seven days' imprisonment. Thomas Gaskins, aged 26, was executed for setting fire to a hayrick at Deerhurst Walton. James Wood, aged 17, was sentenced to transportation on each count for stealing a lock saw and pick-lock keys, and Samuel Lewis was transported for seven years for cutting off and stealing hair from the manes and tails of a colt and gelding. Poaching was ruthlessly punished and game-keepers deeply hated. A man who 'ill-treated' two game-keepers was transported for life. In the year 1834, out of 64 convictions, 29 were for stealing or receiving, 10 for wife-battering, six for keeping a disorderly house or being a 'lewd woman', four for ignoring bastardy orders and for breaking work contracts, and three for poaching, for deserting a family and for refractory behaviour, and one for deserting the army and for re-entering the parish without a certificate. William Hale, a nailer, was transported for life at the age of 33 for stealing £39 from the club box of the New Unity Friendly Society, which met in the Duke of York's, Barton Street. He was a steward at the time.

A similar crime to that of William Hale was committed by the secretary and treasurer of the Chartist Movement in Tewkesbury. This, plus the fact that another member kept a temperance hotel, may have led to lack of support for the Chartists in Tewkesbury. Their demands seem reasonable to us: universal adult male suffrage, secret ballots and the abolition of the property qualifications, but Bennett thought otherwise. When a young Chartist, William Morris Moore, died in the workhouse in 1841 refuting his views, Bennett attributed his earlier errors to a stay in France, which had led to his imbibing the 'fevered notions of "liberty and equality" '.

OPPOSITE LEFT: Tewkesbury's first gaol was the Abbey bell tower. A new gaol was opened in Bredon Road (later the police station) in 1816 and the bell tower pulled down and replaced by the National School. Engraving, 1820. (CAGM) RIGHT: Expenses of the new gaol 1817: Bread was the principal food, each prisoner eating 1½lb daily; no alcohol was allowed, the prisoners drinking milk, buttermilk, whey and occasionally tea or coffee. They were employed at sewing and shoe-making, and a treadmill was introduced in 1828. (GRO) BELOW: Anti-death penalty petition 1819. (GCL)

Borough of Tewkesbury.

A STATEMENT

OF THE

EXPENCES OF THE GAOL,

FOR THE YEAR 1817.

FOOD.

	£	s	d	£	s	d
Bread	£.52	14	11			
Meat	3	3	3			
Cheese	0	11	2			
Oatmeal	1	10	9			
Rice	0	4	3			
Potatoes	0	14	3			
Peas	0	5	8			
Onions	0	0	6			
Salt	0	6	9			
Ginger	0	0	10			
Pepper	0	2	9			
				59	15	1

SALARIES, &c.

	£	s	d	£	s	d
To Thomas Ricketts, Master of the House of Correction and Governor of the Penitentiary House	20	0	0			
.. Ann Ricketts, Matron	10	0	0			
.. Ditto, Laundress	5	0	0			
.. Widow Surman, for shaving Prisoners and cutting their Hair,—three-quarters' Salary	0	19	6			
Gaol Fees	8	1	0			
Weekly Pence to the Prisoners	5	6	8			
				49	7	2

CLOTHING and COALS.

	£	s	d	£	s	d
Three new Prison Dresses	5	8	0			
Six pair of Wooden Shoes	1	9	6			
Sundry Wearing Apparel	3	14	4			
Coals, and Halling ditto	3	18	2			
				14	10	0

SUNDRIES.

	£	s	d	£	s	d
Prison Register, Treasurer's Account Book, and other Stationery	4	17	0			
Brushes and Mops	1	7	2			
Soap	0	10	6			
New Winding Wheel, with Runners, &c.	0	10	6			
Frame Rent, Needles, Oil, &c. &c.	0	15	9			
Sweeping Chimnies	0	0	6			
Itch Ointment	0	2	0			
Milk and other necessaries for Jane Cothers's infant child	1	6	10			
Ditto for Sarah Webb, a child	0	5	0			
				9	15	3
				133	7	6
To Prisoner's Earnings				4	17	6
				£.128	10	0

23

TO THE WORSHIPFUL THE

BAILIFFS

OF THE

Borough of Tewkesbury.

OBSERVING with the utmost satisfaction that a Committee has been appointed by the House of Commons to consider that part of our **PENAL LAWS** which relates to the Punishment of **DEATH**, and conceiving that Offences comparatively small, should not be visited with the same awful Sentence as is affixed to the most atrocious Crimes,---We, the undersigned, do hereby request that you will convene an early **MEETING** of the **INHABITANTS** of this Borough, for the purpose of taking into consideration the propriety of **PETITIONING** the Two **HOUSES** of **PARLIAMENT** to revise the **CRIMINAL STATUTES** of the United Kingdom; and to take such measures as their wisdom may deem meet to abolish the Punishment of Death in all cases where inferior Punishments are applicable, and in fact usually applied.

Tewkesbury, April 30, 1819.

CHARLES WHITE. H. H. FRYER.
WILLIAM PROSSER. CHARLES BANASTER.

ABOVE: The charter granted by William III in 1698. (TM) LEFT: The Town Hall, built by Sir William Codrington MP in 1788 and given to the Corporation, before the paved area in front was enclosed. This was intended for pitching corn, but when, in 1839, the Town Hall was enlarged to include a police station, cells and fire station the outside was made flush with the other buildings in the street. (JB) RIGHT: Richard B. Martin of Martin's Bank, MP for Tewkesbury. Photograph from the supplement to *The City*, 1882. (GRO)

He that would Govern others

The government of Tewkesbury during the Middle Ages was carried out chiefly by the Lord of the Manor, who owned all the Hundred of Tewkesbury, but the Abbot also exercised privileges. The inhabitants of the town attended the Tewkesbury Borough Court, which had view of frankpledge (that is, the male member of the family who paid tithe was responsible for all other members). The court covered items such as trespass, debt and offensive trading, and appointed two bailiffs, two constables, two serjeants, two meat inspectors and two ale conners. The Abbot's court was in Barton Street near his farm, or barton, and he had a prison there. Privileges were granted by William and Robert FitzHamon, Earls of Gloucester, and confirmed by charter in 1314 and 1337. These covered tenure, trading and courts. The burgesses were entitled to buy and sell property, rent, trade, hold courts, pass property on to their heirs, were free of 'death duty' payment to the lord and were free from tolls. They could exclude strangers from becoming burgesses and they held their own court and appointed officers. There were dues to be paid to the lord: market tolls, and fustale and stallage to allow them to erect stalls at market time.

In 1575 the Crown gave the Borough of Tewkesbury its first charter of incorporation, which was confirmed in 1605. The Charter of 1610 allowed Tewkesbury to elect 24 principal burgesses, 24 assistant burgesses, six justices and to return two Members of Parliament. In 1868 the number of Members was reduced to one, and in 1885 the Borough was merged for Parliamentary purposes into the Tewkesbury division. It is now part of the Cirencester and Tewkesbury division. During the Civil War the charter was lost, and Richard Dowdeswell MP obtained a new one at considerable expense to the inhabitants of Tewkesbury. Confusion continued, however, until in 1698 William III granted a new charter. It stated that the charter extended over the whole hundred and liberty of Tewkesbury from Ashton-under-Hill in the north to Barrow and Boddington in the south, and from Forthampton in the east to Bourton-on-the-Hill in the west.

By 1734 a great deal of pomp was obviously indulged in by the Corporation, since draft court rolls list a lord high steward, an under-steward, two bailiffs, two bailiffs-elect, a deputy recorder, principal burgesses, assistant principal burgesses, four constables, bailiff of the hundred, two serjeants-at-mace, keeper of the gaol, beadle and water bailiff. There was also a town clerk, chamberlain and coroner, and later a town cryer.

Until the early 19th century, the Corporation's income came chiefly from tolls, amounting to about £200 a year, raised by charging rent for storing grain in the market warehouses from one market day to the next. Then the custom arose of selling corn by sample, and the warehouses were not needed, so why should the farmers pay? Meetings were held and resolutions passed on both sides. In June 1818 the Corporation took the matter to court and lost. It was left with a debt of about £6,000 and an income of £20! In October 1813 the Corporation threatened to surrender the charter rather than give up its claim to the toll; a public meeting of farmers with John Martin MP in the chair reiterated its determination to resist, and the Corporation gave in. John Edmund Dowdeswell MP and Recorder, advanced a loan of £2,000 and a settlement was made. In 1830 the

Corporation could not afford to pay the Town Clerk his salary of £10 a year. Such income as it had was derived mainly from tolls on livestock sold at fairs and markets.

The Municipal Corporations Act of 1835 saved the day. It left Tewkesbury with a Borough Corporation consisting of a Mayor, Alderman, and Councillors numbering 16 in all, with authority over an area co-extensive with the parish and the power to levy a rate. A Borough Quarter Sessions was granted in 1836, and there were eight justices apart from the Recorder, Mayor and ex-Mayor. In April 1974, under the Local Government Reorganisation Act, Tewkesbury District Council changed its name to Tewkesbury Borough Council and absorbed Tewkesbury Borough, Cheltenham Rural District and part of Gloucester Rural District. The former Borough Council, now a parish council, decided to be called Tewkesbury Town Council. It still elects a Mayor and has a town cryer.

An Act of 1786 allowed Tewkesbury to appoint street commissioners to improve paving, lighting and cleaning and to provide patrolling by watchmen. The streets were drained by large open gutters in the middle of each road, and the alleys were filthy. Some improvement was made by the building of drains and two public privies, but attendance at meetings was poor and the only wages paid were to a surveyor at £12 per annum and a clerk at £10. Lighting was only domestic: in 1608, under a Borough bye-law, the principal burgesses, innkeepers, taverners, chandlers and victuallers were obliged to hang up a lantern outside their house every winter evening when there was no moon.

For Tewkesbury, 21 January 1833 was a big day for it was then that the Tewkesbury Gas Light Company first lit up. The gas works were at the north end of the Oldbury, and the people of Tewkesbury 'had much reason to admire the excellent quality of the gas, the elegant forms of the columns and lamps, the beautiful and novel appearance of the bridge for suspending the gasometers, and the very neat and skilful structure of all the buildings and apparatus'. But alas! at 2am on 10 February the gasometer burst and the cast-iron suspension bridge and columns were destroyed. Fortunately no one was hurt, and Bennett goes on to record that the previous elegant structure was replaced by a more economic one of four brick pillars. In 1931 the Tewkesbury Gas Light Company merged with the Cheltenham Gas Company Ltd. In 1908 the Tewkesbury Electric Light Company was established, which was taken over the the Shropshire, Worcestershire and Staffordshire Electric Power Company. The works were beside Mill Avon at the back of St Mary's Lane.

There are bye-laws for fire regulations dating back to 1608. Viscount Gage's gift of a fire engine in 1734 was followed in 1750 by the purchase of two more fire-engines, bought by subscription. In 1836 the Town Council took charge of the equipment and in 1839, when the Town Hall was enlarged, the fire-engines were housed there. The regulations relating to their use in 1843 make alarming reading. Each parish had to pay a fire rate of between £2 and £4 per annum. Should a parish refuse to subscribe, an individual could do so at a rate of 10s, payable on each New Year's Day. In addition, before any fire-engine left to fight a fire, a levy of £3 had to be handed over, or £13 for a parish which had not paid its rate. A Tewkesbury lady, whose father was a fireman in the late nineteen twenties, says the horse had to be caught and harnessed before the men could proceed to a fire. In 1843 a 'borough engineer' was in charge of each engine, assisted by 10 men selected by himself, and their payment came from the rates and fire levies. A bad fire in August 1847 nearly changed the face of Church Street. It started in a tan-yard near the Hop-Pole, and there were fears for the safety of the inn, but the efforts of the four fire-engines which were able to pump water from the Mill Avon, combined with steady rain, kept the fire confined to the bark-houses, bark-mills and drying lofts. In the late 19th century the fire station was moved to Sun Street, then to the Maltings in Mill Street, and in 1951 to the old Abbey barton in Barton Street which was previously a theatre. It is now in Oldbury Road.

'And from thence we passed to Tewkesbury and Evesham and to Worcester and I never saw the like drunkenness as then in these towns, for they had been choosing Parliament men' wrote George Fox in 1660. Tewkesbury's first MP was Sir Dudley Digges, who was ambassador to Russia in 1618. Sir Baptist Hicks, whose splendid mansion at Chipping Campden was burnt down by the Cromwellians, followed, and then Sir Ashley Cooper, 1st Earl of Shaftesbury, who deserted Charles I in 1643 but found Cromwell even less to his liking, and helped to arrange the return of Charles II. One of the 'Parliament men' elected in 1660 was Richard Dowdeswell of Pull Court, Bushley, and the family over a period of 200 years provided nine MPs for Tewkesbury. The grounds of Pull Court were laid out by Capability Brown, but without the usual lake or stream, and the manor house still stands and is now Bredon School. William Dowdeswell was Chancellor of the Exchequer about 1750. Colonel Thomas Dowdeswell was blinded while on active service in America by the age of 30, but lived at Pull Court, a well-loved figure, supported by his wife, until his death in 1811. His brother William succeeded him as MP, having served 31 years in the army, including duty in France, the Bahamas and India.

In 1734 Robert Tracy was elected as Member for Tewkesbury. He was descended from William Tracy, who was one of the four knights who assassinated Thomas á Becket. The family goes back even further into Saxon times. In 1802 their mansion at Toddington was burnt down and Charles Hanbury Tracy rebuilt it in the monastic gothic style: an astonishing piece of Victorian romanticism and confidence. In 1984 it was in use as a school. In 1838 Charles Hanbury Tracy was created Baron Sudeley of Toddington.

The Martin family provided eight MPs for Tewkesbury from 1741 to 1885, and Overbury Court was built shortly after 1735 by the first representative, John Martin. His son, Joseph, and grandson, James, also represented Tewkesbury, and went into the family banking business in Lombard Street, London, which had been established about 1650. James appeared to be a strong character; often called 'Honest Martin' or 'Starling Martin', the latter because he wished 'there were a speaking starling perched upon the speaker's chair, to sound in the ears of the House, "curst coalition! curst coalition!" ' He was a Whig, and Cobbett called him 'that sensible, honest and constant hater of Pitt and his infernal politics'. A strange marriage took place in 1882 between John Biddulph Martin and Victoria Claflin Woodhull. Mrs Woodhull was 44-years-old, twice divorced and came from a poor American family. She was renowned in the USA for her beauty and for her advocacy of free love, and was the first woman to be nominated as a Presidential candidate, putting up for the Humanitarian Party. The alliance between the Victorian banker and the free thinker from the New World was a happy one. Mrs Woodhull Martin outlived her husband by many years and lived in retirement at the Manor, Bredons Norton, until her death in 1927, held in esteem and awe by the villagers. She was also a great advocate of Anglo-American friendship, as was her daughter, Zulu Woodhull, who gave land and houses to Tewkesbury Abbey.

Sir Christopher Codrington, who was MP for Tewkesbury from 1797 until 1812, came from a family dating back to Henry IV, which took its name from the Gloucestershire village near Chipping Sodbury (now in Avon). The Codringtons made their money in Barbados, and a Christopher Codrington, who died in 1710, was Captain General of the Leeward Islands. He left £10,000 to his old college library at All Souls, Oxford, and also founded a college in Barbados through the SPCK. The rest of his fortune, amounting to £40,000, went to his cousin William and eventually to Sir Christopher Codrington, Tewkesbury MP.

The honour of representing Tewkesbury in Parliament was considered worth paying for. In 1754 Nicolson Calvert and John Martin were elected on the understanding that they paid £1,500 and £2,000 respectively towards the repair of the roads, in spite of Viscount Gage's attempt to oppose what amounted to a sale of votes. In 1774 Nicholas Hyett of Painswick, Recorder of the

Borough of Tewkesbury, wrote to Charles Barrow, MP and a member of the Tewkesbury Borough Council, 'I am very desirous in any reasonable way that my son should get into parliament, as I think it would be the only way to settle him in England, and I believe he would endeavour after reputation if he was in the House'. He offered a bribe of £1,500 but nothing more is known of the case, so either the young man rebelled or the bribe was not accepted. By 1831 the electoral list used was 24 years out of date and some non-residential voters had been dead for years! In 1831 feelings ran high in Tewkesbury about Parliamentary reform; many signed a long letter opposing it, but many more signed a petition to Parliament in favour, which John Martin presented in March 1831. John Martin and William Dowdeswell, the two MPs at the time, were in favour of reform, but they were opposed by Charles Hanbury Tracy, whose election campaign included expenses for two bands, bell ringers, flag bearers, ribbons (£262 worth), inns (£235), printing, summoning non-residential voters and '6d each given to 860 poor women': a total of £1,088 12s 0d. In spite of these efforts he was defeated, but was returned the following year after Martin's death. The usual triumphal procession or 'chairing' arranged for Dowdeswell had to be cancelled because 'dangerous missiles, and filth of the most offensive description, had been conveyed to the tops of some of the houses in Barton Street, for the purpose of annoying that gentleman in his progress'. The Reform Act was passed in 1932, and Tewkesbury celebrated with 'entertainment for the poor', and bread, meat and beer were distributed.

The Martins were a Liberal family, and Tewkesbury's two Members were for many years one Whig and one Tory, but since 1885 a Conservative has always been returned. From 1906 until 1912 it was served by the Hicks-Beach family of Whitcombe Park, and between the Great Wars by W. S. Morrison, who became Governor of Australia.

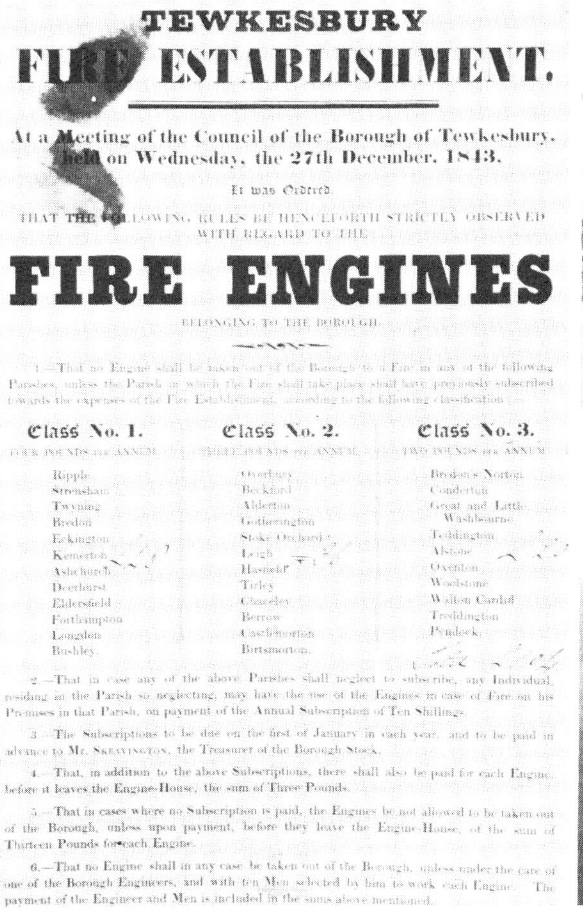

TEWKESBURY

FIRE ESTABLISHMENT.

At a Meeting of the Council of the Borough of Tewkesbury, held on Wednesday, the 27th December, 1843.

It was Ordered,

THAT THE FOLLOWING RULES BE HENCEFORTH STRICTLY OBSERVED WITH REGARD TO THE

FIRE ENGINES

BELONGING TO THE BOROUGH.

1.—That no Engine shall be taken out of the Borough to a Fire in any of the following Parishes, unless the Parish in which the Fire shall take place shall have previously subscribed towards the expenses of the Fire Establishment, according to the following classification:—

Class No. 1.	Class No. 2.	Class No. 3.
FOUR POUNDS PER ANNUM.	THREE POUNDS PER ANNUM.	TWO POUNDS PER ANNUM.
Ripple	Overbury	Bredon's Norton
Strensham	Beckford	Conderton
Twyning	Alderton	Great and Little Washbourne
Bredon	Gotherington	Teddington
Eckington	Stoke Orchard	Alstone
Kemerton	Leigh	Oxenton
Ashchurch	Hasfield	Woolstone
Deerhurst	Tirley	Walton Cardiff
Eldersfield	Chaceley	Treddington
Forthampton	Berrow	Pendock.
Longdon	Castlemorton	
Bushley.	Birtsmorton.	

2.—That in case any of the above Parishes shall neglect to subscribe, any Individual, residing in the Parish so neglecting, may have the use of the Engines in case of Fire on his Premises in that Parish, on payment of the Annual Subscription of Ten Shillings.

3.—The Subscriptions to be due on the first of January in each year, and to be paid in advance to Mr. SKEAVINGTON, the Treasurer of the Borough Stock.

4.—That, in addition to the above Subscriptions, there shall also be paid for each Engine, before it leaves the Engine-House, the sum of Three Pounds.

5.—That in cases where no Subscription is paid, the Engines be not allowed to be taken out of the Borough, unless upon payment, before they leave the Engine-House, of the sum of Thirteen Pounds for each Engine.

6.—That no Engine shall in any case be taken out of the Borough, unless under the care of one of the Borough Engineers, and with ten Men selected by him to work each Engine. The payment of the Engineer and Men is included in the sums above mentioned.

OPPOSITE: Tewkesbury Borough Council coat of arms: in the shield the golden cross engrailed on red in reference to the Arms of Tewkesbury Abbey occupies the place of honour. In the chief of the shield the castle, the Council's emblem from the Corporate Seal and the Mayor's Chain, appears between red and white roses in reference to the Battle of Tewkesbury. In the Crest a great demi lion with two tails from the Arms of Dudley, Earl of Leicester issues from a Saxon crown, denoting a Royal Borough with Saxon origin and holds between the paws a black pear from the Arms of Sir George Dowty. The Supporters are an heraldic Panther from the Arms of the Duke of Beaufort and an Eagle from the Arms of the Earl of Coventry, both families having a long association with the Borough. The Shield and Supporters rest on the compartment in which symbolic reference is made to the convergence at Tewkesbury of the Rivers Severn and Avon. Motto: 'There is wisdom in Counsel'. (TBC) ABOVE LEFT: Rules for the use of the corporation fire-engines in 1843 were strict: engines could not be called out unless the parish in which the fire was situated had paid the fire subscription, or unless the owner of the property on fire had paid his. (GCL) RIGHT: The new fire engine of 1934 superseded a hand pump machine. Manager was D. Bethel and the operator, J. Guy. Alderman Howell denounced it as a waste of money and part of the 'wave of squandermania' which he said was sweeping Tewkesbury! (TR TL) BELOW: One of Tewkesbury's most spectacular fires, September 1908, when Walker's factory behind the Wheatsheaf was burnt down. (TR TL)

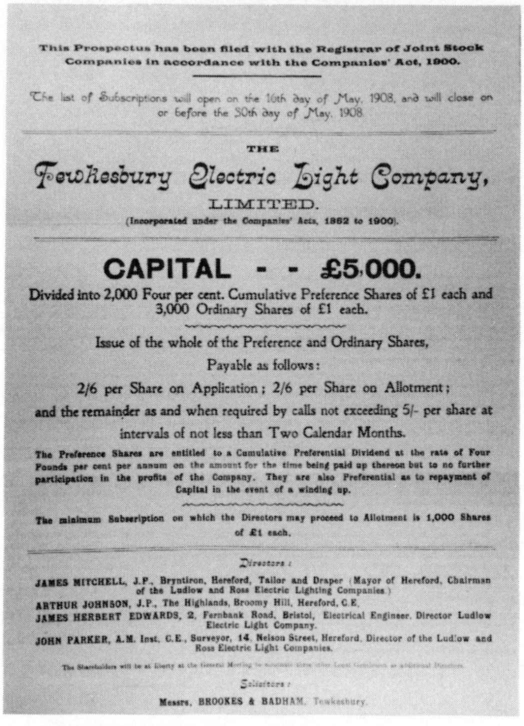

This Prospectus has been filed with the Registrar of Joint Stock Companies in accordance with the Companies' Act, 1900.

The list of Subscriptions will open on the 16th day of May, 1908, and will close on or before the 30th day of May, 1908.

THE

Tewkesbury Electric Light Company,

LIMITED.

(Incorporated under the Companies' Acts, 1862 to 1900).

CAPITAL - - £5,000.

Divided into 2,000 Four per cent. Cumulative Preference Shares of £1 each and 3,000 Ordinary Shares of £1 each.

Issue of the whole of the Preference and Ordinary Shares,

Payable as follows:

2/6 per Share on Application; 2/6 per Share on Allotment;

and the remainder as and when required by calls not exceeding 5/- per share at intervals of not less than Two Calendar Months.

The Preference Shares are entitled to a Cumulative Preferential Dividend at the rate of Four Pounds per cent per annum on the amount for the time being paid up thereon but to no further participation in the profits of the Company. They are also Preferential as to repayment of Capital in the event of a winding up.

The minimum Subscription on which the Directors may proceed to Allotment is 1,000 Shares of £1 each.

Directors:

JAMES MITCHELL, J.P., Bryntiron, Hereford, Tailor and Draper (Mayor of Hereford, Chairman of the Ludlow and Ross Electric Lighting Companies.)

ARTHUR JOHNSON, J.P., The Highlands, Broomy Hill, Hereford, C.E.

JAMES HERBERT EDWARDS, 2, Fernbank Road, Bristol, Electrical Engineer, Director Ludlow Electric Light Company.

JOHN PARKER, A.M. Inst. C.E., Surveyor, 14, Nelson Street, Hereford, Director of the Ludlow and Ross Electric Light Companies.

Solicitors:

Messrs, BROOKES & BADHAM, Tewkesbury.

ABOVE: Tewkesbury Museum occupies a beautiful timber-framed house in Barton Street enlarged c 1660 but of earlier date. The lithograph is by Rowe, 1839. (CAGM) LEFT: Prospectus for the Tewkesbury Electric Light Company, 1908, of St Mary's Lane, later the boat builders Durrant and Vickeridge. (GRO) RIGHT: Mace-bearers, Strawford and Boroughs, in 1897. (TTC)

On Pleasure Bent

There have been many attempts to establish a theatre in Tewkesbury. Our earliest theatrical records are in the Abbey accounts of 1578 and 1585, and these refer to payments for 'sheepe skyns for Christs garments' and 'shippe skines for sinners gears' and 'eight heads of hair for the apostles, and two beards, and a face or vizor for the devil'. The bailiffs' Borough accounts read in 1585 'laid out by them unto players, in wine to the justices, rent for their market-standing and to the clerk of the market and in seneschal [steward] money — £3 15s 8d'. In 1600, plays were held in the Abbey Church to raise money for church repairs. In 1762 a New Theatre is mentioned, which was probably a barn or malthouse in the Oldbury. A few years later there were two buildings used as theatres: one was in Rails Meadow (now a carpark) and the other in a meadow called the Pantry, where Mitton School now stands. The manager was John Kemble's father and the famous actor and Mrs Siddons no doubt played there when in repertory at Cheltenham. In 1823 an 'elegant little theatre' was fitted up by Abbot and Farley of Covent Garden. It extended from the fives court at the back of the Wheatsheaf to the Oldbury. Cheltenham actors used to play there and it was also used by amateurs. Although the great Edmund Kean appeared as Shylock in 1830, it failed to flourish; Bennett in 1836 reported a 'short and unprofitable season' and two years later it was in use as a Sunday School. From 1847 to 1870 it was a silk mill, by 1912 it was a cinema, later a fire station and is now an ambulance station. From 1934 until 1963 the Sabrina Cinema was an attraction near the north end of the High Street. The Roses Theatre was opened on the same site in 1975 for films and live entertainment. It is now leased to Stan Stennett and his two sons.

Races were held annually on the Severn Ham from 1721, when the Prince of Wales gave a gold cup, until 1813. After 1846 the races dwindled away and the last one was held in 1852. Known as the Tewkesbury and Gloucestershire Races, special trains were run from Cheltenham in later years, and there were booths, a temporary theatre, a grandstand and two roulette tables. No race meetings were held at Cheltenham from 1843 to 1845 but, when they were resumed, the competition was too much for Tewkesbury, and the constant threat of floods contributed to the failure to maintain the sport.

To commemorate the Jubilee of Queen Victoria, Tewkesbury opened the Victoria Pleasure Gardens. Part of it is now a carpark and a caravan park, but originally it stretched along the Mill Avon from the Abbey Mill (now called Abel Fletcher's Mill) to Abbey Terrace. It had a splendid yew hedge, described in *John Halifax, Gentleman*, a bandstand, a putting green, a Russian gun and a German gun. The remains of the outer wall of the Abbey shields it from the road. The removal of the guns for scrap metal in the Second World War few will deplore, but it would be to Tewkesbury's credit to replace the iron railings and smarten the gardens when the present economic climate improves.

The bowling green belonging to the Bell Hotel was a great attraction. Artisans used to come from as far away as Birmingham by train and later by charabanc for their annual outing. As many as 200 and a military band arrived in one party in 1886. Tradition says the monks used to play bowls there, and it is sad that the new Tewkesbury Borough Council allowed houses to be built on the site in 1984.

As well as the fives court behind the Wheatsheaf, there was a quoit yard at Upper Lode around 1800, which Bennett says was well used. An annual ploughing match was held at Forthampton under the patronage of Joseph Yorke, from 1837 to 1842.

An enterprising Italian baker named Barsanti, who lived over his shop next to the Berkeley at 9 Church Street, ran what John Moore called 'a dreadful "Italian Tea Gardens" with umbrellas like striped mushrooms shading the tables' on the Abbey Lawn, with his own statues adorning the sward, which had much charm and was certainly well patronised. 'Cycling and motoring were catered for by the local inns, as were those who wished to hire or drive broughams or carriages. The Tewkesbury Corporation Band and the Tewkesbury Volunteer Band enlivened social occasions. The Working Men's Club met in the High Street opposite Quay Street, in what had been the railway station building, where there was a recreation and reading room, and higher up the social scale a Town Club provided similar facilities at the Abbey end of Church Street. The YMCA had a football club, the Tewkesbury Cricket Club was established by 1845 and there was a large Tewkesbury Rowing Club. Bathurst's Docks ran saloon steam launches and had canoes and rowing boats for hire. The Tewkesbury Working Men's Club, in conjunction with the Rowing Club, held an annual regatta from 1890 until World War Two. Races for adults included slow bicycle, blackboard bicycle, egg and spoon, swimming, three-legged, 120 yards sprint, rowing and motor boats. Similar events were held for children from the Abbey, Trinity, Council and British Schools. Many prizes, including the Barlow Cup, were distributed at a 'Smoking Concert' in the Bell Hotel in the evening.

The town swimming pool was opened in 1957 on the site of the old cattle market. Before that the youth of Tewkesbury had learnt to swim the hard way, in the rivers. A favourite place early this century was a backwater known as the Old Severn at Upper Lode Lock. In 1928 this area was rented to the Edgbaston Anglers Club, and swimmers were excluded. The Borough Council therefore supplied huts, raft and diving board, with a paddlers' enclosure, at The Sandy (old sand pits) at the Severn across the Ham. When a swimming club was formed, Stanchard Pit in the Avon was used, and the facilities transferred there from The Sandy, but the Avon had a muddy bottom at Stanchard Pit, so it was not entirely a good move. Jack Fletcher writes 'One facility at Stanchard Pit which attracted the hardy types was being able to dive off the iron road bridge which crossed the water by Bathurst's island; as the water was only some eight feet deep below the bridge, which was at least sixteen feet above, it required more than a little skill and nerve'. Later, a small childrens' swimming pool was opened next to the municipal caravan site and tennis courts, behind Abbey Terrace in Gloucester Road. The old Abbey malt house, later the Fitzhammond Art Centre and now owned by the Bell, was a slipper bath between the wars. There is today a sports centre at Tewkesbury School for the use of townspeople.

Fishing has always been popular in Tewkesbury, as one might expect. Salmon were once so plentiful in the Severn that apprentices had a special clause written into their contracts, safeguarding them from having it served up more than twice a week. Lampreys (large eel-like creatures) were considered a great delicacy; in fact Henry I died from a surfeit of them. Elvers (young eels) are still much esteemed. Bream, chubb, gudgeon and barbel are also caught.

ABOVE: A travelling showman with a dancing bear in Barton Street; after the bear had finished his little dance, the showman would collect pennies and ha'pence and moved on to the next village. Postcard, 1900. (KH)
BELOW: The Boddington Harriers meeting outside the Hop-pole. Stables and kennels were built for them at Boddington Manor in 1890, and in recent times the Cotswold Vale Hunt was housed there. Photograph, c1930. (RFG)

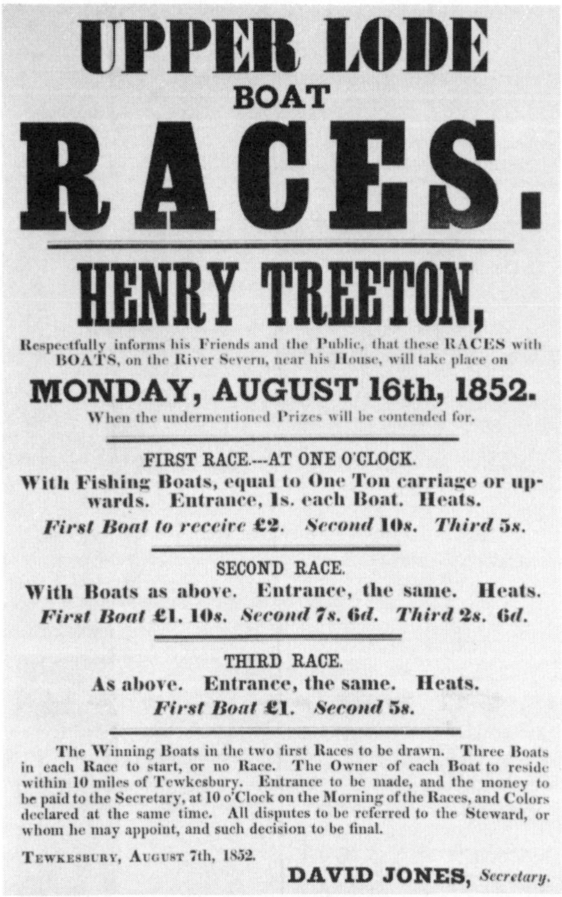

UPPER LODE
BOAT
RACES.

HENRY TREETON,

Respectfully informs his Friends and the Public, that these RACES with BOATS, on the River Severn, near his House, will take place on

MONDAY, AUGUST 16th, 1852.

When the undermentioned Prizes will be contended for.

FIRST RACE.---AT ONE O'CLOCK.
With Fishing Boats, equal to One Ton carriage or upwards. Entrance, 1s. each Boat. Heats.
First Boat to receive £2. Second 10s. Third 5s.

SECOND RACE.
With Boats as above. Entrance, the same. Heats.
First Boat £1. 10s. Second 7s. 6d. Third 2s. 6d.

THIRD RACE.
As above. Entrance, the same. Heats.
First Boat £1. Second 5s.

The Winning Boats in the two first Races to be drawn. Three Boats in each Race to start, or no Race. The Owner of each Boat to reside within 10 miles of Tewkesbury. Entrance to be made, and the money to be paid to the Secretary, at 10 o'Clock on the Morning of the Races, and Colors declared at the same time. All disputes to be referred to the Steward, or whom he may appoint, and such decision to be final.

TEWKESBURY, AUGUST 7th, 1852.

DAVID JONES, *Secretary.*

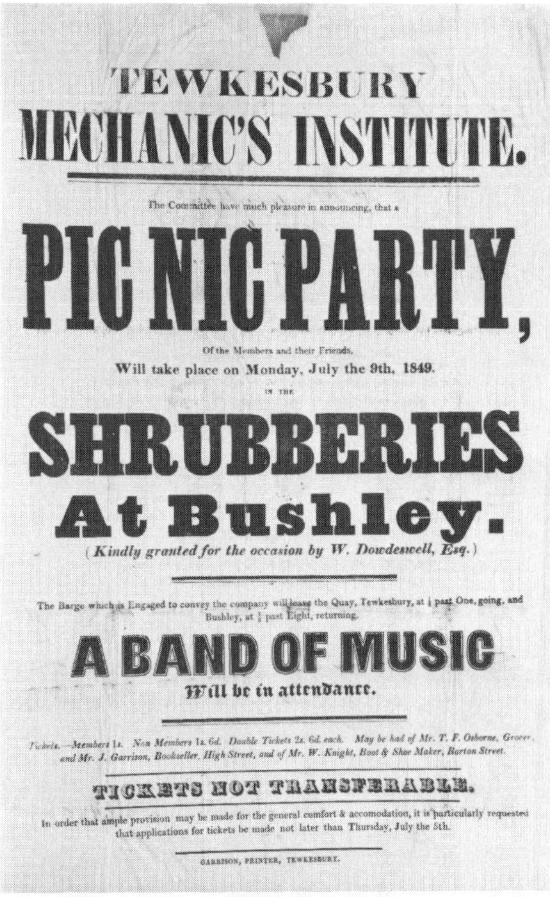

TEWKESBURY
MECHANIC'S INSTITUTE.

The Committee have much pleasure in announcing, that a

PIC NIC PARTY,

Of the Members and their Friends,
Will take place on Monday, July the 9th, 1849.
IN THE

SHRUBBERIES
At Bushley.

(Kindly granted for the occasion by W. Dowdeswell, Esq.)

The Barge which is Engaged to convey the company will leave the Quay, Tewkesbury, at ½ past One, going, and Bushley, at ½ past Eight, returning.

A BAND OF MUSIC
Will be in attendance.

Tickets.—Members 1s. Non Members 1s. 6d. Double Tickets 2s. 6d. each. May be had of Mr. T. F. Osborne, Grocer, and Mr. J. Garrison, Bookseller, High Street, and of Mr. W. Knight, Boot & Shoe Maker, Barton Street.

TICKETS NOT TRANSFERABLE.

In order that ample provision may be made for the general comfort & accomodation, it is particularly requested that applications for tickets be made not later than Thursday, July the 5th.

GARRISON, PRINTER, TEWKESBURY.

OPPOSITE LEFT: 1852 poster advertising boat races on the River Severn at the Upper Lode. (GCL) RIGHT: For many years the Dowdeswell family at Pull Court, Bushley, made part of their grounds available for picnics organised by local societies. This 1849 poster advertises a picnic party of the Mechanic's Institute — they were to leave the Quay, Tewkesbury at 1.30pm and proceed by barge to Bushley, returning at 8.30pm. (GCL) BELOW: Tewkesbury Swimming and Rowing Club at Sandy Point: left to right: two unknown, Ron Bennett, Cyril Allen, Ted Nash, George Packwood, Jack Jones, Len Matty, Arthur 'Petrol' Price, Harold 'Tiny' Bourton, Harry Packwood, Ben Cook. Photograph, c1930. (RFG) ABOVE: Swimming at Sandy Point in the Severn across the Ham. In 1928 the Borough Council supplied huts, a raft and a diving-board, with a paddling enclosure. Photograph, 1930. (GE GCL) BELOW: A men's outing in a charabanc outside the Swan Hotel: above is the balcony from which the Mayor announced election results. Photograph, c1920. (GRO)

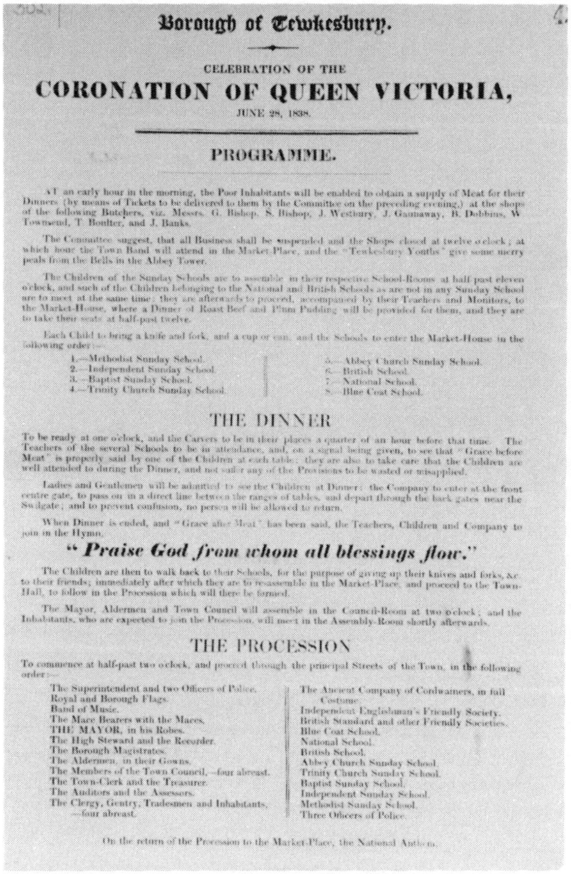

Borough of Tewkesbury.

CELEBRATION OF THE

CORONATION OF QUEEN VICTORIA,

JUNE 28, 1838.

PROGRAMME.

AT an early hour in the morning, the Poor Inhabitants will be enabled to obtain a supply of Meat for their Dinners (by means of Tickets to be delivered to them by the Committee on the preceding evening,) at the shops of the following Butchers, viz. Messrs. G. Bishop, S. Bishop, J. Westbury, J. Gannaway, B. Dobbins, W. Townsend, T. Boulter, and J. Banks.

The Committee suggest, that all Business shall be suspended and the Shops closed at twelve o'clock; at which hour the Town Band will attend in the Market-Place, and the "Tewkesbury Youths" give some merry peals from the Bells in the Abbey Tower.

The Children of the Sunday Schools are to assemble in their respective School-Rooms at half past eleven o'clock, and such of the Children belonging to the National and British Schools as are not in any Sunday School are to meet at the same time; they are afterwards to proceed, accompanied by their Teachers and Monitors, to the Market-House, where a Dinner of Roast Beef and Plum Pudding will be provided for them, and they are to take their seats at half-past twelve.

Each Child to bring a knife and fork, and a cup or can, and the Schools to enter the Market-House in the following order:—

1.—Methodist Sunday School.
2.—Independent Sunday School.
3.—Baptist Sunday School.
4.—Trinity Church Sunday School.
5.—Abbey Church Sunday School.
6.—British School.
7.—National School.
8.—Blue Coat School.

THE DINNER

To be ready at one o'clock, and the Carvers to be in their places a quarter of an hour before that time. The Teachers of the several Schools to be in attendance, and, on a signal being given, to see that "Grace before Meat" is properly said by one of the Children at each table; they are also to take care that the Children are well attended to during the Dinner, and not suffer any of the Provisions to be wasted or misapplied.

Ladies and Gentlemen will be admitted to see the Children at Dinner: the Company to enter at the front centre gate, to pass on in a direct line between the ranges of tables, and depart through the back gates near the Swilgate; and to prevent confusion, no person will be allowed to return.

When Dinner is ended, and "Grace after Meat" has been said, the Teachers, Children and Company to join in the Hymn,

"Praise God from whom all blessings flow."

The Children are then to walk back to their Schools, for the purpose of giving up their knives and forks, &c. to their friends; immediately after which they are to reassemble in the Market-Place, and proceed to the Town-Hall, to follow in the Procession which will there be formed.

The Mayor, Aldermen and Town Council will assemble in the Council-Room at two o'clock; and the Inhabitants, who are expected to join the Procession, will meet in the Assembly-Room shortly afterwards.

THE PROCESSION

To commence at half-past two o'clock, and proceed through the principal Streets of the Town, in the following order:—

The Superintendent and two Officers of Police.
Royal and Borough Flags.
Band of Music.
The Mace Bearers with the Maces.
THE MAYOR, in his Robes.
The High Steward and the Recorder.
The Borough Magistrates.
The Aldermen, in their Gowns.
The Members of the Town Council,—four abreast.
The Town-Clerk and the Treasurer.
The Auditors and the Assessors.
The Clergy, Gentry, Tradesmen and Inhabitants,—four abreast.
The Ancient Company of Cordwainers, in full Costume.
Independent Englishman's Friendly Society.
British Standard and other Friendly Societies.
Blue Coat School.
National School.
British School.
Abbey Church Sunday School.
Trinity Church Sunday School.
Baptist Sunday School.
Independent Sunday School.
Methodist Sunday School.
Three Officers of Police.

On the return of the Procession to the Market-Place, the National Anthem.

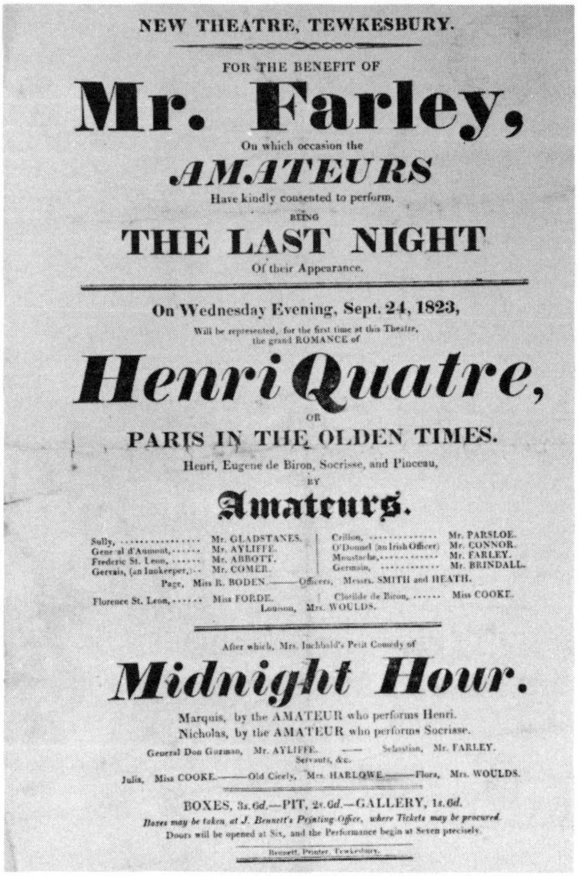

NEW THEATRE, TEWKESBURY.

FOR THE BENEFIT OF

Mr. Farley,

On which occasion the

AMATEURS

Have kindly consented to perform,

BEING

THE LAST NIGHT

Of their Appearance.

On Wednesday Evening, Sept. 24, 1823,

Will be represented, for the first time at this Theatre, the grand ROMANCE of

Henri Quatre,

OR

PARIS IN THE OLDEN TIMES.

Henri, Eugene de Biron, Socrisse, and Pinceau,

BY

Amateurs.

Sully, ... Mr. GLADSTANES.
General d'Aumont, ... Mr. AYLIFFE.
Frederic St. Leon, ... Mr. ABBOTT.
Gervais, (an Innkeeper,) .. Mr. COMER.
Crillon, ... Mr. PARSLOE.
O'Donnel (an Irish Officer) Mr. CONNOR.
Moustache, ... Mr. FARLEY.
Germain, ... Mr. BRINDALL.

Page, Miss R. BODEN.——Officers, Messrs. SMITH and HEATH.

Florence St. Leon, ... Miss FORDE. | Clotilde de Biron, ... Miss COOKE.
Louison, Mrs. WOULDS.

After which, Mrs. Incbbald's Petit Comedy of

Midnight Hour.

Marquis, by the AMATEUR who performs Henri.
Nicholas, by the AMATEUR who performs Socrisse.

General Don Guzman, Mr. AYLIFFE. —— Sebastian, Mr. FARLEY.
Servants, &c.

Julia, Miss COOKE.——Old Cicely, Mrs. HARLOWE.——Flora, Mrs. WOULDS.

BOXES, 3s. 6d.—PIT, 2s. 6d.—GALLERY, 1s. 6d.

Boxes may be taken at J. Bennett's Printing Office, where Tickets may be procured.
Doors will be opened at Six, and the Performance begin at Seven precisely.

Bennett, Printer, Tewkesbury.

OPPOSITE LEFT: Coronation of Queen Victoria in June 1838: 'Poor Inhabitants' were issued with free meat, and Sunday School children were given a free meal of roast beef and plum pudding. There was a tremendous procession accompanied by the town band and 'merry peals' from the Abbey bells. Programme, 1838. (GCL) RIGHT: A New Theatre programme in September 1823 soon after it opened at the back of the Wheatsheaf. It never flourished and was later used successively as a silk mill, cinema, fire station and ambulance station. (GRO) BELOW: The Victoria Pleasure Garden was opened to celebrate the Queen's Jubilee in 1897, and contained a beautiful bandstand, here on a postcard, c1910. (CB) ABOVE LEFT: Architect's drawing of the Sabrina Cinema, opened in the High Street in 1934 by Tewkesbury's MP, W. S. Morrison, and built by Collins and Godfrey. (TR TL) RIGHT: The German gun from World War I outside an arbour in the Victoria Pleasure Gardens (1930) was indirectly responsible for killing a man when it was demolished for scrap in World War II, for the recoil spring was accidentally released and damaged the roof of the house opposite; a workman employed to repair the damage slipped and fell to his death. (GE GCL) BELOW: Tea Gardens on Abbey Lawn, where Barsanti's own statues pleasantly dominated the scene. Postcard, c1910. (CB)

ABOVE: Tewkesbury 'Thursdays' AFC, formed during the thirties. Back row, left to right: Mr Sallis, Jack Underwood, George Avery, Tom Sircombe, Bill Enstone, Bill Lockhart, Cyril Fellows, Frank Bennett, ? Booth, Mr Cook?, 'Salmon' Moss. Middle row: Ted Collins, Alf Wagstaffe, Ralph Carter, Bill Sammons, Bill Smith. Front row: Ron Dickinson?, Hawker?, Dave Booth?, Digby?, Eddie Furley. Photograph, c1930. (RFG) BELOW: Twyning Cricket Club: Tewkesbury Hospital Cup winners, 1950. Back row, left to right: Alf Clements, Bill Young, Geoff Healey, Jim Bourton, Jim Healey, 'Rimbo' Green, Ron Etheridge, Mr Sidwell (umpire). Front row left to right: Arthur Beale, Lewis Townsend, Mrs Bowles (scorer), Dick Brookes (Captain), Ron Stew, Dennis Bowles, Bert Smith. Seated: Dick Sidwell (mascot). (RFG)

ABOVE: Twyning FC and mascot. Back row, left to right: G. Merrick, F. Allen, F. Wakefield, H. Nicholls, W. Cartwright, S. Niblett, A. White. Front row: N. West, J. Jeynes, J. Meadows, F. Pates (Captain), T. Bayliss, H. Shakespeare, J. White (Secretary). Photograph, c1930. (RFG) BELOW: Tewkesbury Town Band in 1983. (TTB)

Racing took place every summer on the Severn Ham 1721-1813. Flooding, and competition from Cheltenham Race Course closed it down, the last race was held in 1852. (TTC)

River, Road and Rail

Until 1800 Tewkesbury was largely dependent upon its rivers for transport. The Severn had its trows and barges. Bow-hauliers used to pull the barges along the Severn to and from Tewkesbury until around 1832, in which year men lost their employment to horses, because the wages and subsistence of the eight men needed to haul a 20-ton barge were more than the cost of the single horse and driver which replaced them.

There was no bridge over the Severn at Tewkesbury until Telford's was opened at the Mythe in 1826. The river was crossed by the ferries at Upper and Lower Lode, the latter linking the Abbey with its estates at Forthampton. The ferry continued in use for goods until about 1920, and for passengers a few years longer. In 1668 there was a coal wharf near the Quay and passenger travel to and from Gloucester was established by 1703. In 1810, during the canal boom, it was proposed to link Tewkesbury to Cheltenham by canal, but this was dropped as too expensive. In the 13th century, malt, mead, hides and grain were sent from Tewkesbury to Gloucester and Bristol, and to the west country, and grain has continued to be important. In 1517 the town slipway was repaired and two new ones made. Now there is only one, near the remains of Bill Shakespeare's boatyard in Smith's Lane. In 1857-8 the Severn Navigation Company built the Ham weir, incorporating a salmon leap. Bennett claimed that attempts to improve navigation 10 years earlier had caused the river to sink two feet, thus cutting communication between the two rivers and making it difficult for barges to get to the Quay, but this seemed to be only a temporary set-back, as we hear no more of it.

The Avon rises near Naseby and runs past Warwick Castle, Strensham, Bredon, Twyning and Mitton to Tewkesbury. The Mill Avon was probably cut by the monks to power their mills, although there is a tradition that associates it with the Duke of Clarence. Richard Beauchamp, Earl of Warwick, whose monument is in the Abbey, tried to make the Avon navigable, but could not get the necessary legislation passed. However, in 1636 William Sandys of Miserdine spent £20,000 on providing sluices at Tewkesbury, Strensham, Nafford, Pershore, Piddle, Fladbury, Evesham and so on up to Stratford. This venture left him almost penniless, but created much wealth for others. The lock 200 yards to the north of Healings Mill joins the Avon to the Severn. In the mid-19th century, grain barges used the Mill Avon to reach the Abbey Mill. In 1950 the Lower Avon Navigation Trust Ltd was set up to maintain navigation from Tewkesbury to Evesham for recreational purposes. Healings Mill still uses grain barges.

Leland, describing the Swilgate River in the early 16th century, wrote 'There is a little broke caullid Suilet cumming downe into Avon from Clive [Bishops Cleeve] and entereth into Avon at Holme Castelle by the lifte Ripe of it [left bank]. This, at sodayn rayns, is a very wylde brooke, and is fedde with water faulling from the hilles thereby'. This, together with the difficulties experienced by the fleeing Lancastrians after the battle of 1471, suggests that the river was wider and deeper than it is today. Before entering the Avon, the Swilgate is united with the Tirlebrook, which rises above Winchcombe, runs north to Teddington and then through Pamington,

Ashchurch and Walton Cardiff. The Carrant Brook rises just east of Ashton-under-Hill and flows through Beckford, north of Ashchurch and Northway, and through Mitton to join the Avon just above King John's Bridge.

Bridges have always been of vital concern to Tewkesbury. There was a bridge over the Avon at the north end of the town back in 1202. Leland states that King John made a stone bridge over the Avon and a wooden causeway over the Ham. Until 50 or 60 years ago this was known as the Long Bridge — well named because it was nearly half a mile in length. Leland states that John authorised tolls from the Wednesday and Saturday markets to pay for its upkeep. This was not always done, and in 1638 the County Assizes forced Tewkesbury to see to the reparation and maintenance of the bridge, complaining that 'divers of his majesties subjects travelling that way have been unfortunately drowned'. For centuries frequent disputes broke out between County and Borough, concerning how much each authority should pay. The *Victoria County History*, describing King John's Bridge in the early 20th century, says it was 'a miscellaneous collection of stone and brick arches on stone piers, with brick parapets, an iron side walk, and a roadway as narrow as 16 feet in places. There were four arches over the Mill Avon, six over the Old Avon and seven between the two'. In 1962 'the whole was rebuilt in stone and concrete, retaining some of the old features . . . as two distinct bridges, King John's Bridge over the Mill Avon and Beaufort Bridge over the Old Avon'.

The old Quay, or Key, Bridge was originally a drawbridge, with red sandstone supports, and those who favour the theory that the Duke of Clarence cut the Mill Avon believe he also built this bridge. It was repaired and altered in 1592, but by 1808 was unusable, and a temporary bridge of boats was in use from the bottom of Smith's Lane until a new, light, single-arched iron bridge was opened in 1822.

There was a bridge over the Swilgate, sometimes called Holme Bridge and sometimes Swilgate Bridge, from 1540. It was once a drawbridge, but was replaced by a stone one, widened in 1757, probably to accommodate the new road to Gloucester. Later it was widened again and parapets erected. There was a wooden footbridge across the Swilgate at Ganders Lane called Priests Bridge by 1540, which the Earl of Essex replaced with a stone one in 1791, and that still stands. There was a third bridge over the Swilgate in the 16th century, the location of which is uncertain.

The Bredon Road bridge over the Carrant Brook was mentioned in 1592 when it was called Carrant Bridge, and it has been widened several times over the centuries. Salandine's Bridge over a tributary of the Carrant on the former Tewkesbury-Ashchurch boundary also existed in the 16th century, and has also been rebuilt since.

Tewkesbury's most famous bridge is, of course, the Mythe Bridge over the Severn, designed by Thomas Telford. It is made of cast iron in a single arch of 170 feet; a 24 feet wide roadway, plus three feet six inches each side for a footpath. The open arches on the banks are not only graceful but allow flood water to pass through. 'And as this is the first instance in which this mode has been adopted, as well as some other improvements,' wrote Telford in 1828, 'I reckon this must be the handsomest bridge which has been built under my direction.' The ironwork was by William Hazeldine of Shrewsbury and the masonry by Hugh M'Intosh. It cost £36,000, of which Telford received £250. It was opened in 1826, freed from tolls in 1891, and reinforced with concrete in 1923. The toll house is still there.

The laying of the foundation stone of the Mythe Bridge on 8 September 1823 caused tremendous interest in Tewkesbury, and was celebrated by Bennett in seven pages of his most purple prose. The ceremony was conducted by the Provincial Grand Lodge of the County of Gloucester with masonic ceremonies. There were peals of bells, flags, a long procession, and an even longer sermon in the Abbey on the principles and practice of Masonry. The procession then re-formed and, attended by a band, proceeded to the Mythe Tute 'which from its brow to its base was covered by an incalculable assemblage of well-dressed persons, prominent amongst whom were a great number of elegant and beautiful females'. There were prayers, a blessing, the laying of the stone, more speeches and then the procession re-formed to return to the Abbey for numerous votes of thanks. An 'elegant dinner' later took place at the Hop-pole, and some less elegant celebrations at other inns. Sadly, there were two anti-climaxes to these festivities: contemporary coins buried under the foundation stone were dug up that very night and stolen, and the architect who attended these ceremonies and whose name appeared on the brass plate, George Moneypenny, later had his design turned down in favour of Telford's.

Tewkesburians have always lived with floods. The winter floods, when not too severe, have been beneficial, enriching the fields with fertile river sludge. The summer floods were often disastrous. A flood in August 1484 was known as Buckingham's Water, because it stopped the Duke of Buckingham from crossing the Severn with his forces to oppose Richard III. His men, lacking pay and provisions, deserted him, and he was captured, brought to Richard and executed. In 1640 there were eight floods between midsummer and Michaelmas and all the hay was lost. In July 1839 the Mythe road was nearly covered and the town surrounded with water; all the hay was lost and the sheep and cattle only saved by being herded onto higher ground.

On 17 November 1770 Neast Harvard, the Tewkesbury Town Clerk and a solicitor, wrote an account called *Mr Harvard's Voyage round Tewkesbury in the time of the High Flood.* He took a boat from the Black Bear and rowed over Oldbury Field, Ashchurch Road, passed the Plough, up Gander's Lane into Church Street, through Abbey Orchard into Gloucester Road (where he records five feet of water) to the Bell, down St Mary's Lane, back into Church Street, sculled *over* the Long Bridge to the Upper Avon Ham and back to the Plough. Two days later he noted that most of the south aisle of the Abbey Church was under water, but that the nave was dry. The cause of the flood was heavy snow, followed by three days of rain. The worst flood recorded this century was in 1947, when the Ham was under six feet of water, but other bad ones occurred in 1924, 1943, 1960, 1968 and 1982. Eric Wynter, a Bushley farmer, recalls: 'More than three feet of rain fell in one night in July 1968. Roads, paths and farmyards turned into torrents of water roaring down into the valleys, and as usual Tewkesbury Ham and Severnside meadows sank under the flood . . . Haymaking had been in full swing that week but as the water rose across the fields there were bales by the score to be seen floating in the tops of hedges, while the windrows that had been mown and left to dry in the sun rose slowly to the surface. As the flood water drained away, they settled back, faintly green with a scum of duckweed, ruined'. The Severn River Authority over the next few years raised river banks and provided one-way sluice-gates on ditches. Mr Wynter continues 'Since then the 300 acres in the village which had always been permanent pasture because of inundation, have made suitable for mixed farming. The whole face of the countryside has changed with the growing of corn as have local farmers' fortunes'.

Tewkesbury has been on a trading route since prehistoric times. The great salt way ran from Droitwich *via* Ashton-under-Hill and Hailes Abbey down into Hampshire, and Ryknield Street ran from the north *via* Birmingham and Alcester, Sedgeberrow and Tewkesbury, to Ross and into Wales. The Western Trackway came down from Worcester to Gloucester *via* the Gupshill side of Tewkesbury. The Romans built roads upon these tracks and made others. Traces of Roman roads can be seen at the Mythe and Ripple. Until about 1750, the only way to travel to Worcester from Tewkesbury was on horseback, as the roads were too bad for carts. There were two routes out of Tewkesbury in this direction: the lower went from Paget's Lane by way of Bow Bridge and Ripple, where it joined the other in Ripple Field. The upper road ran from Mythe Hill over Shuthonger Common, passed near Twyning Church and Twyning, and then turned west over Brockeridge Common to Ripple Field and became the present A38 to Worcester. The road running east through Ashchurch was called Salandine's Way. There were two roads running south from Holme Bridge. The east fork led past Gupshill and then on to Cheltenham. The west fork went to Gloucester *via* what is today Lower Lode Lane.

In 1755, under a turnpike act, the road to Cheltenham was rebuilt, and in 1792 a road club was formed to improve the Ashchurch road. Under an act of 1818 the Lower Lode road was abandoned and in 1825 the Mythe Hill road was lowered and widened. The materials used were a mixture of Bristol stone, brought up on the Severn, and local gravel. The money was raised by tolls. Many turnpike houses are still in the area, and can be distinguished by their tall, narrow shape, with windows giving a good view of the road in each direction. There is one opposite Holm Hospital, and another on Mythe Hill.

By 1830 the improved roads were paying rich dividends to the townspeople, as 30 stage coaches a day passed through Tewkesbury. The Swan and the Hop-pole were posting houses where the coachmen changed horses and took refreshment, and Key House, next door to the Swan, was a ticket office. Numerous inns opened in Tewkesbury in the early 18th century to provide food and lodging. The most famous coach was probably *L'Hirondelle,* which once covered the run of 122 miles from Birkenhead Ferry to Tewkesbury in nine hours.

At the height of the coaching era mail travelled in a four-horsed coach by night from London *via* Oxford, Gloucester and Cheltenham, reaching Tewkesbury at 8.45am and continuing on to Ledbury, Hereford and South Wales. It left Tewkesbury for Cheltenham and London at 5.45pm. The Bristol-Birmingham mail coach passed through about midnight to these cities and a reply could be received in 24 hours. But in 1845, after the railways had come, the London-Hereford route was changed to go direct from Gloucester to Ledbury, and in that year the last four-horsed coach passed through Tewkesbury. A postman's job was well-paid, but it was hard work. Mrs Sarah Dyer, a widow who died in 1837, was a letter-carrier for 16 years. Her round consisted of Beckford, Conderton, Kemerton, Westmancote and Bredon, so she walked at least 16 miles a day with a heavy postbag. She left over £200 to her eight children. Before 1820 there was a post office in the High Street, but by 1909 the main office was at 98 Church Street, now the shop called Brass Tacks. The Post Office moved to its present site in the High Street in 1971.

The Cheltenham-Bromsgrove line of the Birmingham and Gloucester Railway opened on 24 June 1840, with a station at Ashchurch, and the next month the branch line from Ashchurch to Tewkesbury was opened. This is how Bennett describes it: 'Passengers are conveyed between the stations at Tewkesbury and Ashchurch in a handsome and convenient carriage, drawn by one horse, at a good speed; the body of the carriage is divided into compartments for first and second-class passengers, those of the third-class riding on the outside, and it is so constructed as to run on the rails with perfect steadiness and security'. The gauge was four feet eight and a half inches. The frequently held view that local landlords were opposed to the main line coming to Tewkesbury appears to be based on a misunderstanding. The objection to the railway lay in the fact that there was to be no station at Tewkesbury in the original plan; the nearest was to be at Ashchurch. This was obviously bad for trade, and in 1836 William Dowdeswell MP, a principal landowner, presented a petition from the people of Tewkesbury to the House to stop the railway bill. The petition failed, so Lindsey Winterbotham, G. E. Williams and John Moore personally lobbied against the bill in the Lords. At this the railway company agreed, as a compromise, to run a branch line from Ashchurch to Quay Lane and later to the end of the quay. This was done in 1844 and the line also became steam-powered as far as Tewkesbury town.

The depôt and station were completed at Tewkesbury in August 1839. The station house at the corner of old Sun Street faced the High Street, was 38 feet long and 34 feet high and built in stone to a gothic design. The platform was 160 feet long. The Birmingham and Gloucester Railway Company built a wooden bridge across the Avon at the bottom of Quay Lane, extended the railway to the end of the Quay and made a strong wall alongside the water. In 1861 the Malvern and Tewkesbury Railway Co built a branch from Ashchurch *via* Tewkesbury through the Mythe, travelling under the Tute. It crossed the Avon by a cast-iron bridge designed by William Moorson, which is now destroyed. The new line necessitated the re-siting of the station, and a new one was built immediately to the east. It was an impressive, gabled, stone structure and its destruction is to be regretted, especially as the station at Ripple, which has been converted into a most attractive house, shows what could have been made of it.

The railways continued to use horses for many years for delivery. Jack Fletcher recalls four magnificent shire horses which were stabled near the entrance to Station Road, where the telephone exchange now stands. They were in the charge of Jimmy Perks, and they were used to draw railway trucks up and down the special line, which ran from the engine sheds across Oldbury Road and the High Street to the Quay.

There was a crossing in Chance Street which was looked after by a woman who lived in the crossing cottage, now demolished. She would control the traffic passing along Chance Street with two flags, red and green. There was a four-storey malthouse near the Chance Street crossing, and barley trucks would pass to sheds adjacent to it. Until recently it was used by Dowty Electrics, but now there are plans to convert it into flats.

The goods vans between the wars carried anything from mail to racing pigeons. Consignments of boxes, fruit and vegetables, crates, parcels and newspapers were unloaded under the supervision of the Station Master, Mr Alldridge, imposing in his uniform of gold-braided cap and frockcoat. Horses arrived in a special goods van which was switched to a quiet siding for them to be collected by grooms.

Another way the railway used horses was for parcel delivery by dray. This was supplemented by some eight 'common carriers'; one of them, Green, in East Street, later used a T model Ford van. He and his son delivered and collected parcels to and from Cheltenham and Gloucester two days a week. The Bristol and Midland Red 'bus companies also collected and delivered parcels to and from agencies. This enabled parcels to reach their destination the same day.

In 1841 Bennett summed up the effects of the coming of the railways: 'The effects of rail-roads . . . has hitherto been one of almost unmixed evil to the inhabitants of Tewkesbury . . . Of six and twenty stage coaches which, only 12 months ago, passed through this town to or from the west alone, not one conveyence of the kind now exists upon the road, nor is there even a single stage coach running through the place to Gloucester, although there were formerly nearly a score a day'. He speaks of the isolation of villages like Kempley not on the railway and of 'inns and posting houses shut up or conducted unprofitably'.

This bird's eye view was produced to promote tourism in the nineteen thirties, and shows the town's three main streets and the confluence of the rivers Avon and Severn. (GRO)

ABOVE: Tewkesbury from the Severn, looking north east; the Abbey tower centre background, c1870. (GRO) BELOW: Upper Lode Lock in 1950, then the biggest river lock in Britain, with a dumb barge entering it. (TR TL)

ABOVE: 'Tewkesbury Canal 1870': a Yorke family photograph of the Old Severn at Upper Lode, a backwater formed by the cutting of the lock and, between the wars, a favourite place for swimming. (GRO) CENTRE: Lower Lode Ferry with horse drawn carriage and equestrian, and the Abbey tower in the distance. Photograph, 1870. (GRO) LEFT: Key, or Quay Bridge was a mediaeval bridge pulled down in 1808; the present iron bridge was opened in 1822. (JB) RIGHT: King John's Bridge before widening showing the slipway, and on the right Bayliss and Merrill and Gaze's Dairy. Photograph, c1920. (GCL)

ABOVE: Telford's Mythe Bridge, showing the high arches which allow flood water to pass through easily, and with horses crossing the bridge. Photograph, c1920. (GCL) LEFT: River Swilgate from Gander Lane in 1985, probably with much less water than when the Lancastrians were cut down trying to cross it after the Battle of Tewkesbury. The bridge was erected by the Earl of Essex in 1791, but has since been widened and reinforced. Drawing by Hilary Swan. RIGHT: One of the first cars in Tewkesbury: a T model Ford outside Lion House, 38 Barton Street, driver: Fred Green; passenger: Dick Green, c1920. (RFG)

ABOVE: View up Mill Street with the Tudor cottages on the left, the Abbey tower in the background, and Abel Fletcher's Mill, named after the stern old Quaker tanner in *John Halifax, Gentleman*, on the right. Photograph, c1920. (CH) BELOW: 1947 floods on King John's Bridge, which was then only 16 feet across in parts: the vessel on the left is level with the bridge. (DV)

ABOVE: Church Street flooded in 1947, showing Abbey Lawn house standing where the Crescent lies today: in the distance a fire engine pumps out water from the basement. (DV) BELOW: View from Mansard House, Lock Court, in winter during the floods of 1968 which followed heavy snow: the lock gates are almost submerged. (HB)

Tewkesbury and Ashchurch Junction Stations, photographed by J. M. Rogers (16), Marling School, Stroud in 1964. (GL GCL)

ABOVE: Tewkesbury today, from the Abbey Church tower, looks down Mill Street to Abel Fletcher's Mill with the Bell on the left. BELOW: Mediaeval merchants' cottages on the left, Hanover Court flats behind and Healing's Mill in the distance: a view that spans six centuries. Above the roof of Holy Trinity Church, Bredon Hill fills the horizon on the right. (RR)

Between the Wars — and After

Industrially speaking, Tewkesbury stagnated from the close of the nineteenth century until 1940. Most of the land was down to permanent pasture for Hereford cattle, and cheese was an important product as well as milk. Double and Single Gloucester, Cheddar and Stilton were all produced. There was more timber then, chiefly elm. Fruit growing was general as was the manufacture of cider and perry. Basket-making still took place at the Mythe by the Red Pools. Market gardening was important at Twyning and is still a considerable industry.

For the unemployed as well as those who preferred not to be tied down to an employer there was odd-jobbing. John Moore wrote: 'In Tewkesbury at any rate the class of odd-job man included some of the best elements in the community . . . These were the adventurous and the imaginative men . . . These were the jacks-of-all-trades'. They would turn to sprout-picking, rabbit-trapping, carpentry, boat repairing, salmon-fishing, osier-cutting, hay-making, fruit-picking as the season dictated, and make a good living out of it all. But unemployment was a blight on the community. An epidemic of foot-and-mouth hit the farms and farmers had to lay off yet more workers, and in 1934 there were 333 unemployed out of a workforce of 1,190 — about 28%. The Mayor of Tewkesbury set up a Work Fund to raise money in order to set men to work on useful projects. The response was slow but, out of a population of 4,700, £360 was raised and some men set to work on a new carpark in Wyatt's Meadow (now the Gloucester Road carpark). Wages were low. A messenger and delivery boy, working a 50-hour week with a half day on Thursday, got 8s. A grocer's assistant (male) received £2 10s 0d. The unemployment 'dole' was 30s a week for a family man and prices were not all low: a bicycle cost £3 19s 6d.

A report on Gloucestershire published under the auspices of the County Council in 1940 stated that Healing's employed 120, boat-building firms 100, building contractors 300 and there were many small firms employed in milling, cattle cake manufacturing, seed cleaning, malting, milk distribution, agricultural implement-making and custard making. The report listed the disadvantages of Tewkesbury as an industrial site as flooding, distance from a large centre of population, housing shortage and the 'lethargy of local workers'.

The Second World War brought prosperity to Tewkesbury. In 1940 George Dowty flew over Tewkesbury looking for space in which his firm could repair planes salvaged from the Battle of Britain. He saw the brick building beside the railway station at Ashchurch, originally used as a forage shed for railway draught horses and later by Birds Custard, and this was speedily adapted. In 1947 it became Ashchurch Seals Limited and later Dowty Seals. Next year Dowty Mining Equipment Ltd was formed; it developed the hydraulic roof support for mines known as the Roofmaster, and later as the Rolf system (remotely operated long-wall face). This revolutionary equipment has provided work for thousands of Tewkesburians in the last 40 years. Sir George Dowty received the Freedom of the Borough in 1964. This ancient honour derived from the mediaeval law that it was illegal for anyone but a freeman to follow a trade. It could be passed on to the firstborn son of a freeman after he had become free, or could be bestowed after an apprentice had completed his indentures. By 1639 it could be purchased for the minimum sum of 20s, or bestowed as an honour. In Sir George's case it was certainly an honour well deserved. In 1985 the forage shed where the Tewkesbury firm of Dowty's began life was taken over by George Bence, timber and builders' merchant.

Tewkesbury's popularity as a tourist centre continued. As many as 2,000 anglers a day would pour off trains or charabancs between the wars, and works outings from Birmingham and Coventry continued to arrive in 30 or so motor coaches per firm. As well as bringing trade to the public houses and tea shops, the outings also provided pocket money for Tewkesbury's lads by way of collecting empty bottles and finding bait for fishing. The first 'Municipal camping ground' was opened by 1953, 64 Barton Street was opened as a museum in 1960 (and has an information office adjoining), and the John Moore Countryside Museum was opened in 1980 at 45 Church Street. The latter is run by a charitable trust to promote concern about conservation, and as a tribute to the memory of John Moore. It displays farm tools, domestic bygones, and exhibitions explaining the countryside to the town-dweller. Ray Goodwin's tapes of country life sounds provide an appropriate background. The museum works closely with the Gloucestershire Trust for Nature Conservation, who run the Mythe Railway Nature Reserve, Paget's Lane, which they bought from the Tewkesbury Town Council for £1 in 1984. It is a haunt of butterflies; wild strawberries grow there and stonechats tic-tac among the gorse bushes, while swallows and martins nest in the old railway tunnel, and in winter redwings and fieldfares feed on the hawthorn berries. The elm trees died of Dutch elm disease and were cleared, but a fine walnut and a spindle tree are among the many trees left.

Sadly the swan, like the curlew, nightingale and redshank, is now seldom seen around the Avon. Its chief enemies are the lead weights and nylon lines of anglers, oil pollution and disturbance by motor boats. The otter, which John Moore used to delight in watching, has gone from Gloucestershire. The mink is a new pest with no natural enemies and a voracious and carnivorous appetite.

Victoria Pleasure Gardens in 1904, showing Abel Fletcher's Mill and, on the right, the Russian Gun and beyond that an arbour. (KH)

ABOVE: Church Street from the Cross c1928: Warwick House (behind lamp-post), Abbey Lawn in the distance, where the Crescent is today, on the opposite side of the road the Riverside Hotel (not yet incorporated into the Hop-pole next door), the Post Office (now Brass Tacks), and nearest to the camera (right) part of the Willow Cafe (now the Co-op). (EP) LEFT: John Moore, well-known writer and broadcaster, inaugurator of the Tewkesbury Literary festival, and member of the distinguished Tewkesbury family. Photograph, c1960. (LB JMM) RIGHT: 'Sally Watkins' Cottage', Bedford Court, opposite Tudor House and now demolished, believed by some to be the cottage where John Halifax had his attic room in Mrs Craik's novel, while Ursula Marsh is reputed to have lived in Tudor House. Photograph, 1921. (GE GCL)

LEFT: Watercolour by A. Phipson, of Bank Alley, between 99-100 Church Street, which has been demolished. Between c1841-1923 Lechmere and Hartland's Bank stood at 99 Church Street, after which the alley got its name. (GCL) RIGHT: Cross House from Tolsey Lane. The same view today would demonstrate that its condition has deteriorated a lot in the last 50 years. Photograph, 1932. (GRO) OPPOSITE ABOVE LEFT: Cross House, after restoration by Thomas Collins and before conversion into shops. Photograph, 1932. (GRO) RIGHT: Tudor stairway in Cross House after restoration by Collins. Photograph, 1932. (GRO) BELOW LEFT: Walls Alley, now Walls Court, at the northern end of the High Street. Photograph, 1965. (HB) RIGHT: 3-4 High Street being demolished in order to erect Woolworth's, now lying empty. A great deal of demolition has taken place in Tewkesbury this century, some of which may have been unnecessary. Photograph, 1934. (TR TL)

PDA

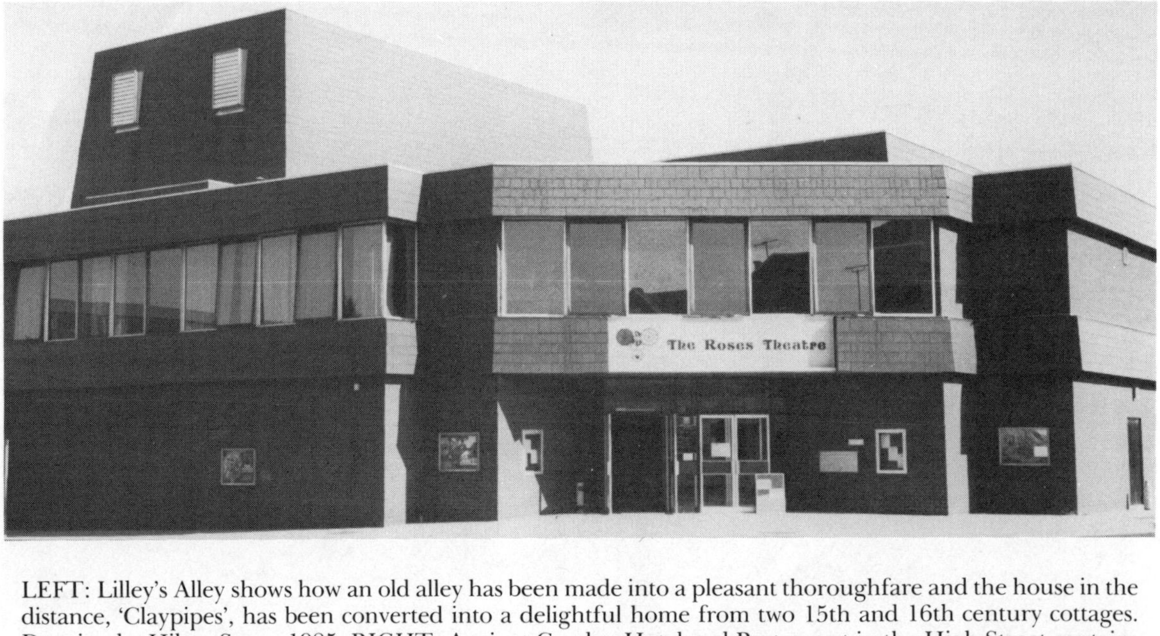

LEFT: Lilley's Alley shows how an old alley has been made into a pleasant thoroughfare and the house in the distance, 'Claypipes', has been converted into a delightful home from two 15th and 16th century cottages. Drawing by Hilary Swan, 1985. RIGHT: Ancient Grudge Hotel and Restaurant in the High Street contains some of the best linenfold panelling in Tewkesbury. The initials 'R P' in the spandrels above the great fireplace may refer to Abbot Richard, Prior of the Abbey 1481-1508. The Hotel's name is believed to have been chosen because in the last century it was situated between two cafés, one called the 'White Rose' and the other the 'Red Rose'. (RR) BELOW: The Roses Theatre was opened in 1975, a comfortable, well appointed theatre and cinema, but is this the architecture which Tewkesbury wants? It occupies the site of the Sabrina Cinema. (RR)

Round about Tewkesbury

A whole book could be written on the charming and interesting estates and villages around Tewkesbury. Tewkesbury Park, now a country and golf club, is the site of a house used by the Clares as a hunting lodge, and lived in by the lord of the manor, Edward le Despenser, in the late 14th century. In 1553 Queen Mary leased it to the Jermingham family for 20s per annum and they later bought it. They leased it to John Nanfan of Birtsmorton, who employed Cardinal Wolsey as a family chaplain when he was a young man. It was eventually bought by Sir John Popham, who was accused by Aubrey in his *Brief lives* of accepting the manor and estate of Littlecoat, in Wiltshire, as a bribe to acquit a knight named Dayrell of the murder of his bastard baby. If so, the family was punished, for Sir John's son Francis and his wife led such a dissolute life that they 'died from excess and luxury' leaving a debt of £100,000. The Tewkesbury Park estate passed by marriage to the Wall family, and in 1817 Rev Joseph Shapland, a distant relative, bought it and left it to his daughter Fanny. She married James Primatt Sargeaunt; her daughter Violet inherited and lived there until recent times with her husband Lt-Col H. M. B. Salmon. The 'fair manor house of timber and stone' which Leland described has long since disappeared, and the present building is believed to have been erected by John and Mary Brilliana Wall in the late 18th century. When Rev Joseph Shapland owned the house he built on two galleries for his picture collection, but on his death in 1837 the pictures were sold and the galleries pulled down.

At one time there was a fair-sized hamlet at Gupshill; 21 houses in 1662 and 23 houses two centuries later, with another hamlet at Lincoln Green just south of the new housing estate. In 1707 Gupshill Manor was bought by William Ransford, and stayed in the Puritan and Baptist family until they emigrated to America in 1835 and sold the house to Mrs Ann Nash. Until this time the manor house had consisted of two converted old houses; now one was pulled down and the present property is all that remains. George Hone, the cattle auctioneer, was living at Gupshill in 1910, but by 1931 it had become an hotel, as it is today. Most of the house is 16th century, but parts date from 1438, and there is a tradition that Queen Margaret spent the night there before the Battle of Tewkesbury.

Southwick Park was auctioned about 1820 and the advertisement provides an interesting description of a typical country gentleman's residence of the period. The estate consisted of 120 acres, with curtilage, granaries, stable, harness room, coach house, cart-horse stable, cider house, barns, stalls and sheds, brewhouse, wash-house, dairy and cheeseroom, yet the house had only seven bedrooms and, of course, no bathroom. This demonstrates how independent each estate still was, and how much employment a wealthy family gave to those who lived on it. A further asset was the sporting facilities, with three packs of foxhounds and the Whitefield Harriers within reach, 'and the partridge shooting is most excellent'. In 1887 the house was 'rebuilt and restored at great expense' to include 15 bedrooms, two dressing rooms, and also bathrooms, but the estate had been cut to 80 acres. Tewkesbury Grammer School occupied it from 1952 to 1972, and it is now in the possession of the Severn Trent Water Authority. Southwick Farm, not far away, is a most attractive 18th century three storey brick building with later additions. Samuel Healing bought it about 1860 and members of the Warner family have lived there since.

The Mitton Farm housing estate on the Bredon road was built about 1965 but there is a record dated 841 stating that Beorhtwulf, King of Mercia, gave the manor to Worcester Cathedral. Among subsequent owners were the Beauchamps, the Grevilles and the Earls of Coventry. A chapel was mentioned in 1287, when Sir Nicholas de Mitton was lord of the manor, and later the estate was bought by Giles Read, whose imposing early 17th century monument is a feature of Bredon Church. The manor house still stands, an attractive late 17th century building, which in 1946 had 93 acres of pasture and orchards. The house was used as a Red Cross hospital in World War I. It has now been converted into flats.

Rev Witts, visiting Tewkesbury in May 1825, to preach in the Abbey, recorded his impressions of Mythe Hill: 'As we walked over the confluence of the Severn and Avon we greatly admired the sweet meadow verdure, and the diversity of cheerful objects presented to our view. Mythe Hill is much improved, and the neat villas on its summit greatly ornament the bank. At its foot are the abutments of the proposed projected bridge nearly in a state of completion, and ready for the iron arch to be thrown over the Severn; beyond is the straight road, marked out, but as yet not made, which will lead to Ledbury'. The Mythe was not in the Domesday book, but by 1327 it was recorded as having 10 taxable inhabitants. King John's Castle is a recent name for the Mythe Manor House, which belonged to King John and which became the property of Gilbet de Clare, 6th Earl of Gloucester. When he died in 1230 he left the manor to the Abbey of Tewkesbury, and it was used as a rest home for the monks of Tewkesbury, Fairford and Thornbury until 1539. Then John Wakeman, the wily Abbot of Tewkesbury, succeeded in establishing his brother Richard there just prior to the dissolution, and it remained in Wakeman hands for the next 300 years. All the original buildings of the manor house, including the chapel, were pulled down, except for the large staircase tower. The building is now mostly Tudor, one of the most interesting and delightful of Tewkesbury's buildings. The most attractive of the 'neat villas' on the Mythe was Mythe House, a fine mansion built in 1756 and later the home of Charles Grove, who gave so much to the Abbey. Alfred Healing of the milling family lived there in 1936. The mansion was used as a hospital for American troops during the Second World War, fell into disrepair and was demolished in 1955.

In 1889 Cheltenham Corporation built the water works at the Mythe, and the tower is now being converted into a residence. The views from the top will surely rival those from the Abbey Church tower.

The mound at the top of Mythe Tute is man-made, probably by the Saxons, and no doubt used as a look-out post. King George III with his Queen and the three princesses visited Mythe Tute in 1788 more than once while staying at Cheltenham to drink the waters, and were reported to be delighted with the view. During the 19th century it was often called 'Royal Hill'. The ancient salt-way, called Kyvehull Way by the Saxons, ran close to the river to Droitwich; indeed, some of it is now *in* the river, owing to soil erosion. Paget's Lane runs past King John's Castle and joins Kyvehull Way. The railway track is now a nature reserve.

In the Middle Ages the parish of Ashchurch was part of the parish and manor of Tewkesbury, but soon after the dissolution it became independent. Until 1882 it contained 4,284 acres; it lost and gained some land to Kemerton and Tewkesbury in 1935. It included Aston-on-Carrant, Fiddington, Natton, Northway, Newtown, Newton, and Pamington. Until the mid-19th century the population was between 500 and 700 but, after the building of the railway, it increased somewhat. It was still agricultural land until after World War II. In the 10th century the east-west road was called Port Street; it was turnpiked in the 18th century and the turnpike cottage is still there on the corner of the road to Walton Cardiff. After the opening of the railways, Ashchurch became a small railway centre, with two terraces of railway cottages and a large brick storehouse for provender, serving the south-west Midlands. Three large houses were built: Ashchurch House, formerly called Southfield, and two at Northway. The focal point for Northway was the railway bridge south of the station: the Church was close at hand and here a school, village hall and police station were built. After World War II the Dowty works expanded, owing to the proximity of the railway and the plan for the M5 motorway, a council housing estate was built by Cheltenham RDC in the late forties and the fifties, and private housing in the sixties. The army camps, established in World War II, extended from Aston Cross to the railway line. Another new industrial park is now being developed.

At the time of Domesday, most of Ashchurch Manor belonged to Tewkesbury Abbey, but some to the Abbey of Bolbec in Normandy. In the mid-16th century it was sold by the Crown to Sir Ralph Fane. The parish remained almost unchanged through the ages. In 1740 it was mostly grassland, but also grew wheat, peas, oats, barley, clover and vetches. Enclosure in 1816 made little difference to the number of farms, which continued to be small: 27 in 1829 and 31 in 1939. Early this century cider apples, hops and osiers were also grown. Most non-agricultural jobs were connected with the railways. At one time there were six mills in Ashchurch, of which one survives: Northway Farm and Mill, standing near the motorway, a fine monument from the past, with a 14th century stone doorway attached to a 17th century house.

Among the remaining interesting old buildings in Ashchurch parish is the Church, dedicated to St Nicholas. In 1147 it was a chapel-of-ease to Tewkesbury Abbey; the south wall of the nave is late 12th century and the rest dates from the 13th to 16th centuries. A Quaker burial ground marked with trees is all that survives of the early 18th century Meeting, but a small Ebenezer Methodist Chapel at Isabel's Elm, between Aston and Aston Cross, dating from 1846, is still there though deserted. Northway House, built by William Woodward, a major local landowner in the mid-19th century, is still in use as an hotel. There was no manor house at Northway.

Ashchurch Church has a monument to William Ferrars, founder of the Grammar School at Tewkesbury. Another important name in Ashchurch parish is that of Elizabeth Smithsend. Her father, Nicholas, built Walton House and left it to his four daughters, of whom Elizabeth was the last to survive. When she died in 1833 she gave 120 acres of her estate to the living of Ashchurch, which until then had been a poor one. Elizabeth also founded a Sunday School, and left £400, the income from which was to maintain the school and provide a blanket fund for the poor. Walton House and all that was left of the estate, 44 acres, was bought by the incumbent of St Nicholas, Francis Henry Romney. George Ruddle, Commissioner for Peace for Tewkesbury, rebuilt the house in red brick about 1860. In 1946 it became a children's home, and in 1983 it was re-opened as a home for the mentally handicapped.

There were some quaint charities in the parish of Ashchurch. An early one to provide a lamp in the church was diverted in the 16th century to distribute 23d among the poor. William Ferrars left a £20 rent charge: £10 for the minister and £10 for the poor, which was later distributed in the form of coal. Charles Parsons of Bredon left a rent charge of 20s for the distribution of bread on Christmas Day, which earlier this century took the form of biscuits.

Walton Cardiff was part of Britvic's estate and was owned by William of Cardiff in 1166, and nearly 500 years later by Sir Baptist Hicks of Chipping Campden, as part of his Tewkesbury estate. The villagers used the Abbey Church until their own Chapel was built in 1658; they then refused to pay Tewkesbury rates. This led to considerable illwill in Tewkesbury, but by 1683 the town had given up trying to enforce the debt, and Walton Cardiff became a separate parish. It was nevertheless included in the 1686 town charter. The chapel has since disappeared.

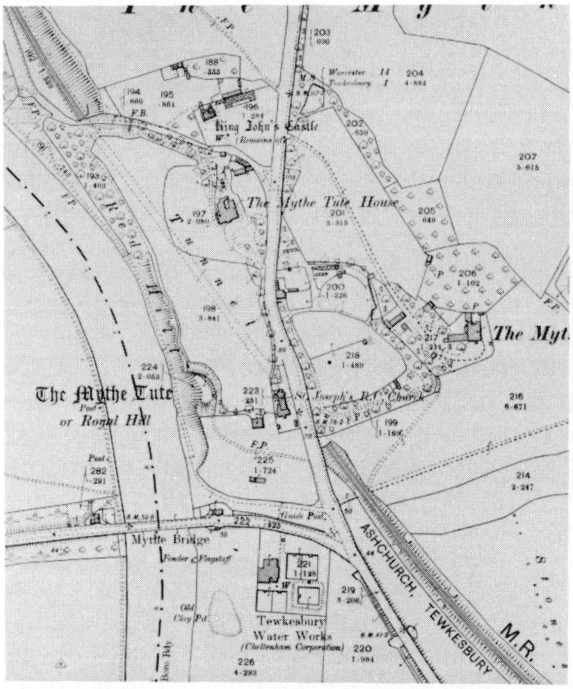

LEFT: 1903 OS map of Tewkesbury 6" = 1 mile, 2nd edition; marking King John's Castle and other houses with their gardens, the Roman Catholic Church, Mythe Bridge, railway line and water. (GCL) RIGHT: Putting green at Tewkesbury Park Golf and Country Club, which was opened July 1976. The course was designed by the famous golfer and course designer, Frank Pennick. The building was erected in the late 18th century, but there had been a house there at least as early as the 14th century, when Edward le Despenser was Lord of Tewkesbury manor, and the Clares used it as a hunting lodge. Photograph, 1976. (GAL GCL) BELOW: The Saxon Duke Oddo built the chapel at Deerhurst in 1056. Later it became incorporated into a farm house but it was discovered in the late 19th century and the nave restored. Photograph, 1901. (GE GCL)

ABOVE LEFT: Brass of Sir John Cassey and his wife Alice, who has at her feet her dog Terri, 1400. This is the only example of an animal named on a mediaeval brass. Engraving by Lysons, c1795. (GRO) RIGHT: Fiddington, although less than half a mile from the M5, is a peaceful hamlet with a fine 16th century timber-framed manor house, once the home of William Ferrars, who founded Tewkesbury's Grammar School. Nearby stands this large 17th century stone dove-cote. (RR) BELOW LEFT: Shuthonger Manor, near Twyning, is an 18th century brick house made into a country club c1960 and later enlarged and converted into flats. Photograph before conversion, 1962. (HS) RIGHT: Southwick Park it was rebuilt in 1887: Tewkesbury Grammar School occupied the house from 1952-1972, and it is now in the possession of the Severn-Trent Water Authority. The engraving is by George Rowe and is from a sale catalogue, c1840. (GRO)

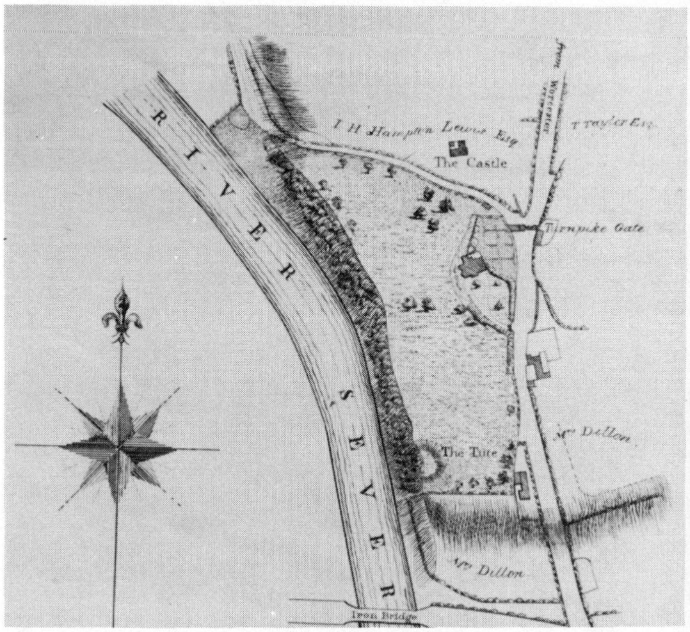

ABOVE LEFT: This engraving by George Rowe shows Mythe House, built in 1756, home of Charles Grove and later of the Healing family, which was used by Amnerican troops as a hospital during World War II. It was demolished in 1955. BELOW: The plan of Mythe Tute, also by George Rowe, shows the position of King John's Castle and the turnpike gate. The turnpike cottage is still there on the eastern side of the Worcester road. c1840. (GRO) ABOVE RIGHT: Mythe Manor House, now known as King John's Castle. The staircase tower may be 12th century and can be seen on the right; the rest is Tudor. Drawing by V. Holland, c1980. (CH) BELOW: Paget's Lane, leading to Salt Way and the old road to Worcester, was named after one of the speculators who sold monastic property at the dissolution, and now leads to a nature reserve. The old bridge in the photograph (1903) was demolished c1920. (GCL)

ABOVE: The Tracy family of Toddington and Stanway went back to Saxon times, and William Tracy was one of the knights who assassinated Thomas à Becket. In the early 19th century Charles Hanbury Tracy MP rebuilt their Toddington mansion in the monastic gothick style, a grandiose gesture of self importance. Until recently it was in use as a school. Drawing from *The Mirror*, 1832. (GCL) BELOW: This aerial view from the Ham, looking up Mill Street, shows the old Grammar School with the demolished rear wing, Abbey School on one side and the Bell bowling green on the other, and a more extensive Victoria Park Gardens in the foreground, c1930. (CB)

Names

For those who enjoy words and are curious about their meaning, the following is a selection of personal and place names connected with Tewkesbury, and their meanings. Old English (O.E.) refers to the period before about 1150 and Middle English (M.E.) to the period 1150-1500.

Ashchurch: Church near the ash tree.
Ashleworth: Aescel's enclosure. *Woro* is O.E. for enclosure.
Avon: O.E. word for river.
Bredon: on the hill. *Don* is O.E. for hill.
Birtsmorton: low lying farm belonging to the Le Bret or Le Brut family from Brittany. *Mor* is O.E. for low lying and *ton* is O.E. for farm.
Bushley: forest clearing. *Bysc* is O.E. for bush and *leah* is O.E. for clearing.
Carrant Brook: sluggish water. *Ar* is Gaelic for water and *on* is sluggish. In the early 19th century the brook was called the River Carron.
Chandler's Court: a chandler made candles, soap etc.
Deerhurst: wooded hillock frequented by deer. *Hyst* is O.E. for wooded hillock.
Fiddington: farmstead associated with Fita (a Saxon personal name).
Fletcher's Alley: a fletcher was an arrow maker.
Forthampton: Farmstead associated with Forthelm (a Saxon personal name).
Gupshill: Guppa's Hill (a Saxon personal name).
Ham: water meadow (O.E.)
Lode; passage over the river (O.E.)
Mythe: river confluence (O.E.)
Natton: either from *naet,* meaning wet farmstead or from *neat* meaning cattle (O.E.)
Newton: new farmstead. *Niwe* meaning new (O.E.)
Newtown: a recent name referring to a new suburb which grew up round Walton Cardiff.
Northway: Northern enclosure. From *nore* meaning north and *haeg* meaning enclosure (O.E.)
Oldbury: Old fort or manor house from *bury,* O.E. for fortified building.
Pamington: Poefen's farmstead (O.E.)
Perry Hill: Pear tree on a hill (M.E.)
Puckrup: Goblin-haunted farmstead, or Puca's farmstead (O.E.)
Saladin or Saladine: from *salden* meaning a willow valley.
Severn: at one time spelt Havren, from Sabrina, a river name in Tacitus' *Annals*.
Shuthonger: wood on a steep slope, from the Norse words, *scyte,* meaning a steep slope, and *hangra,* meaning wood.
Southwick: South dairy farm or dependent farmstead from *wic,* O.E. for a small farm.
Stanchard Pit: probably from a stone gap, referring to the weir (M.E.)
Swilgate: to wash or rinse, from the O.E. verb *swillan,* and the gate was probably a flood gate.
Tirlebrook: previously called Turlebrook, either from O.E. for aperture or Celtic for descent.
Toddington: farmhouse associated with Tuda (O.E.)
Tolsey or Tolzey Lane: from *tolley* or tollbooth, M.E. for courthouse.
Tute: Look-out place, from O.E. *tot.*
Twyning: two meadows, from *twii,* meaning two and *ince,* meaning a meadow (O.E.)
Walker's Lane: the fullers' (cloth-dressers') lane. *Walker* was O.E. for fuller.
Walton Cardiff: farmstead belonging to Robert de Cardiff (who lived at the end of the 12th century) with a wall or embankment, or farmstead belonging to the Welshmen. Welshmen could also be used to mean strangers (O.E.)

Bibliography

Atkyns, R. *The ancient and present state of Gloucestershire* (1712).
Bennett, J. *The history of Tewkesbury* (1830).
The Tewkesbury Register. Vols I and II (1830-1849).
Bristol and Gloucestershire Archaeological Society *Transactions*.
Brooke, D. *The Saxon and Norman Kings* (1963).
Burrows, E. J. *The 'Borough' pocket guide to Tewkesbury* (1908-9).
Cheltenham Chronicle.
Clifton-Taylor, L. *Six English Towns* (1978).
Cobbett, W. *Rural rides* (1982 edition abridged by E. R. Chamberlain).
Cotswold Life.
Davies, W. *Official guide to Tewkesbury* (1903).
The Tewkesbury Academy (1898).
Domesday book for Gloucestershire (1983).
Fox, G. *Journal* (1975 edition) abridged by J. L. Nickalls.
Gloucestershire and Avon Life.
Gloucestershire Notes and Queries.
Gloucestershire Society for Industrial Archaeology *Industrial archaeology in Gloucestershire* (1975).
Gough, L. *The Abbey Church of St Mary the Virgin, Tewkesbury* (1959).
Hammond, P. W., Shearing, H. G. and Wheeler, G. *Battle of Tewkesbury* (1971).
Harger, R. *Public libraries in Tewkesbury* (c1976).
Harris, M. *Alan, Abbot of Tewkesbury* (1980).
Harte, G. W. *Souvenir of the one hundred anniversary of the Baptist Sunday School at Tewkesbury* (1910).
Healings Flour Mills *Healings of Tewkesbury* (1981).
Henson, G. *History of the framework knitters* (1831).
Hilton, C. *Tewkesbury in old picture postcards* (1982).
A short history of the Mythe, Tewkesbury (1985).
Langland, W. *Piers the Plowman* (c1379, Penguin ed. in modern English 1959).
Leland, J. *Itinerary of England and Wales* (c1530; 1945 edition).
Linnell, B. *Public houses of the Tewkesbury Borough* (1972).
Tewkesbury battles and soldiers (1975).
The Tewkesbury Volunteers: 1750-1950 (1972).
Theot, Guppy and Wulf (1978). A study of names and their meanings. (Very informative on alleys in particular).
MacLagan, D. W. *A popular guide to Tewkesbury Abbey* (1979).
Marples, M. J. *The founders of Tewkesbury Abbey* (1982).
Mulock, D. M. (Mrs Craik) *John Halifax, Gentleman* (1856).
North, W. *The Battle of Tewkesbury* (c1900).
A handbook and guide to Tewkesbury (c1912).
Notes on old Tewkesbury (c1900).
Old houses of Tewkesbury (c1900).
Tewkesbury Abbey (c1900).
Oxford Dictionary of English Placenames.
Payne, G. E. *A survey of Gloucestershire* (c1940).
Piggott's *Directory of Gloucestershire* (1844 and 1863).
Rammell, T. W. *Report to the General Board of Health . . . into the . . . sanitary conditions . . . of Tewkesbury*.
Reddell, E. *A history of the Abbey Church . . . at Tewkesbury* (1816).
Rolt, L. T. C. *The Dowty Story. 2 Vols* (1962 and 1973).
Rudder, S. *A new history of Gloucestershire* (1779).
Seymour, J. *The countryside explained* (1977).
Smyth, J. *Men and armour for Gloucerstershire* (1608).
Tewkesbury Borough Council *Beneath Tewkesbury's buildings* (c1980).
Official guide (1984).
Old Baptist Chapel (c1980).
Tewkesbury Borough Council and Tewkesbury Chamber of Commerce *Tewkesbury: official guides* (1952 and 1960).
Tewkesbury Register (1858-1964).
Verey, D. *Gloucestershire: the Vale and the Forest of Dean* (1970. Buildings of England series).
Victoria History of the County of Gloucestershire. Vols II and VIII (1907 and 1964).
Witts, F. *The diary of a Cotswold parson* (1978).

Index

Figures in *italics* refer to illustration

Subscribers

Presentation Copies

1 Tewkesbury Town Council
2 Tewkesbury Borough Council
3 Gloucestershire County Council
4 Tewkesbury Library
5 Tewkesbury Abbey
6 Tewkesbury Museum
7 The John Moore Museum
8 Rev Michael Moxon

9 Reg & Kathleen Ross
10 Clive & Carolyn Birch
11 Ruth Turnbull
12 Paul Sandback
13 Frank Stokes
14 Mrs D.M. Massey
15 Miss R.F. Holmes
16 E.H. Davis
17 S. Avery
18 Mrs R. Hogan
19 Mrs E.M. Knoyle
20 Mrs S.M. Schofield
21 Mrs N.G. Brown
22 B.G. Murray
23 Mr & Mrs Peter Griffin
24 Mr & Mrs B.J. Beecher
25 Mrs J.M. Sklenar
26 Mrs J.A. Raggatt
27 Mrs J.A. Raggatt
28 E.F. Potter
29 Miss H. Milton
30 Mr & Mrs J.A. Stedman
31 Mrs W. Snarey
32 A.E. Malpas
33 R.W. Mills
34 Mrs D. Hartland
35 Rev Rowland W. Heming
36 J.W. Birch
37 Mrs J.L. Spencer Futter
38 R.C. Woodard
39 Victoria & Albert Museum
40 London Guildhall Library
41 Mrs B.J. Fedrick
42 F.R. Sollis
43 Mrs N. Fowler
44 D.N. Avery
45 Alan Smith
46 Mrs Joan Lock
47
48 Mrs Daisy O'Beirne
49 Mrs J. Stew
50 Mr & Mrs T. Riccalton
51 Mrs M. Turner
52 Miss Grace Powell
53 Mrs J. Taylor
54 Mrs S. Piff
55 R.F. Green
56 R.C. Stanford
57 Mrs L. Henshall
58 Mrs Y. Wakeling
59 Mrs M. Turner
60 K. Wignall
61 D.M. Willavoys
62 Mrs P. Brooke
63 Mrs E. Bird
64 Mrs A.C. Hayward
65 Mrs P. Evans
66 D.G. Carter
67 C. Price
68 C. Burford
69 Mrs M.D. Brixey
70 Peter J. Brown
71 Miss M.J. Clark
72 P. Wagstaff
73 Mrs C. Romeo
74 H. Innocent
75 C.A. Nightingale
76 Joy Everitt
77 Mrs M. Weatherly
78 Mrs B. McEwan
79 P.A.J. Culver
80 Mrs R.C. Grimshaw
81 Mrs L.M. Whittaker
82 G.N.L. Nimmo
83 Isabel Masters
84 Mrs Beryl O. Williamson
85 R.B. Horne
86 Mrs D. Walker
87 Mrs S.J. Hobbs
88 Mrs S. Toms
89 Frank Peachey
90 Mrs M.E. Devereux
91 Mrs Wendy Harrison
92 Graham Pollock
93 A.L.J. Page
94 R.D. Walker
95 Mrs L.S. Culross
96 Monica Prole
97 Mrs C.A. Lloyd
98 R.C. Mavin
99 Mrs H. Castle
100 Mrs R.H. Collier
101 William J. Llewellyn
102 Miss O. Grace Powell
103 Betty Ellis
104 D.B. Smith
105 Mrs D. M. Cole
106 F.S. Askew
107 John Melhuish
108 Mrs Jane Swindail
109 Mrs C. Carter
110 D.W.H. Watts
111 Mrs M. Calveley
112 Mrs G.E. Northey
113 Mrs Mary Avery
114 J. Fletcher
115 Mrs J.A. Ross
116 Miss Elizabeth Melling
117 Mrs E. Grant
118 Mrs J.A. Gascoyne
119 Mrs M. Pitman
120 Mrs S. Pitts
121 Mrs M. Turner
122 Katie Thomson
123 Mrs E. Taylor
124 Mrs V.M. Fowkes
125 Mrs P.C. Goddard
126 N. Balster
127 Noel G. Slaney
128 A.F.J. Fogden
129 Mrs C. Silburn
130 R.B. Elmes
131 Allen Moorhouse
132 Mrs K. Hall
133 C. Dobson
134 Mrs G. Barker
135 Mr & Mrs A.E. Bell
136 A.H. Cole
137
138 Beryl Barnes
139 Janet Yvonne Woods
140 Mrs P.E. Smith
141 Roger M. Martins
142 R.W. Panter
143 R.F. Green
144 Pam Hall
145 K.A. Follett
146 Mrs E. Cumberlin
147 C.J. Stephens
148 Mrs P. McQuillan
149
150 Mrs I. Pearse
151 N.H. Plester
152 Miss M.F. Purden
153 L.A. Cameron
154 G.F. Carter
155 V.L.J. Hanks
156 Mrs Carol M. Nicolle
157 Frank Holley
158 Mrs P.M. Tamlyn
159 J.V. Garrett
160 J.M. Beard
161 Mrs W.M. Nunn
162 M.S. Candler
163 A.J. Hall
164 Miss J. Hamblett
165 R.G. Collett
166 L.J. Halling
167 Peter E. Holland
168 P.E. Ricketts
169 Simon D. Williams
170 Dr & Mrs Steven Blake
171 Simon F. Wilson-Chalon
172 T. Bruce Bayley
173 Dr A. N. Crowther
174 D.N. Hodges
175 F. Richmond
176 Mrs A. Gardener
177 L.W. Buchanan
178 Robert J. Haines
179 M.W. Trott
180 Mrs Dora Bond
181 Mrs Wardle Robinson
182 Elizabeth & Peter Mills
183 Stuart Benley
184 Inett Homes
185 Barbara Tyler
186 Mrs Parsons
187 Frank Stokes
188 Mrs Hilary Swan
189 Phillips Pickford
190 M.J. Marshman
191 John R. King
192 K.G.W. Household
193 Oxstalls Campus Library
194 Newtown W.I.

195 Ms R. Turnbull
196 R.G. Otter
197 Michael J. Fisher
198 N.H.K. Coleman
199 E. Mylrea Dickson
200 Alan Saville
201 Mrs M.R. Shephard
202 Mrs W. Rowe
203 M.W.H. Shephard
204
205 Mrs Brenda Ilott
206 P.A.S. Aldridge
207 Michael J. Mulrenan
208 The Vicar of Tewkesbury
209 Miss J. Crawford
210 R.W. Panter
211 Roy Smith
212 Mrs Lawrence
213 Anne S. Lloyd
214 T.R. Wollatt
215 Harry Lewis
216 Lena M. Clarke
217 G.A. Crofts JP
218 Kenneth Lloyd Hodges
219 R. Pitt
220 Miss M. Clarke
221 N.E. Sprackling
222 Harry Oliver Workman
223 Roger Hewins Workman
224 Michael J. Bailey
225 Mrs D. Wagstaff
226 Eric Sydney Phillips
227 Mitton Manor
232 School
233
235 Miss S. Gomm
236 Mrs Yvonne Wakeling
237 S.J. Boskett
238 Christine Stokes
239 A.E. Fowler
240 Mrs Winifred Page
241 Mrs A.F. Woodward
242 W.P. Miles
243 S.R. Reynolds
244 J.I. Peachey
245 R.G. Price
246 W.A. Gidley
247 Mrs Carrol Sherlock
248 A.P. Bluck
249 Tewkesbury Borough Council
250 E.G. Russell
251 Mrs Kay Duck
252 Mrs C. Cresswell
253 D.M. Griffiths
254 Mrs J. Coombes
255 A.W. Lewis
256 Mrs E. Raggatt
257 S.R.S. Rhymes
258 A.W. Lewis
259 P.R. Strickland
260 E.O. Bright
261 Mrs B.D. Dudfield
262 Mrs M. Wilkes
263 G.C. Beaumont
264 R.A. Dauncey
265 G.P. Edyvean-Walker
266 Lynne Cox
267 H.W. Nash
268 Judy Short
269 Mr & Mrs J.W. Rennison
270 Mr & Mrs R.D. Taylor
271 Amanda Jane Graham
272 R.C. Merchant
273 Kerrie David Workman
274 Richard Allan
275 Willian L. Pitt
276
277 H.R.W. Roberts
278 Arthur Charles Hawker
279 Ellen Moore
280 Michael James Waddell
281 Leslie Compton
282 Mrs Judith Hird
283 Lt Col J.O. Endall
284 W.S. Cooper
285 Barbara Joy
286 G.C. Spry
287
288 H. Didcote
289 Richard G. Turner
290 Mrs A.R. Langford
291 J.A. Thompson
292 G. Mills
293 Michael J. Andrews
294 David H. Aldred
295 Mrs Sheila Jillian Parry
296 Diana Parke
297 Ninian Johnston
298 Stephen W. Stokes
299
300 Dr G.A. Fletcher
301 Stanley Greenland
302 Lindsay Allinson
303 A.T. Hendry
304 R.J. Pates
305 Alan Goose
306 J.E. Hallmark
307 G.F. Carter
308 Jean Watson Fenwick
309 C. Burd
310 D.J. Mace
311 Mrs M. Glenn
312 Colonel W.H. Blakemore
313 Mrs Susan Wright
314 Mrs S. Ridgeon
315 Mrs E. Robertson
316 Rev Brian Underwood
317 Grahame Buckland
318 R.D. Pitt-Stewart
319 Mrs A.C. Allum
320 Ann Mathie
321 F.W. Chescoe
322 Mrs K.A. Overton
323 M.J. Buckland
324 Graham Sanders
325 O.F. Thomassen-Telle
326 Robert J. Bowers
327 K.R. & H.I. Taylor
328 M.W. Peachey
329 W.J. Sandy
330 Barry J. Hall
331 Robert Lewis
332 Miss J.E. Bagg
333 Eric R. Cox
334 June Evans
335 Sheila Crosby
336 Mrs L.J. Thomas
337 J.E.P. Kibble
338 A.L. Morgan
339 J.R. Round ISM
340 Mrs V.F. Smith
341 Mr & Mrs A. Brazier
342 Mrs J.D. Start
343 H.O. Workman
344 Ian Bartlett
345 Mrs A. Devaney
346 A.G. Rogers
347 Mrs A.V. Butler
348 Mrs Shirley Turner
349
350 Mrs Mary Pollard
351 Charles Henry Allchurch
352 J.W. Shakles
353 M.W. Thompson
354 Mrs P. Burns
355
356 Michael Walsh
357 M. Oxford
358 Mr Redfern
359 Mrs D. Shakespeare
360 K. Sutcliffe
361 J. Fletcher
362 Mrs A. Taylor
363 Joan Sharman
364 Mrs A. Morris
365 Mrs E. Williams
366 A. Craven
367 Mrs E. Sargeant
368 Mrs J. Herbert
369 Miss M. Steel
370 Mrs F.E. Wagstaff
371 C. Allen
372 G. Campbell-Browning
373 A. South
374 Mrs W. Matty
375 Mr & Mrs L.M. Davies
376 Alan David Whitby
377 Mrs E.M. Moses
378 Frank Treen
379 Mrs Jem Davis
380 H. Harris
381 C.N. Richards
382 Mrs J. Monaghan
383 Mrs Elizabeth Swan
384 Miss F. Fisher
385 W.C. Walker
386 Handyman Centre
387 Mrs R. Parnham
388 Mrs M.J. Jarvis
389 Miss Margaret J. Pyman
390 Mrs J.C. Wilding
391 Mr & Mrs H.C.E. Lovejoy
392 Joyce Clements
393 Mrs M.J. Jarvis
394 James Lewis
395 Gloucestershire
416 County Library
417 Archie Mew
418 Charles Frederick
419 Mrs K.W. Long
420
421 G. Caudle
422 Mavis D. Ricketts
423 Edward G. Cook
424 John Pocock
425 Andrew M. Kidd
426 J.W. Cooper
427 John Richard Copper

Remaining names unlisted.

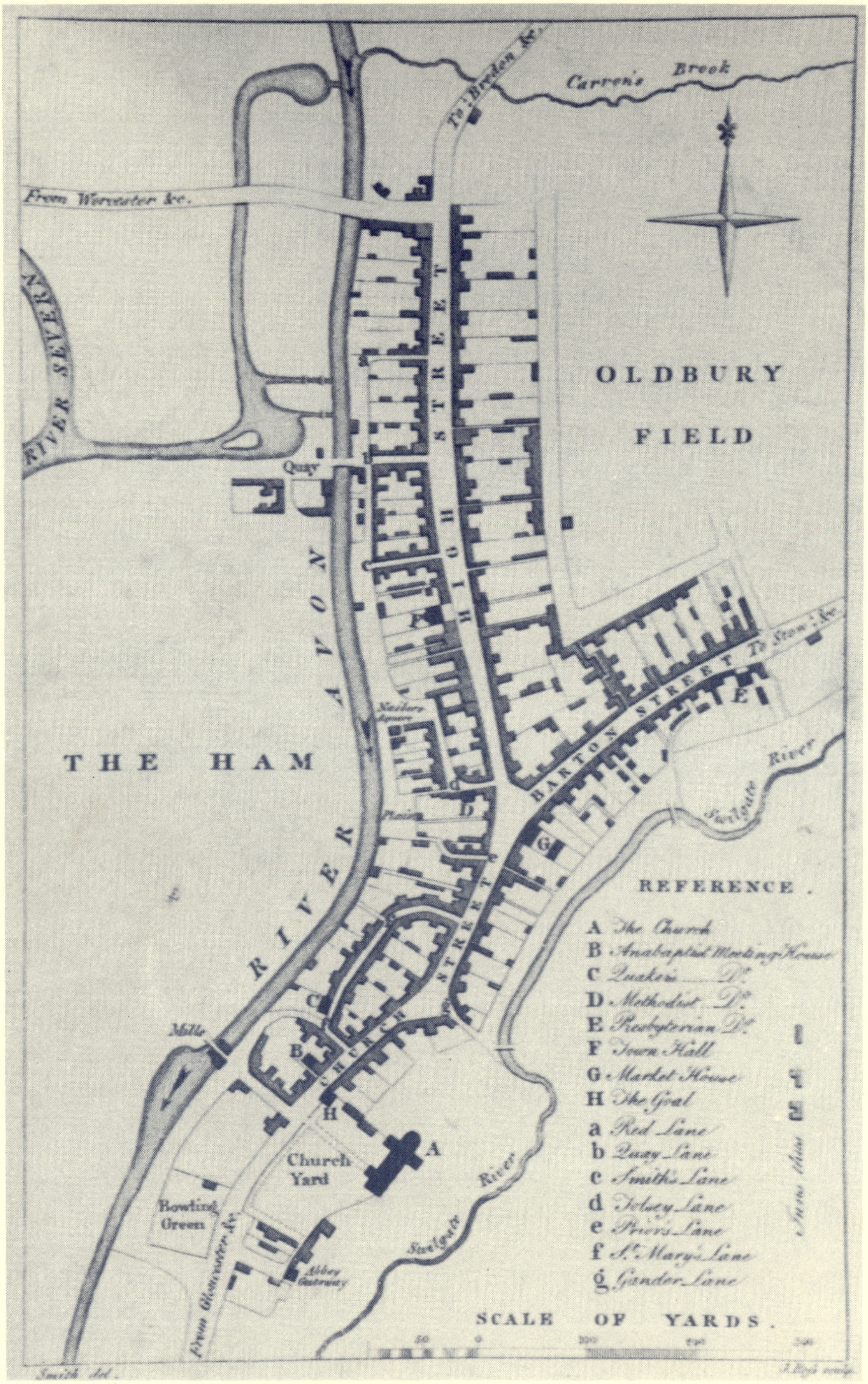
Carren's Brook
To Breden &c.
From Worcester &c.
RIVER SEVERN
OLDBURY FIELD
HIGH STREET
Quay
RIVER AVON
THE HAM
BARTON STREET
To Stow &c.
Swilgate River
CHURCH STREET
Mills
Church Yard
Bowling Green
From Gloucester &c.
Abbey Gateway
Swilgate River
REFERENCE.
A The Church
B Anabaptist Meeting House
C Quaker's ..... D°.
D Methodist .. D°.
E Presbyterian D°.
F Town Hall
G Market House
H The Goal
a Red Lane
b Quay Lane
c Smith's Lane
d Tolsey Lane
e Prior's Lane
f S^t. Mary's Lane
g Gander Lane
SCALE OF YARDS.
50 0 100 200 300
Smith del.

ABBA annual

£ 1·30

the abba story

The Abba story really begins as far back as 1966. At that time, the group which has become world famous, and perhaps the most popular in the world, had not been formed.

In the summer of that year young Bjorn Ulvaeus, working with the Hootenanny Singers, one of the best known Swedish pop groups, met Benny Andersson, at that time playing organ and writing songs for another group called the Hep Stars. They met at a party at Linkoping held because three Hootenanny Singers had been called up for military service.

Firm attachments were not formed at once, but a couple of months later at another party, this time in Vastervik, Bjorn and Benny found themselves together again.

During a long conversation they found out that they had similar views on music and one of them said, "Right, let's write a song together".

Immediately, they drove off in the middle of the night to a paper mill where Bjorn's father was working. Quickly they took over an office, hauled up an organ, guitars and amplifiers and started composing.

The result was a song called "Isn't It Easy to Say" and eventually it was recorded by the Hep Stars.

For some years after that, Benny and Bjorn followed separate careers, and then Bjorn became discontented with the type of music played by the Hootenanny Singers.

He wanted to do something more demanding and when the Hep Stars guitarist Janne Frisk failed to get home from Spain on time for a Swedish tour, Bjorn was delighted to be asked to stand in for Janne.

The tour brought Benny and Bjorn closer together and when the Hep Stars split up in 1969, they had a chance to collaborate even more.

Benny and fellow Hep Star Sveene Hedlund decided to put on a floor show cabaret style act with Sveene's wife Lotta. Bjorn made up the fourth member of the group and they played some of the finest clubs and restaurants in Sweden.

Bjorn met Agnetha Faltskog around the same time as Benny met Anni-Fred Lyngstad. In 1970 the four teamed up in the Festfolk Quartet and put on a show at Tragarn in Gothenburg on 1st November. This was Abba's first stage performance . . . but of course, the famous name was some way away.

Benny and Bjorn slowly emerged as the best writing team Swedish pop music had seen and their compositions began to take on importance outside Sweden.

On July 7th, 1971 Bjorn and Agnetha married in Verum parish

church in the southern province of Skane. The same day, Bengt Bernhag, friend and partner to Stig Anderson died after a long illness.

Bengt and Stig had formed the music publishing and recording business which had become the most dynamic in Scandinavia and had recorded the hits of the Hootenanny Singers. With the tragic loss of Bengt, Stig was forced to take a realistic approach and asked Bjorn if he would become the producer at Polar Music.

Bjorn agreed but insisted on Benny being also employed, and they split the salary between them. Success followed quickly as Bjorn's and Benny's talents were developed more and more by Stig until many top singers were having substantial hits with the boys' compositions.

Then in 1972, a record called "She's My Kind of Girl" established a pattern for the future. Bjorn and Benny recorded the song and used Agnetha and Frida as the backing choir.

The next couple of records carried only the names of the two boys, but the girls' voices were beginning to dominate the vocal content and before very long the label read: "Bjorn, Benny, Agnetha and Frida".

The quartet grew in recognition, mainly in Sweden, and in the Autumn of 1972 Swedish Television invited them to compete for the Swedish element of the Eurovision Song Contest.

Bjorn, Benny and Stig went to their hide-out on the holiday islands near Stockholm and emerged with the song "Ring Ring".

The previous year, Lena Anderson had pulled off a third place with a song called "Better to Have Loved", written by Bjorn, Benny and Stig. This time it was agreed that Bjorn, Benny, Agnetha and Frida would sing the new song, although Agnetha's presence was very doubtful because

she was expecting a baby on February 2nd and the selection contest was to take place on February 10th.

Agnetha managed to get through the contest, her daughter Linda arriving a week or so later.

"Ring Ring" was voted by the 'panel of experts' into third place, much to the fury of the fans and TV viewers. The newspapers agreed with the fans and that was the last occasion 'experts' were used in the judging.

Third place was at first a disappointment, but before long "Ring Ring" became a firm international success even without Eurovision help. In Sweden it broke all records and achieved greater success than the Beatles had done in their hey-day.

About this time, the name Abba began to emerge in the Swedish newspapers.

"When I spoke to journalists", explains Stig Anderson, "I couldn't be bothered with the four individual names, so I started using their initials, ABBA. Soon the newspapers were using this name all the time.

"Bjorn and Benny were not happy at first because Abba is something like the name of a well-known brand of pickled herring in Sweden, but very soon we all agreed that it was a first class name for international purposes; it's easy to pronounce in any language".

It was realised that if Abba was to gain the international success for which each member of the group hoped, it would not come as easily as their choice of name. It was announced that the group would have the chance to represent Sweden once more in the Eurovision Contest. Firstly they needed to make sure they could gain those extra votes needed to top the Europoll. But the Eurovision Contest is

notorious for creating one-hit-wonders. Abba wanted to remain a success. And that meant much hard work and careful planning.

To start with, Bjorn and Benny decided to write in English and, together with Stig, they wrote the pop masterpiece "Waterloo", which they then performed with crispness and perfection at the 1974 Eurovision contest in Brighton. In the end they were easy winners, but only Abba will know just what effort went behind the eventual success.

Abba's Eurovision win took the Western world by storm, and "Waterloo" soon became a British number one. The record also topped the charts in just about every European country, as well as achieving considerable success in America.

"Waterloo" was to prove an almost universal key to the charts, but there was one country in which Abba were unable to consolidate the success – Britain!

As we know, Abba was to bounce back into the British charts before too long, but in today's fast changing music world, it seemed like a very long time indeed. When "SOS" was high in the charts, Benny Andersson explained how he felt about the absence from the British scene.

"In England, we didn't get the image we deserved. Because we won Eurovision, we got the image that goes with Eurovision, and it's not really correct. We just happened to be in the contest – for example, I think we'd prefer the sort of reputation that the Mamas and Papas had.

"In Sweden, we have a similar status to that of Elton John in Britain. We're practically the only group that reaches outside Sweden".

Abba might have distinguished themselves at Brighton by being the first group to achieve a Euro win, but the British record buyers did not seem concerned about the group's follow-up records.

"Ring Ring" was released for a second time in Britain – it had previously been issued at the time of the 1973 contest – but the song, jointly written by Benny, Bjorn, Stig, Phil Cody and Neil Sedaka, only made the top fifty for a couple of weeks. In addition, Abba's "Waterloo" album was only a moderate success.

For the next year Abba continued to build a reputation as international hitmakers, following their 5 million plus worldwide sales of the single "Waterloo"

Usually, when singles are taken from albums, diminishing success is expected for each subsequent release, but with the "Abba" LP it was to be a very different story.

The third single release from the album was "SOS", which changed many a critic's regard for Abba's musical ability, and the Super Swedes were delighted to see it high in the British Top Ten.

Everyone was acclaiming "SOS" when "Mama Mia" sent Abba back to the top of the charts in January last year.

That success and later 1976 hits put Abba on the road to becoming Britain's top group.

The January number one was followed by two more chart toppers, "Fernando" and "Dancing Queen", and a fourth single, "Money, Money, Money" only just failed to make the top slot. "Knowing Me, Knowing You" smashed to the top recently keeping the ABBA momentum going. Add to their single successes two top selling albums, "Abba's Greatest Hits" and "Arrival", and it is easy to see why Abba has achieved more than any other group or artist since the Beatles.

As the album says, Abba have "Arrived", but the acclaim of being the world's number one recording artists hasn't changed their way of living, working and enjoying themselves, which is best summed up with Stig Anderson's four rules for success and happiness.

"Always work very hard — do your best and don't forget a thing". And the fourth and most important rule? "Don't take life too seriously".

Bjorn, Benny, Anna and Frida get a great deal of pleasure out of their work, but they get even more out of sharing their happiness with their fans through their music.

BJORN ULVAEUS

Bjorn was born in Gothenburg in the west of Sweden on April 25th, 1945. He had his first taste of music and performing in the town of Vastervik where his family had moved to when he was eleven.

Vastervik literally translated means "West Bay" and that is what Bjorn's first group was called. He formed it with some school friends and they sang numbers like those performed by the Kingston Brothers and Brothers Four.

"We copied our American idols shamelessly", Bjorn recalls. "Our whole programme consisted of material with English lyrics".

Then Stig Anderson came along. In America the craze for Hootenanny singing developed and Stig looked around for likely recording talents who could produce a similar style for the Swedish market.

He persuaded the boys to sing more folklore songs of Swedish origin, and next there was a smash hit group called the Hootenanny Singers.

Many hits followed, but Bjorn wanted to do other things . . . know more about the music industry. He was still a student studying corporative law, but he knew that he would have to move to Stockholm if he wanted to achieve his real ambitions.

In 1968 Bjorn made his first solo record and had considerable success. Then he turned his hand to song writing and producing quickly followed. The professional background was complete. A veteran at the age of 23, Bjorn was ready to begin the pop revolution known as ABBA.

Birth date:	July 25th, 1945
Birth place:	Gothenburg
Height:	1.76 m
Weight:	60 kg
Colour of eyes:	Blue
Colour of hair:	Dark Blonde
Instruments played:	Guitars
Age entered show business:	17
First hit:	"Jaguantar"
Hobbies:	Reading, boats, music
Favourite singers:	John Lennon, Elton John
Favourite actor:	Jack Nicholson
Favourite actress:	Liv Ullman
Favourite food:	French
Favourite drink:	French wines
Favourite colour:	Blue
Favourite band:	Beatles, Beachboys
Favourite composer:	Lennon/McCartney
Likes:	Honesty, humour
Dislikes:	Hypocrisy
Real Name:	Bjorn Christian Ulvaeus
Nick Name:	

abba's eurosound

On a cool April night in Brighton three years ago, the Eurovision Song Contest underwent a change—one from which it will never recover. For the previous eighteen years, predictable ballads and jolly sing-a-long songs had won first place in the contest, but on Saturday, April 6th, 1974, they were forgotten.

Four young people dressed in glitter, a contrast to the usual evening dress, swept the board with a song that was pure pop. The group: Abba. The song: "Waterloo".

Before the contest, Abba had thought that they had a good song, but they had also thought that it was a little out of style to be a Eurovision winner. Even so, they backed themselves to win at 20 to 1 and picked up a cool £500!

"Waterloo" was regarded by many as being a clear head and shoulders above the general Eurovision standard. The song had a strong melodic content and a vitality that the rest of the entries couldn't match.

Abba's win marked the first triumph by a group in the contest. They romped home six votes ahead of the rest of the field, looking like silver-booted visitors from another planet in their futuristic gear. Apparently, the glitter wasn't their usual style of dress, but it certainly set the Brighton Dome sparkling! Even their musical director, Sven-Olof Walldoff, joined in the fun by wearing a complete Napoleonic outfit to conduct the orchestra!

Abba's manager, Stig Anderson, who co-wrote "Waterloo" with Benny and Bjorn, said that they had written the song deliberately choosing a name — Napoleon — that everyone, whether Japanese, Indian or American, would recognise.

Stig had already tried the song out on a worldwide music audience at the Midem '74 music festival in Cannes, and it received a very encouraging response.

"Waterloo" had originally been written as album material, and Abba chose it for the contest because it

seemed the most fresh and lively tune amongst their numbers. It was submitted as the Swedish entry, along with the songs of nine other composers who were invited to take part. For the first time that year, Sweden's way of selecting its song was left up to the television viewers — and they obviously knew a winner when they heard it!

The year before, Abba had come third in Eurovision with "Ring Ring", which went on to become a big international hit. They were determined that 1974 was going to be **their** year, and that they would finally make their mark on the British pop public. And to make doubly sure of success, the group came armed with their own secret weapon!

A few months before, Anna had been given a large stuffed toy donkey as a mascot, and she insisted on bringing it to England for Eurovision, convinced that it would bring Abba luck. Despite the others' appeals to leave the donkey behind, Anna did bring it with her. Maybe it was even luckier than she thought, though, for the day after winning Eurovision, Anna went down with a sore throat and the doctor ordered her to bed. It would have been a different story — one of disaster rather than success — had it happened a day or so earlier!

The contest itself was watched by 500 million viewers who tuned in throughout Europe. The silver and black stage, which turned pink, turquoise and yellow throughout the show, cost £5,000.

The organisers of Eurovision that year were worried about possible incidents, and the whole affair was shrouded in a heavy security blanket. Guests were checked on arrival with airport-style metal detectors and special rods for examining the inside of jacket seams. But they needn't have worried. The evening passed off peacefully — unless you count Abba's explosive performance on stage, that is!

For the first time, there were four genuine pop groups appearing in the contest, complete with drums and backing tracks. Second place that year went to a haunting Italian song, while Britain's entry, "Long Live Love" sung by Olivia Newton-John, came joint fourth.

One amusing moment came when the awards were presented. Abba had difficulty in convincing the people concerned that they had actually written "Waterloo", too, and consequently they weren't given the composer's award until after the show.

After their win, Abba were, needless to say, absolutely delighted. Commented Benny at the time: "It's great that we have helped to bring more up-to-date music to the contest.

"I'm amazed at our success", he added. "I'm so surprised and pleased that I can hardly talk. We thought perhaps Holland would win. We really didn't think that we would.

"One of the nicest things about it was that almost every country voted for us, it wasn't a big vote from one country that gave us the decision".

It was champagne all the way the day after Eurovision. There was an official party first, and then Abba got down to some celebrating of their own! They even drank champagne with their breakfast.

A few days later, their British record company, CBS, held a big reception for them with smoked salmon and strawberries and cream. It's a wonder Abba didn't go home weighing half a stone more than when they arrived!

In just a few short days, "Waterloo" rocketed to victory. It topped the charts in Sweden, Norway, Denmark and Holland, and was selling 20,000 copies a day in England, to give them another number one. Abba received offers from just about every television station in Europe; their future was secure. They were destined to become more than the usual Eurovision one-hit-wonders, and it was a success that the talented foursome deserved.

AGNETHA FALTSKOG

Born in Jonkoping in the middle of Sweden, Agnetha Faltskog was encouraged to take to the stage very early in life. Her father used to run local amateur revues and by the time Agnetha was eight years old she was composing her own songs.

At fifteen, Anna started to sing with a local dance band and in 1967 CBS records played some test tapes she had made.

Immediately she was signed for a long term contract and after that Sweden took Anna to its heart. Germany also responded to her fabulous looks and great singing talents and before long the blonde beauty was a very valuable pop star in her own right.

On the subject of her relationships with the other members of the group Anna has this to say:

"People think you have to be pieces of the same cloth to be able to work successfully together.

"Not so! As people, we are really very different couples. Bjorn and I are what I would call "morning people". Benny and Frida prefer to sleep late. We don't like to hang about much, eating fancy food in late night restaurants for example. Benny and Frida almost always disappear when we are on tour, sampling small restaurants till the small hours of the morning.

"But we work well together, and that's the most important thing of all".

Birth date:	April 5th, 1950
Birth place:	Jonkoping
Height:	1.72 m
Weight:	56 kg
Colour of eyes:	Blue-green
Colour of hair:	Light blonde
Instruments played:	Piano
Age entered show business:	17
First hit:	"I Was So in Love"
Hobbies:	Swimming, reading, dancing
Favourite singer:	Stevie Wonder
Favourite actor:	Jack Nicholson
Favourite actress:	Liv Ullman
Favourite food:	Chinese, French
Favourite drink:	Whisky, milk, champagne
Favourite colour:	Blue, red
Favourite band:	10cc, Eagles Beachboys
Favourite composer:	Lennon/McCartney, Ulvaeus
Likes:	Children, summer
Dislikes:	War, falseness
Real Name:	Agnetha Ase Faltskog
Nick Name:	Anna

SUPER ★ STAR

abba at work and play

Whether they're at work or play, Abba always make sure of one thing — that they're enjoying themselves!

It's a well-known fact that they dislike touring intensely and do as little of it as possible. The tiring life on the road, hanging around in airport lounges and living out of suitcases from one hotel to the next is not for them. Instead, they prefer to rely on films to promote their records.

They have supplied highly professional video films, arranged and produced by themselves, to television companies all over the world, each film fitting perfectly with the mood of the record it is promoting.

Said Bjorn, "When we go on the road, we need about forty people plus a whole mass of equipment to ensure that we get the results on stage that we want. We've relied on films to boost our record sales, rather than undertake the high cost and problems involved in doing a tour".

"Touring can make you mad", Bjorn continued. "It's the most anti-social life you can lead. You don't live like normal people and it's difficult to get both feet back on the ground after a tour has finished. A lot of groups do almost three hundred dates in a year, living in a strange world of unreality".

Another problem is finding the time to fit in all their commitments — it would be extremely difficult for Abba to take on extended concert tours even if they wanted to. Benny and Bjorn are still the principal producers for Polar Records and both Anna and Frida still record solo material for release in Scandinavia.

Writing their songs is considered a 9 to 5 routine job for Benny and

Bjorn — 10 am to 10 pm if they're recording. Then there is the business side to be organised, plus producing. It all makes for a hectic life!

Benny and Bjorn start their day by deciding exactly what they're going to write, and then they get on with it. They try to eliminate songs that they know won't work as they go along, rather than record fifty numbers and then waste all but ten of them. And they only write what they want to write! Abba refuse to be dictated to about their music, where and when they work — and they defy anyone to drag them away from Sweden for more than two weeks at a time.

Because of their individually successful careers, Abba don't rely on the group for their existence, which means that a lot of the pressures facing other top groups are removed. In many ways, Abba admit that the group is more of a hobby to them.

They work together because they want to — and they enjoy it. Frida commented: "Unlike some groups, we all like being together. Despite the fact that we're all paired off romantically, we all genuinely like each other"!

Added Benny: "It's much more fun working together than it ever was working apart. We're all enjoying ourselves enormously".

The four prefer a quiet life to the hectic pop world. They have homes in Stockholm, in an exclusive suburb a mere five minutes from the sea, where they work and relax. They make plans in the comfort of their own living rooms, working on new

ideas and creating songs in an atmosphere that they love.

The four also have holiday homes on the Island of Vittso, a small island in one of the numerous fjords that surround the Swedish coastline, where they escape as often as possible for some rest and privacy. As Anna said, it's the one place where they can go and not be hounded by fans!

Anna and husband Bjorn have a very special reason for wanting to spend as much of their time at home as possible. She's called Linda, and she's their little daughter! They tried taking her to America once but she didn't enjoy it. They flew from Stockholm straight to California, but it was just too much for her.

Bjorn explained that Linda obviously enjoys herself most at home. She wants to stay there, because that's where she feels happiest, and so, when he and Anna have some free time, they obviously want to spend it with their daughter.

It's not possible for them to be with her every minute of the day, and Bjorn and Anna have a nanny to take over when the need arises. And of course, Linda's grandparents are only too pleased to help out!

Linda isn't really aware of the fact that her parents are famous pop stars. She thinks it's quite normal to have a mummy and daddy who are always appearing on the television. And she's word perfect on all the Abba songs!

As you can see, the lives of Bjorn, Benny, Anna and Frida are hectic, full . . . but happy. And that's what counts!

BENNY ANDERSSON

Benny's full name is Goran Bror Benny Andersson and he was born in Stockholm on December 16th, 1946.

Benny's father and grandfather played the piano accordion and on his sixth birthday young Benny was given an instrument to tinker around with. Tinker is the wrong word. Very quickly he could copy some Swedish folk songs verifying the fact that he had a good ear for music.

Since those early days, Benny has proceeded in similar manner, for he says, "I never took a formal music lesson in my life. Perhaps a few hours piano in school – but it bored me stiff. Music to me should be fun".

Close to the Andersson home was a teen club. Soon Benny was occupying the piano in the intermissions, pounding out boogie woogie rythms.

Talent will find a way out and before long, Benny was featured with a group called the Hep Stars which, during the sixties was rivalling the Beatles for Swedish popularity on the rock scene.

The group's days, however, were numbered for tax problems and financial difficulties forced the Hep Stars to disband. Benny does not regret the problems.

"It took me four long years to pay all my tax debts", he says, "but I did it . . . and all from my own writing and composing".

Birth date:	December 16th, 1946
Birth place:	Stockholm
Height:	1.8 m
Weight:	75 kg
Colour of eyes:	Blue
Colour of hair:	Blonde
Instruments played:	Piano, accordion, guitar
Age entered show business:	16
First hit:	"Cadillac"
Hobbies:	Modern Art, Music, Reading
Favourite singer:	John Lennon, Rod Stewart
Favourite actor:	Richard Burton
Favourite actress:	Liv Ullman
Favourite food:	French
Favourite drink:	Beer
Favourite colour:	Blue, red and yellow
Favourite band:	Beachboys
Favourite composer:	Tchaikovsky
Real Name:	Soran Bror Benny Andersson
Nick Name:	

abba + stig = success

Behind every great pop group, often there is one man who has guided and advised it to stardom. For Abba, that man is Stig Anderson.

Stig is one of Scandinavia's major music publishers and his company, Polar Music, has achieved success on an international level far in excess of any other Scandinavian company in the business.

And Stig is a very definite part of the team that produces Abba's records. He writes some of the lyrics and is used as a sounding board for Benny and Bjorn's ideas. They try out new songs on him and, depending on his reaction, decide what is going to be used.

Stig's story really starts when he was a teenager. At 16, he asked a girl to dance and she turned him down, so he went straight home and composed a song about her! Later, he performed the song in public — much to the embarrassment of the girl who happened to be in the audience — but it helped him to discover that he could write songs and sing them rather well.

Stig had his first song published in 1950, when he was 19, and he went on to success, writing song after song and performing them in Sweden. He also wrote songs that were recorded by other artists.

The money he earned from his songs was put to good use. It paid for his years at college and, in 1957, he graduated from the National Training College for Teachers in Stockholm.

In 1960, Stig's career took a dramatic turn. He wrote a song for a famous Swedish singer, Lill-Babs. The song was called "Klas-Goran" and it became a huge hit, not only in Sweden but the whole of Scandinavia, also earning a gold disc in Holland. By this time, Stig had realised that, instead of giving his songs to other people to publish, it made sense for him to publish.

He borrowed some money, had the sheet music of "Klas-Goran" printed and, towards the end of 1960, he formed his own publishing company, Sweden Music.

The song brought enormous success to the new company, attracting interest from foreign publishers anxious to publish the song in their own countries. It was through "Klas-Goran" that Stig met a Belgian publisher who asked him to set up a branch of his

company in Stockholm, covering the whole of Scandinavia. It was that Belgian publisher, Robert Bosmans, who taught Stig what the music publishing industry is all about.

The first foreign copyright that Stig Anderson published in Scandinavia was an American number called "You Can Have Her". Stig wrote a Swedish lyric for it and the song became a big hit for Anita Lindblom.

It was a great start for the young music publisher and his company went from strength to strength, with Stig's combined talents as composer, lyricist and translator.

Stig was determined not to stop there. It took him just four years after the formation of Sweden Music for him to expand into records. Polar Records was formed in 1964, with Stig operating in partnership with one of the most successful producers in Sweden at that time, Bengt Bernhag.

Polar Records got off to a big start, just as Sweden Music began life with a hit. The first release was by a group called the Hootenanny Singers, and it was an instant winner.

And so it went on for the next six years, a string of hits bringing success to Stig and Polar Records.

When Bengt Bernhag died in 1970, Stig took over full control of the company. At the time, there were two very promising young men working in Stockholm, Bjorn Ulvaeus and Benny Andersson, combining their talents as artists, songwriters and producers. Bjorn had already worked with Stig as lead singer with the Hootenanny Singers, and Benny had made himself a name in Sweden as a pianist and composer with a highly popular group called the Hep Stars. Both Bjorn and Benny had record production experience, but neither had worked independently — so Stig signed them up.

He predicted a big future for the pair, and teamed them with two girl singers Anni-frid Lyngstad and Agnetha Faltskog. Originally, the group was called simply Bjorn and Benny, with the girls acting as back-up vocals, but as Anni-frid and Agnetha became increasingly important in the musical identity of the group, the name was extended to Bjorn & Benny, Anna & Frida.

But Stig soon realised that the string of four names was both ungainly and difficult for people to remember, so he reduced the group's title to the initials of their names . . . Abba!

From that moment, Abba has enjoyed a fairytale success. Bjorn and Benny are still the principal producers for Polar Records, and Stig is heavily involved in their careers. But he still finds time to produce other artists, including some of the most popular in Scandinavia.

abba • abba • abba • abba •

How much do you know about Abba? Find out with this fun quiz.

1. In which year did Abba win the Eurovision Song Contest?
2. What was their winning song titled?
3. Name the famous general mentioned in the song.
4. Who is Abba's manager?
5. One member of Abba was not born in Sweden. Can you name him/her and where he/she was born?
6. How many British number one did Abba have in 1976?
7. Which was Abba's first big international hit?
8. What is the name of Abba's Swedish record company?
9. Name the capital of Sweden.
10. What was the name of Benny Andersson's first group?
11. Which two members of Abba are married?
12. Anna's first Swedish hit was a self-penned number. Can you name it?
13. Which Abba song was about a distress signal?
14. Can you make the title of an Abba hit from this anagram?

    NEARFOND
15. For which record label do Abba record in Britain?
16. What colour are Bjorn's eyes?
17. Name Benny's favourite group.

Answers on page 46.

abba • abba • abba • abba •

Lois
Lois
JEANS & JACKETS

ANNI~FRED LYNGSTAD

Frida, as Anni-fred has become known, was born in Norway in the small iron exporting town of Narvik situated in the land of the midnight sun.

When she was two, her family moved to Eskilstuna, south-west of Stockholm, another iron town.

When she was very young Frida would sing word for word all the popular songs of the day and it was obvious that she would emerge as a singer.

She made her first stage appearance in an amateur talent contest when she was ten, and entered show business at the age of thirteen.

An early marriage failed and to support her family she began her own dance band singing songs by the Gershwin Brothers, Cole Porter, Rogers and Hart.

The band wasn't a roaring success, but Frida made a living and more importantly, she was singing.

By the time Frida met Benny, she had moved to Stockholm, and there she was invited to appear on a Swedish TV talk show.

Her presence, good looks and obvious talent went down well. The press gave her good credits and almost overnight she was a star with offers for work flooding in from near and far.

Two years of touring with other established Swedish artists, making records, travelling around the world fashioned Frida for the success which was just around the corner . . . the success that was soon to be known as ABBA.

Birth date:	November 15th, 1945
Birth place:	Narvik, Norway
Height:	1.72 m
Weight:	57 kg
Colour of eyes:	Green/brown/blue/ yellow
Colour of hair:	Red
Instruments played:	Piano
Age entered show business:	13
First hit:	"Min Egen Stad"
Hobbies:	Reading books, music
Favourite singer:	Stevie Wonder
Favourite actor:	Jack Nicholson
Favourite actress:	Faye Dunaway
Favourite food:	French
Favourite drink:	Whisky
Favourite colour:	Green and yellow
Favourite band:	Rufus
Favourite composer:	Tchaikovsky
Likes:	Modern Art
Dislikes:	Torture
Real Name:	Anni-Fred Lyngstad
Nick Name:	Frida

just for the

record

If you are a real Abba fan, then you probably have all their records. But if you have any gaps in your collection — or just want to make sure that you haven't — here is an Abba discography, complete with catalogue numbers and release dates. "Ring Ring", Abba's 1973 Eurovision entry was re-released by Epic following the success of "Waterloo".

Ring Ring/Rock 'n' Roll Band	EPC 1793	12/10/73
Waterloo/Watch Out	EPC 2240	5/4/74
Ring Ring/Rock 'n' Roll Band	EPC 1793	21/6/74
So Long/I've Been Waiting for You	EPC 2848	29/11/74
I Do I Do I Do I Do I Do/Rock Me	EPC 3229	4/4/75
SOS/Man in the Middle	EPC 3576	19/9/75
Mamma Mia/Intermezzo No 1	EPC 3790	14/11/75
Fernando/Hey Hey Helen	EPC 4936	5/3/76
Dancing Queen/That's Me	EPC 4499	6/8/76
Money Money Money/Crazy World	EPC 4713	12/11/76

Waterloo: EPC 80179 17/5/74
Waterloo; Sitting in the Palm Tree; King Kong Song; Hasta Manana; My Mama Said; Dance (While the Music Still Goes On); Honey Honey; Watch Out; What about Livingstone?; Gonna Sing You My Love Song; Suzy-Hang-Around; Ring Ring.

Abba: EPC 80835 6/6/75
Mama Mia; Hey Hey Helen; Tropical Loveland; SOS; Man in the Middle; Bang-a-Boomerang; I Do I Do I Do I Do I Do; Rock Me; Intermezzo No 1; I've Been Waiting for You; So Long.

Greatest Hits: EPC 69218 26/3/76
SOS; He's Your Brother; Ring Ring; Hasta Manana; Nina Pretty Ballerina; Honey Honey; So Long; I Do I Do I Do I Do I Do; People Need Love; Bang-a-Boomerang; Another Town Another Train; Mama Mia; Dance (While the Music Still Goes On); Waterloo; Fernando.

Arrival: EPC 86018 12/11/76
When I Kissed the Teacher; Dancing Queen; My Love My Life; Dum Dum Diddle; Knowing Me Knowing You; Money Money Money; That's Me; Why Did It Have to be Me?; Tiger; Arrival.

abba • abba • abba • abba •

Here's another chance to quiz yourself with more Abba questions.

1. **Abba came third in the 1973 Eurovision Song Contest. Can you name their song?**
2. **Where is Abba's holiday home?**
3. **Who is Abba's musical director?**
4. **What was the date of the 1974 Eurovision Song Contest?**
5. **Which country came second that year?**
6. **What is the name of Anna's and Bjorn's daughter?**
7. **On which television programme did Frida make her career breakthrough?**
8. **Can you name the year?**
9. **Where was Bjorn born?**
10. **In which year did Abba get together?**
11. **What is Frida's full christian name?**
12. **What was the toy mascot that Anna insisted on taking to Eurovision in Brighton?**
13. **When was Abba's album, "Abba", released in England?**
14. **What was the name of Stig Anderson's partner in Polar Records?**

Answers on page 46.

abba • abba • abba • abba •

ANSWERS TO PAGE 38

1, 1974. 2, "Waterloo". 3, Napoleon. 4, Stig Anderson. 5, Frida was born in Norvik, a small town in Norway. 6, Three — "Mama Mia", "Fernando", "Dancing Queen". 7, "Ring Ring". 8, Polar Records. 9, Stockholm. 10, The Hep Stars. 11, Bjorn and Anna. 12, "I Was So In Love". 13, "SOS". 14, "Fernando". 15, Epic Records. 16, Blue. 17, The Beatles.

ANSWERS TO PAGE 44

1, "Ring Ring". 2, Isle of Vittso. 3, Sven-Ollof Walldoff. 4, April 6th. 5, Italy. 6, Linda. 7, "Hyland's Corner". 8, 1967. 9, Gothenburg, Western Sweden. 10, 1972. 11, Anni-frid. 12, A stuffed donkey. 13, March, 1975. 14, Bengt Bernhag.

presence

Images of Christ for the Third Millennium

A LINKED SERIES OF EXHIBITIONS
IN SIX CATHEDRALS
THROUGHOUT BRITAIN IN 2004
CELEBRATING 150 YEARS
OF BIBLE*LANDS'* MINISTRY

FEBRUARY TO SEPTEMBER 2004

presence
Images of Christ for the Third Millennium

Exhibition Curator Meryl Doney

Catalogue Editor Tom Devonshire Jones

Designer Carol Marsh

Exhibition coordinators Aileen Campbell, Paul Bayley, Ellie Doney

Bible*Lands* 150th Anniversary Co-ordinator Jean Hatton

Special thanks for invaluable help and support to:

The Dean and Chapter of St Paul's Cathedral, Martin Fletcher, Vicki George, Liz Washford, Anthony Reynolds, Terry Denzinger-Miles, John Erle-Drax, David Tregunna, Cynthia Corbet, Jane England, Anthony Mould, Paul Stolper, The Dean and Chapter of Canterbury Cathedral, Angela Prior, Cathy Martin, The White Cube Gallery, Irene Bradbury, Alexandra Bradley, Isobel King, James Parsons, Alan Thomson, Matthew Dipple, The Very Revd Griff Dines, Alistair Fulton, Alan Kean, Norman Stone, Sally Magnusson, The Dean and Chapter of Worcester Cathedral, Jean Armstrong, The Dean and Chapter of Lincoln Cathedral, Anne James, The Usher Gallery, Jeremy Webster, Janita Alton, Flowers East Gallery, Ben Lawrence, Milly Liverton, Dan Flowers, The Dean and Chapter of Durham Cathedral, Canon Bill Hall, Anne Heywood, Scottish Arts Council.

This exhibition has been made possible by the generous support of the following:

The Christian Arts Trust, The Drapers' Company, Juliet & Andrew Gibbs, The Gibbs Family Trust, Greenbelt Communion Fund, The Hope Scott Trust, The Jerusalem Trust, St Mary's Cathedral, Glasgow, Scottish Arts Council New Project Fund, friends and trustees of Bible*Lands*.

Selective use has been made of the text and images that artists were invited to supply. All works are in the collection of the artists unless otherwise stated.

Front cover *Vigil*: light installation by Willie Williams for Canterbury Cathedral

Published by Bible*Lands* to accompany the exhibition *Presence: Images of Christ for the Third Millennium* – a linked series of exhibitions in six British cathedrals in 2004

ISBN 0-9546914-0-7

Catalogue produced by Trinity Communications

BibleLands

Hugh Boulter, Chairman of Bible*Lands*

2004 sees the 150th Anniversary of Bible*Lands*. In marking this event we have two main aims. First, to celebrate work that God has done through Bible*Lands*, its supporters and partners over the last 150 years. Secondly, at a time when the needs in the Middle East are as great as ever, we would like to make our vital work more widely known, not only among the Christian community, but throughout Britain.

To this end, we have planned a series of events which underline the Christian ethos and inspiration for our work as we address the changing needs of our partners in the Middle East and develop a wider constituency of support.

Presence: Images of Christ for the Third Millennium is a key part of our 150th Anniversary Celebration. We are particularly indebted to Tom Devonshire Jones of Art and Christianity Enquiry (ACE), who has advised us throughout the planning process, and has edited this accompanying volume to the Exhibition. Also to Meryl Doney, our Curator, who has planned the whole exhibition series and brought together a remarkable range of artists and works of art. We are also grateful to the Deans and staff of the cathedrals where *Presence* is being featured. Without their support, encouragement and co-operation, *Presence* could not have taken place. The distinguished authors of the two essays that follow also deserve our special thanks. While the opinions which they express are entirely their own, I believe that they help us to understand both theologically and artistically what artists are trying to achieve when they engage with the person of Christ today.

Presence: Images of Christ for the Third Millennium is a particularly fitting title, not only because it describes well the theme of the exhibitions, but also because it symbolises our work in the Middle East where we join our partners in demonstrating the compassionate nature of Christ especially in the fields of disability, health and education. We work with Christian-led projects of all denominations, especially in Lebanon, Egypt and Palestine/Israel. We provide, though our partners, support and help to all those in need, regardless of race or faith. In a part of the world where retaliation and vengeance often seem to be more important than forgiveness and reconciliation, Bible*Lands* believes that it is vital to support an indigenous presence that demonstrates the love of Christ for all.

Nazareth is the site of our 150th Anniversary project and Bible*Lands* aims to raise £300,000 towards the cost of building a new School of Nursing. Over the last 75 years, the Nazareth School of Nursing has trained hundreds of nurses to serve, either in the Hospital itself or throughout the community in Galilee. It is a vital area of work. If you would like to support this Anniversary project or find out more about our work, please contact us at:

Bible*Lands*, PO Box 50
High Wycombe, HP15 7QU

Tel: 01494 897950 Fax: 01494 897951
email: info@biblelands.org.uk
website: www.biblelands.org.uk

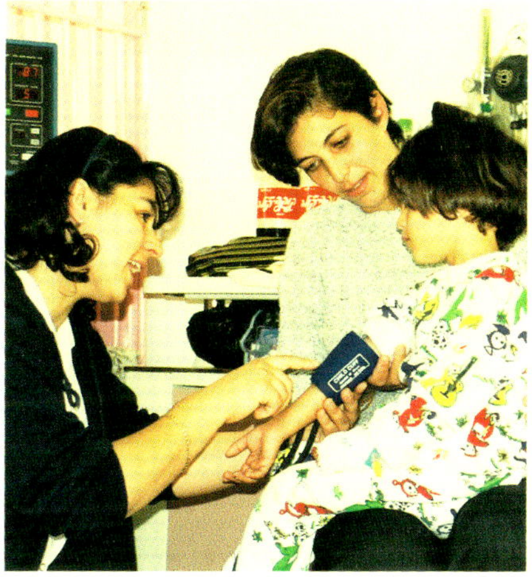

A nurse-in-training at the Nazareth School of Nursing takes the blood pressure of a young patient.

Contents

Presence

Rowan Williams

What are people doing when they try to make images of Christ? Forget the obvious answers for a moment; there have never been utterly obvious answers in the history of Christian art, even though we might think there have. The very earliest representations have a sort of anonymous quality: the young man staring into the distance with a lamb over his shoulders, one of the commonest early Christian images, could be a routine piece of classical decoration. The simple catacomb paintings of gospel miracles show, again, an anonymous youth, marked out only by a kind of magic wand, in scenes that are anything but self-explanatory. All these images inhabit an imaginative world in which an ordinary figure is put into a context where it is clear that some sort of extra meaning attaches to him – but there is no clear way of saying what that extra is. As has sometimes been said, there is something both prosaic and uncanny about these depictions. What they say to us is not so far from what they must have said to the non-Christian Roman viewer: here is something important, and you will only know what it is by sharing the life of the people who made this image. The image will not tell you its own importance; there is no rhetoric, as you might say, of power and significance. You are invited to sit alongside people for whom this matters and discover why. If you don't, the image simply remains. So all you see is an anonymous youth? Then that's all you see.

Kierkegaard wrote in the nineteenth century that there was a sense in which all Christian theology and proclamation boiled down to someone saying to someone else, 'Once God walked the streets as a human being'. No story, no way of identifying where God is (because that would break God's self-imposed concealment); we simply know that it was true and so everything is different. I'm not convinced that Kierkegaard said all that needs saying – but he encapsulates something of what the catacomb paintings of Jesus say. Here is an anonymous figure, of which we say that his actions change our frame of reference: how? The picture will not tell you because that would be to suggest that the change can be represented – and so would cease to be the kind of change we are trying to talk about, something that has become an object for viewing. Perhaps a distant analogy might be Bellini's *Ecstasy of St Francis* in the Frick Gallery: level evening light, the grass very exactly lit, a single human figure exposed to the light in a slightly awkward half-theatrical posture. Everything is normal, and nothing is. Somehow the light itself has to do the work of showing that things are changed; as perhaps in the catacombs the blank backgrounds and half-sketched faces have to suggest significance.

Some of the history of Christian art is about the tension between recognising that the change associated with Jesus is incapable of representation and recognising that for the change to be communicable it must in some way be represented. The violent controversies of the seventh and eighth centuries over iconoclasm reflect this conundrum; and some of the most subtle and interesting strands in Greek theology were deployed to secure a resolution, whose effects are still to be seen in the continuing tradition of classical Eastern iconography. What I have described as anonymity is one strategy to cope precisely with the ingrained tensions of representing a divine event in human narrative record. But another strategy is irony, the irony – regularly missed or misread – of much of this traditional Eastern iconic representation of Jesus. Here is a figure in the imperial position, enthroned at the 'royal' end of the meeting hall, often sitting on a cushioned stool of the kind reserved for royalty; but he is a long-haired, bearded exotic, dressed as a teacher of philosophy, usually pointing to a book. What is 'royal' or imperial in the order of the universe? Wisdom. Who is the emperor's emperor? A wandering scholar. It is another way of representing a change, putting a figure in a position that is in some way uncanny. And the whole set of conventions that surround iconographic practice are interwoven with similar if less direct ironies and 'uncanny' elements (famously, the reversed perspective typical of most icons, and the deliberately exaggerated elongations and stylisations of human physique).

Once the irony has been lost or forgotten, once a tradition has become 'obviously' the way to depict Christ, the image can retain power of a kind, but its witness to change becomes less evident. Or it can be systematically robbed of irony by modification: the late mediaeval eastern version of the Eastern icon of Christ which shows him robed as bishop and crowned as emperor flattens out something of the complexity of earlier types – though it is worth pondering that this only becomes a common image when there is no longer a Christian emperor. Western pictures of Christ the King or of the triple-crowned God the Father (van Eyck) and so on also risk losing the ironic; though the crowned and vested Christ on the cross sometimes retains it.

There are artists who have tried to show the change of the world around Jesus in more narrative and dramatic ways. Raphael's *Transfiguration* comes to mind; or, more startlingly, the resurrection picture that forms part of Grunewald's Isenheim altarpiece with its unsparing crucifixion. Why are these images so uncomfortable (not uncanny but uncomfortable, false-note uncomfortable)? Surely because the picture tries to 'include' the difference, to render it in a way that can only say, 'What is different is that a familiar experience is raised to the highest possible degree by Jesus'; so let us have blinding brightness and levitation, an extremism of effect and emotion. This is a personal view, obviously, but it is why I find Baroque religious art both brilliantly inviting and exhilarating and spiritually flat. Something of the difference that is *God* is absent, and what remains is a world of extremity which may or may not precipitate a beholder into the radical presence of what is not of this world. This is an art that eschews irony and so denies itself one of the subtler tools for evoking what is distinctive about the figure of Jesus.

The same absence of irony is of course present even more conspicuously in later modern religious art – the German Nazarenes, the Pre-Raphaelites, the historical realism of Tissot or Hole. What has come to matter is the record of things that have happened; but the very mood of the painting already declares that this is a story you *know*. The figure of Jesus is anything but anonymous; robed and radiant, calm, stately, how could anyone fail to see that he matters, that he is holy? What kind of monster of insensitivity could fail to respond, within the narrative depicted, to the pathos and dignity portrayed? The style is the very opposite of ironical or transforming; it renders visible the obviousness of religious sentiment of a certain kind, and so makes practically unthinkable any perception other than that already familiar. That is not to say that it cannot operate as religious art of a kind, as what you might call casual reinforcement of shared piety; but it fails, once again, as a depiction of difference or distinctiveness, and so as a depiction of the divine importance, the reference-changing character, of Jesus.

All in all, it is no surprise that the contemporary depiction of Christ is so complex a task. In some areas, the problem is, if not solved, at least modified by the requirements of a genre – the Stations of the Cross, for example, which have produced some powerful modern renderings like those of Peter

Howson. These are traditionally figural, but it is a genre that does not demand this, and there are also fine instances of something far less representational. Here it is the associated *practice* that displays transforming meaning. Works that do not have this clear liturgical role face very taxing challenges. But it is intriguing to see how variously the 'uncanny' has been handled. Mark Wallinger's work stands out here, especially the now well-known *Ecce Homo*; this is a piece which still provokes debate, and on which I personally find myself both admiring and querying. But its installation in Trafalgar Square produced, I think, exactly the sort of double-take that catacomb art induces (and probably induced at first): here is an ordinary representation that clearly has extraordinary significance, but a significance that does not show itself as an element in the actual physical composition. Prose made poetic by being put in a particular place.

The ironic use of familiar or half-familiar images casts light on the performance art of Michael Gough, walking the streets dressed as the Jesus of representational cliché; but also on the use of fractured or otherwise distorted reproductions of actual classical images in collage or comparable mode. The New York artist, Jim Morphesis, has produced some striking work in this mode (see the article on his work in *Image*, Spring 1994); and Yuri Titov, active in the sixties and seventies, used pictures of broken or vandalised icons of Christ against stylised urban Soviet backgrounds to say something about the persistence of the image in and through apostasy and social devastation. Something even beyond irony is evoked by the extraordinary work of Roger Wagner, with his fusion of Jewish and Christian symbols and narratives with the cooling towers of Didcot power station – Jewish victims of the Shoah wandering in the neighbourhood of a distantly seen, conventionally depicted crucifixion, the background dominated by the immense towers exuding gas, arranged in the pattern of the ceremonial candlestick, the Menorah which gives this 1993 painting (in the artist's own collection) its title. This is very dense imagining indeed, but it manages a representation of the creatively and theologically uncanny that is haunting.

The contemporary artist trying to represent Jesus is not, then, confined to modernistic recycling of iconic forms; the challenge is to create a frame of visual reference which prompts the question of how and why a whole landscape is altered by the presence of the single provoking figure. Again, I have Bellini's *Ecstasy* in mind, though you might also want to think of the teasing way in which, say, Caravaggio's *Calling of St Matthew* obliges you to search out the almost obscured figure of Jesus as the source of whatever it is that turns the rest of the composition in one direction. Presumably, any contemporary artist – other than a professional illustrator – trying to represent Christ is unlikely to be seeking to portray a figure from two thousand years ago. And the statistical prevalence of practising artists who are conventional Christians is not high, so we can probably assume that they will not be seeking to produce a devotional image either. What might prompt such an artist to undertake this difficult task is likely to be just the tension we have been sketching: how do you *show* transcendent difference in the representation of earthly events? Once again, it is the question of the iconoclastic controversy, how do you depict a humanity that is inseparably united with divine action? For the artist as artist, it is a formal rather than a theological challenge, but all the more provocative for that.

What makes it absorbingly interesting to the theologian, or indeed the reflective Christian in general, is that it is one way of focusing and expressing the central issue of all talk about Jesus Christ. To say that Jesus is God made flesh is, strictly, to say that you cannot represent God as something added to the flesh, or as 'flesh' somehow strained to extremity – that is, by making flesh unfleshly (I

Mark Wallinger
Ecce Homo, 1999

regard the Eastern canons of iconography as something other: not exaggerating a basic realism of depiction but adopting a whole idiom of representation which works with the relations of line and colour in a flat space). This is simply to paraphrase the formulae of traditional doctrine: Jesus is complete in divinity, complete in humanity. To show divinity in such a context has just the same problems as to speak of it: it is not an added element in a compound but a characterisation of the whole. And thus it is speakable or tangible only as perceived in the changes it effects. The divinity of Christ cannot be shown in a depiction of Jesus 'alone' – uninterpreted, unthought; not in a photographic historical portrait. The attempt to do this in nineteenth century religious art by a rather specious realism coloured by devotional emotion is not going to work for just the reasons that revisionist doctrines of the same period have not worn well: divinity is not a particularly fine and inspiring instance of the human, the human with inspirational extras. So we are driven back to looking for the ways in which this ordinary human identity (which did not walk the roads of Galilee with a soft radiance and a spotless robe any more than it/he walked the roads of Galilee in the two-dimensional frame of the icon or sat on an imperial stool or wore a chasuble on the cross) alters the lines of force in the field – spiritual, moral, visual.

If this is right, the Christian will learn something of major importance by watching how the artist deals with the challenge of representing divine action in the historical world. And perhaps too the artist's continuing fascination with the challenge of depicting Christ is because there is something of almost paradigmatic seriousness in the challenge. Any artist is going to be in the business of showing the world differently. The most committed realist cannot but 'show differently', in the physical medium chosen. The question is always how that showing creates an environment, a continuous world, in such a way that it makes still more difference possible in the world it started from. Or, in plainer English, how it communicates sufficiently to enlarge the world.

The event of Jesus Christ is for the Christian tradition the unsurpassable enlargement of the world; nothing could take us further. It makes possible what had been impossible. And it does so without tearing the fabric of history and matter. Put like that, it becomes clear why representing miracles is pretty hard, and representing the Resurrection the most difficult thing of all (how many effective pictures are there of the Resurrection? I'm inclined to say only one, Piero's in Borgo San Sepolcro – by refusing to dramatise, to show a series of happenings, but offering a single moment of monumental and timeless relation between God and sleeping humanity, and a face of incomparable stillness, a pivot on which all movement moves). How does presence alter things? That is what the artist tackling this most impossible of tasks is after; it is both the extreme case of every artistic challenge and something that cannot be addressed except in relation to these particularities, these stories, this face and figure. We watch expectantly as the artist searches for the appropriate form of the uncanny, waiting to see if our world becomes strange as a result of having this particular stranger, Jesus, introduced into it.

Rowan Williams
is Archbishop of Canterbury

Moments of Intimation

Richard Cork

When Mark Wallinger's quiet yet potent *Ecce Homo* arrived in Trafalgar Square, just before the twentieth century came to a close, the response was extraordinary. Many onlookers expressed surprise that the religious reference seemed so overt. After all, few leading contemporary artists could be described as Christian. But this modest white sculpture, standing so precariously on the front edge of the otherwise empty Victorian plinth, had undoubtedly sprung from Wallinger's response to the martyrdom of Jesus. Presented without rhetoric as the embodiment of Everyman, this suffering Christ had a poignancy that impressed many who came to view the statue after its unveiling. Wallinger's decision to place a defiantly small image of the bound and humiliated figure took everyone by surprise. Blanched and resigned, he was the quintessence of vulnerability. And his straightforward, life-size humanity spoke to many who might have found a more conventional, elevated statue of Christ unbearably pious.

Not that modest dimensions are guaranteed in themselves to arouse admiration. Towering on a hilltop near Gateshead, Antony Gormley's *Angel of the North* is unashamedly colossal. Spreading his wings as if to bestow benediction on everybody around him, this mysterious titan has managed to lodge himself securely in the affections of the locality. But his appeal arises from Gormley's ability to escape from the blandness afflicting so much contemporary religious art. We do not know who this enigmatic 'angel', really is. And he could easily be seen in a tragic light, as someone who yearned for the liberty of flight even as he remained frustratingly earthbound. If those wings ever did make him airborne, he might well succumb to an Icarus-like fall. Intimations of this kind lend complexity to the sculpture, helping to explain why it has become cherished by many of those who, whether walking beneath the sculpture or driving past on the nearby motorway, encounter his gaunt, grave presence.

Sometimes, the act of placing secular art in a religious setting enhances its significance without imposing an excessively spiritual meaning on the work. In 1999, around the time when Wallinger's *Ecce Homo* appeared on the empty plinth, the First Liverpool Biennial was staged. Its organisers took the inspired decision to place Doris Salcedo's contribution in the city's Anglican Cathedral. The sunken space at the west end of the nave provided an ideal arena for her sculpture. Salcedo, a Colombian, produces memorials to the victims of repression. But no portraits could be detected in this sombre work. Instead, she took wardrobes and other, equally domestic furniture as her starting-point. They should have been reassuringly intimate presences. Salcedo, though, showed a chair half-buried in cement with metal bars thrusting from its raw surface. A large bed, stripped of mattress and springs, was invaded by a cupboard. And a group of small tables rested on legs so fragile that they scarcely seemed able to remain upright. Most of the furniture was old, and looked as if its owners had abandoned it in an emergency. But the cracks were all sealed up, like witnesses whose ability to give evidence had been silenced.

Showing such work in a cathedral intensified Salcedo's role as a memorialist: her art looked appropriate there, in a building where tombs and inscriptions likewise testified to the need for remembrance. Some contemporary artists, however, are willing to explore religious themes in the most unexpected of secular settings. At the Millennium Dome in 2000, Rose Finn-Kelcey was among the artists invited to instal work in the North Meadow stretching between the building and the Thames. Her response, quite unpredictably, centred on providing spiritual reassurance to the Dome's

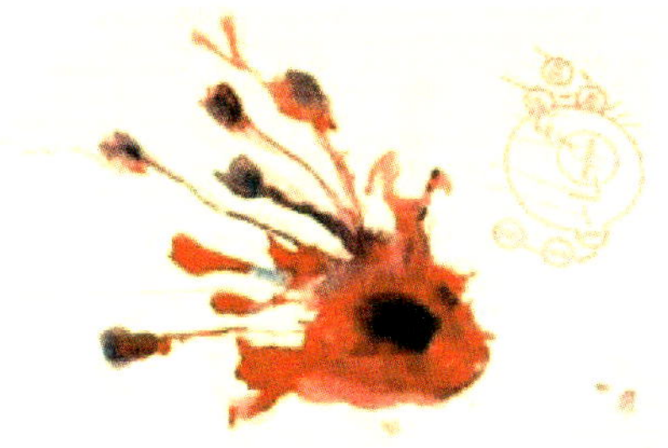

Conrad Atkinson
Drawing, 2002

visitors. She turned four chocolate vending machines into sources of prayer. After putting a twenty-pence coin in the slot, the 'customer', could select a non-denominational prayer from a list of fourteen. The titles used words associated with chocolate bars, including Wispa, Ripple and Milky Way. Then, after the prayer's words flashed and whirled round a circular LED screen, the coin was returned. Sprayed a metallic, sparkling blue, the machines offered a verbal sustenance radically removed from the familiar phrases chanted in church. But Finn-Kelcey's faith in her alternative offerings was summed up by the overall title she gave them: *It Pays to Pray.*

Humour, whether wrily ironic or frankly playful, can be turned to eloquent account when dealing with religion. Take Braco Dimitrijević, whose *Triptychos Post Historicus* project lifts even the most venerable art-works out of the context they normally inhabit. By juxtaposing them with other, more everyday objects, either man-made or as natural as fruit or vegetables, Dimitrijević aims at generating a fresh response to everything assembled in his provocative tableaux. Cultural hierarchies are dispensed with, and in their place a more open-minded understanding is encouraged.

Rose Finn-Kelcey
It pays to Pray, 2000

In 2001, he was let loose on the outstanding collection owned by the Barber Institute of Fine Arts, Birmingham. Among the pictures Dimitrijević selected was Gaudenzio Ferrari's *The Madonna and Child with St Mary Magdalene and a Bishop.* Here, secure in his mother's grasp, the naked Christ child turned his head to grin across at Mary Magdalene. She smiled back, holding an ointment jar as if ready to anoint his feet. The only grave face in this faint yet heartfelt drawing was the unidentified bishop in the centre, who gazed sadly at the group as if preoccupied with thoughts of the suffering and martyrdom to come. He may have commissioned Ferrari to execute the cartoon around 1543, in readiness for a painted altarpiece. But Dimitrijević placed a real cooking-pot and onion in front of Mary Magdalene, blocking out her body and the jar alike. So the bishop now appeared to be staring down at the pot, and sniffing its contents with an air of pious disapproval. Dimitrijević's choice of vegetable suggested that it might be onion soup, a staple meal as popular at the sixteenth-century dining-table as the Madonna and Child were in Italian churches. Now that so much of the drawing was obscured by the pot, they became the focus of attention. And we realised how blithely Ferrari had defined the unaffected warmth of the relationship between mother and offspring.

On the whole, though, today's artists are more likely to be drawn to the elements of suffering in religious themes. No one more unnervingly than Conrad Atkinson, who was invited to become Distinguished Visiting Professor at the Courtauld Institute of Art in 2002. Looking with fresh eyes at the Courtauld Collection's medieval and Renaissance paintings, he became preoccupied with images of martyrdom. Focusing on the idea of 'beautiful mutilations', he realised that the bloodiest and most tortured Courtauld paintings related to his long-standing involvement with the imagery of modern war. Atkinson aimed at 'breaking open the collection, like a wound', and visitors found his work dramatically intervening in the normal gallery display. 'Aesthetics can be a pretty ugly business', announced a digitalised embroidery inscription on a Daniel Hechter wool suit. As if to bear out the truth of this paradoxical assertion, Atkinson extracted the gash in Christ's side from a Fra Angelico predella panel. Transferred to a jacket, the blood-soaked wound made the garment resemble evidence discovered at the location of a murder. He even borrowed the leaves covering Adam and Eve's genitals in a Cranach painting. They were turned into vine-leaf motifs ornamenting the base of a glazed and gold-lustre ceramic. But any suspicion that Atkinson had turned the leaves into decorative devices was allayed by our realisation that the seductive, glinting ceramic took the form of a land-mine.

Sam Taylor-Wood is equally unafraid to reinterpret the most anguished of biblical subjects. In 2001 she made a filmed homage to Michelangelo's early *Pieta* carving in Rome. The artist herself adopted the role of the mourning Madonna, seated on a wide flight of steps as she strives to hold the inert body of a man sprawled across her lap. She looks as coolly composed as the Virgin in Michelangelo's carving. But the body she supports gradually falls lower. Although he is still breathing, and his right arm shifts uneasily on the steps, he is unable to help himself. She attempts to raise him at one point, but he slumps back. As she tries again, and turns away as though looking elsewhere for help, the image fades. We are left wondering how long this slender young woman can continue to cradle him – and wondering, too, why Taylor-Wood cast the Hollywood actor Robert Downey Jr in the man's part. Maybe she equates him with the subject of her photographic piece called *Bound Ram*. Condemned to stand in its own urine, the hapless animal is trussed and doleful. It looks like a sacrificial victim waiting to be slaughtered, and Taylor-Wood awakens memories of the Lamb of God whose Christ-like death redeemed the world. She is unafraid of such references, and her involvement with Renaissance art undoubtedly enriches her work.

A similar fascination has also transformed Bill Viola's art. In 2000, he brought video into the National Gallery with his installation *The Quintet of the Astonished*. Taking as his springboard Bosch's macabre painting *Christ Mocked (The Crowning with Thorns)*, he showed five men and women transfixed by overwhelming emotions. But unlike the vicious, cackling tormentors in Bosch's painting, they seemed caught up in a slow-motion drama of ever-shifting feelings. Three years later the same work returned to the National Gallery, as one of the exhibits in a full-scale Viola exhibition called *The Passions*. The work on show benefited from this supremely appropriate context. For Viola had been studying the old masters with great intensity, and his art now thrives on its proximity to painted images from the past.

Apart from a single corpse, the people in his show were able to speak, shout or cry. But we could not hear them. In the first room, an unshaven man in a denim shirt was seen from head to shoulders on a single screen. Filmed in silent and exceptionally slow motion, he moved from left to right and back again, fighting the urge to weep. Tears ran down his cheeks and he opened his mouth to sob. Although he then succeeded in closing his lips and controlling himself, the victory was short-lived. He kept breaking down and, as we speculated about the cause of his misery, the two National Gallery pictures flanking him suddenly appeared revelant. On one side, a *Man of Sorrows* by an unknown Umbrian master crossed his pierced hands against a backdrop of hysterical angels and a crucifix. It was a ferociously distraught image, while on the other side Bellini's *Dead Christ supported by Angels* seemed even more heartbreaking. For Jesus was now slumped and oblivious, and all the angels could do was prop up his limp body and mourn his loss.

By placing his own distraught man between these two Italian paintings, Viola openly declared his sources of inspiration. He even called his own work *Man of Sorrows*, as if determined to make the influence clear. But the titles of his other exhibits were more removed from overt Christian references. Zen teachings, which have influenced Viola for many years, stress the importance of releasing the rational mind in order to gain self-understanding. In a tall, single-screen work called *Observance*, everyone was bent on scrutinising an object we could not see. Forming a line, they moved forward at a funereal pace. When reaching the front, each of them gazed down sorrowfully at something below the frame's edge. It could well be a figure lying in a coffin, for everyone took it in turn to stare with a sense of utter desolation. We ought to have felt frustrated by Viola's refusal to identify the source of their grief. But his dramatisation of their reactions was so absorbing, and painful to behold, that we ended up accepting the element of mystery. They tried to comfort one another, clasping hands in an attempt to gain mutual support. But each mourner ended up looking very isolated, and unable to cope with the unbearable sorrow for more than a few seconds.

Perhaps it was just as well that the reason for their distress remained invisible. Later in the show, Viola explored equally distraught feelings in a work called *Emergence*. But this time we were able to see precisely why two women, seated by a marble cistern with a cross on its side, became so upset. After a while, a naked young man rose up from the water. Judging by his glacial flesh, he was dead. And at first, the women's astonishment seemed to be fired by the hope that he might regain life. The parallels with the resurrection were self-evident, but the man proved unable to move. He slumped into the women's outstretched arms, and they laid him out carefully on the ground. The most moving moment occurred when the older woman struggled fiercely to prevent her companion from pulling a sheet right over the dead man's face. She needed to see and touch him, and the work ended as she cradled his head tenderly on her lap. The whole event was performed with understated gravity, yet I found it excessively theatrical and self-conscious.

To everyone's surprise, the autumn of 2003 turned out to be a memorable moment for artists openly tackling religious themes. Damien Hirst's exhibition at White Cube2 was transformed into an arena where the twelve apostles had been assembled. But no trace of their figures could be discerned. We were presented instead with a sequence of steel and glass cabinets ranged along the side walls. They recalled, at first sight, the chilling pharmaceutical world that Hirst explored in many of his earlier works. Even so, clinical purity was replaced, here, by a relentless preoccupation with suffering and destruction. Although plenty of the vessels and tubes resting on these shelves were still intact, they had become besmirched with blood.

This was far and away the most expressionist show that Hirst has ever mounted. The bell jars, crucibles and flasks were accompanied, now, by surgical scissors, knives and crumpled tissues soaked in gore. Peering in at these sacrificial objects was alarmingly akin to examining the aftermath of illicit medical operations. The longer we stared, the more they reminded us of the torture inflicted by dictators in so many unstable countries where power is only achieved through fear. Here and there, specific references could be found to an apostle: St Peter was represented by his cluster of keys, while the thick rope in another cabinet referred to the suicidal hanging of Judas. On the whole, though, these gruesome receptacles testified to a larger vision of a modern world where pain and brutality flourish ever more ruthlessly.

True, the centre of the end wall was dominated by a thirteenth cabinet, where the glass shelves remained bare and the clean vessels above were surmounted by a stuffed dove. Flanked by two large paintings where dead butterflies floated in lucid blue skies, this pristine cabinet was clearly intended to symbolise the resurrection. But the promise it strove to provide, through the ascension of Jesus, was outweighed by evidence of anguish and devastation elsewhere. Most of the room was closer in mood to a charnel-house. Holes were cut in some of the glass fronts, allowing the blood to emerge and run down the cabinets before splashing in droplets on the floor below. In one particularly unnerving work, a gore-drenched vessel dangled outside a hole like an organ wrenched wholesale from a body. Beneath, blood-soaked plastic tubing was coiled in a clotted mess, suggesting that no one had bothered to clear up after some heinous act of brutality.

Each cabinet was named after a saint, and the carefully inverted glass vessels in one of them referred to St Peter's fate when he was crucified upside-down. But looking at the contents of the other cabinets, where a skull, a bone, a hammer and a bloody axe could be detected, we did not think of Bartholomew, John, Simon, Matthew and the rest of Christ's beleaguered disciples. Rather were we forced to meditate on the darkest aspects of our own time, and this harsh imperative ensured that Hirst's exhibition could not simply be seen as a return to religion. The main room also contained two large paintings called *Devotion* and *Rapture*, where hundreds of butterfly wings were assembled in mandala-like patterns saturated with radiant colour. But their impact was countered by the gruelling sight of a cabinet pierced, vertically and horizontally, by spears. The damage was even more grievous in another cabinet, which had been completely split in two. Blood had coursed down both sides of the sundered pieces, and nothing appeared capable of bridging the void between them.

As if to ram home his obsession with mortality at the expense of transcendence, Hirst also represented the violated disciples as a series of cows' heads marooned in their own glass tanks. There they rested, swimming in formaldehyde and exposed in all their blanched, skinned rawness. They lay on the floor in lowly, abject positions that accentuated their plight. Each one related to its neighbouring wall-cabinet, and we could identify Judas as the blindfolded black cow who faced the other way. In the main, however, these pallid remnants smacked of the abattoir rather than the temple. Hirst seemed to be insisting that he was still concerned with mortality in general, not religion in particular, and the outraged response of some Anglican clerics to this exhibition proved how far he remained from conventional Christian faith.

The overall mood of Hirst's show could hardly have been more removed from a masterpiece by the artist with whom I began this essay: Mark Wallinger's slow-motion video called *Threshold to the Kingdom*. Filmed in the millennium year at City Airport in London, it concentrates on the double doors marked International Arrivals. They seem welcoming. But when opened for the first time, they only admit a bald man in a black coat. He comes through, and they shut soundlessly. It is a simple start, yet Allegri's charged and sublime choral music *Miserere* alerts us to the possibility that the solitary traveller will soon be succeeded by far more emotional encounters.

So indeed it proves. Presided over by an impassive official behind a desk, several figures arrive. Their limbs are slowed down so much that they seem to be floating. Some look expectant and alert, busily finding their bearings after the passive fatigue of flight. Then, as the doors open once more, Allegri's chorus swells and a young woman detaches herself from the group to smile and wave at an unseen friend. The text for *Miserere* is Psalm 51, which begins with a plea: 'Have mercy upon me, O God, according to thy loving kindness: according unto the multitude of thy tender mercies blot out my transgressions'. And, by a miracle, the same heartfelt level of feeling is achieved by Wallinger's video. For an older woman has been waiting on the left, and she advances towards a white-haired woman among the latest batch of arrivals. They embrace with ecstatic delight, kissing each other on both sides of their faces, while another woman of a similar age looks on beatifically. She, in turn, is given an enthusiastic hug and they disappear.

Their meeting provides *Threshold to the Kingdom* with a powerful sense of epiphany, confirming the supposition that these passengers have arrived at the gates of heaven. But by no means all of them savour the bliss experienced by the elderly women. A cluster of men appears, looking around apprehensively before succumbing to yawns and disappointment. Although bystanders walk forward in search of someone, they fail in their task and leave one late arrival stranded. The cabin crew appear, with deadpan faces registering no thought of an emotional meeting. Then, finally, a solitary man enters, pushing a trolley containing only a yellow bag inscribed 'See Buy Fly'. He pauses, and scrutinises a piece of paper while a stewardess runs past him without a glance. As he lingers there, looking uncertain and lonely, this strangely moving video fades to a close. It seems a melancholy ending, and yet Wallinger leaves us in little doubt that *Threshold to the Kingdom* offers, for the most part, a redemptive experience.

Richard Cork is an art critic, historian, broadcaster and exhibition organiser. A four-volume selection of his writings on modern art, 1970-2000, was published recently by Yale University Press.

Photograph courtesy Gerhard Haupt

Draco Dimitrijević
Le Dernier Chemin vers le Paradis, 1997

Introduction

Meryl Doney, Exhibition Curator

Early in 2002 I was given the exciting task of curating an art exhibition in the cathedrals of Britain, which would review the response of contemporary artists to the person of Christ.

It was commissioned to mark the 150th Anniversary of Bible*Lands*, a charity working with local partners in medical, educational and developmental projects across the Middle East. In looking for something that would reflect the spirit of Christ that inspires their work, the Trustees decided to draw upon the vision of a broad spectrum of contemporary artists. The result is *Presence: Images of Christ for the Third Millennium*. It is not a travelling exhibition, but a series of linked events involving the work of different artists in six cathedrals – Canterbury, Durham, Lincoln, Worcester, St Paul's in London and the Episcopal Cathedral, Glasgow.

An encouraging aspect of this initiative has been the willingness of the cathedrals to take an active part in the project. In each place artists have been invited to contribute work that engages with both the worshipping life of the cathedral and with its many visitors, pilgrims and tourists. The series has been shaped by this approach, and the exhibition designed to follow the events of the Christian year. It is hoped that people will visit most of the cathedrals, planning to make them the focus of a pilgrimage during the period from Epiphany to Whitsun in 2004.

This approach has resulted in some exciting collaborations. In Worcester Cathedral, for instance, seven new paintings by Martin Rose will accompany a performance of Haydn's *Seven Last Words* by the Lindsay Quartet for Palm Sunday evening. In Lincoln, the city's Usher Gallery and the Cathedral have worked together on a two-location exhibition of sculpture and video.

Equally exciting has been the ready response from artists. My experience in putting together this exhibition belies the perception that the art of our day is largely secular, concerned only with human identity and with referencing art history itself. The new century has been marked by a continued interest in spirituality. As the millennium dawned, Mark Wallinger's *Ecce Homo* was installed on the plinth in Trafalgar Square. *Seeing Salvation* at the National Gallery surpassed all expectations in attracting over three hundred thousand visitors. Many artists continue to find depth and new inspiration in Christian iconography – in particular the cross and passion of Christ that speak of injustice, suffering and redemption.

In choosing work for this exhibition, I have been delighted by the quality and diversity of the material available. I am pleased to be able to show recent video pieces by Bill Viola, Mark Wallinger and Sam Taylor-Wood, sculpture by Antony Gormley, Nicola Hicks, Jill Sim and Fenwick Lawson, drawings for his new *Stations of the Cross* by Peter Howson and a survey exhibition of painting by twenty-six artists.

I have also involved rising artists and commissioned some innovative projects as part of the series: Michael Gough and Barry Jenkins will be restaging their performance piece, *Iconography* in the City of London; a group of five young, Glasgow artists have been invited to respond to the theme of *Presence* and to site work in the body of St Mary's Episcopal Cathedral; in Canterbury, the specially commissioned installation, *Vigil* by Willie Williams, will fill the cathedral with light for Holy Week and Easter.

It is my hope that *Presence* will provide an opportunity for as wide an audience as possible to celebrate Bible*Lands* over the last 150 years through seeing what is being done by working artists today, as they create forms and images that will carry meaning and inspiration into the future.

St Paul's Cathedral, London

The Messenger, a video/sound installation by Bill Viola was commissioned for Durham Cathedral by the Chaplaincy to the Arts and Recreation as part of the celebrations for UK Year of the Visual Arts in 1996. It is a profound example of presence. Though not itself an image of Christ, *The Messenger* presents the primal themes of birth, death and the eternal cycle of renewal also associated with the Christian tradition. It will be shown in the north west aisle of the cathedral.

At the same time, an exhibition of work by twenty-six contemporary painters, on the theme of Presence, is presented in the north and south transepts.

Photograph courtesy of Kira Perov

1 **Bill Viola**
The Messenger, 1996
Single-channel colour video and stereo-sound installation, continuous loop

Though not itself an image of Christ, The Messenger presents the primal themes of birth, death, and the eternal cycle of renewal that we associate with the Christian tradition.

A large image is projected on a screen mounted onto a black wall. The image sequence begins with a small, luminous, abstract form shimmering and undulating against a deep blue-black void. Gradually the luminous shape begins to get larger and less distorted, and it soon becomes apparent that we are seeing a human form, illuminated, rising towards us from under the surface of a body of water. The water becomes more still and transparent and the figure more clear on its journey upwards towards us. We identify the figure as a man, pale blue, lying on his back rising up slowly. After some time, the figure breaks the surface, an act at once startling, relieving and desperate. His pale form emerges into the warm hues of a bright light, the water glistening on his body. His eyes immediately open and he releases a long held breath from the depths, shattering the silence of the image. This forceful primal sound of life resonates momentarily in the space. After a few moments, he inhales deeply, and with his eyes shut and his mouth closed, he sinks into the depths of the blue-black void to become a shimmering moving point of light once more. The image then returns to its original state and the cycle begins anew.

Contemporary painting on the theme of Presence

Photograph courtesy of Timothy Taylor Gallery

2 Norman Adams RA
Man of Sorrows, 1998 (shown *Ecce Homo*, 1999)
Gouache and watercolour on paper
126 x 102 cm

3 Craigie Aitchison CBE RA
Crucifixion, 1999/2000
Oil on Canvas
142 x 112 cm

4 Phillip Archer
The Narrow Doorway, 2003
(not shown)
Oil on canvas
60 x 75 cm

'Ordinary things reveal those forms of simplicity that tell us of a higher state of being, which constitutes all the richness of the secret of art.'
Scuola Metaphysica

For some time now, I have been possessed by the necessity to paint religious subject matter. The way of the cross and the passion of Christ have taken me over. A few years ago I worked on a commission to paint the fourteen Stations for the Roman Catholic Church of St Mary in Manchester, known as the Hidden Gem. These were large canvases, most of them six feet high, and monumental in structure. In most of them, the head of Christ almost filled the canvas.

In *A Man of Sorrows* the structure is softened. The imagery is more natural than in the Manchester *Head of Christ,* and there is a feeling of growing. There are leaves and fragments of the natural world. This present painting is not the start of another sequence. I feel it embodies a certain sort of truth. I don't know that I can really name what it is.

I hesitate to call myself a Christian, but I don't know what else I am; and I don't think it is important. The work is not to do with me, but stands on its own feet, and I hope people will find some affinity with this image. I still strive to clarify my language of colour and structure, and to stir people's sensitivity so that they find my paintings moving and, in their own way, also beautiful.

5 **Dr John Bellany CBE RA**
Requiem for Ella Percy, 2002
(not shown)
Oil on canvas
178 x 203 cm

6 **Matthew Burrows**
Heavenly Messenger, 1999
Oil on board
25.5 x 30.5 cm

Heavenly Messenger is one of a series of paintings, which takes as its starting point a passage from Dante's, *The Divine Comedy*. At the beginning of *Inferno IX*, Dante and his companion Virgil, are met by a heavenly messenger who opens the gates to Dis (the central city of hell), which Virgil had failed to open with his earthly wisdom. The messenger approaches the weary travellers through a mist, which he wipes away with his left hand. He stands before the gates of Dis, which is pictured here as Brighton Pier, promising everything but delivering nothing. The revelation of identity and grace through the density of moisture creates a sense of material reverie. The liquid paint, which will in time evaporate and leave only the evidence of movement, is more than the picture itself – it creates an imaginative synchronisation and empathy, one in which we attempt to repeat its speed and weight.

Collection of John and Elizabeth Gibbs

7 **Mark Cazalet**
Christ Sentenced, 1999
Oil on Linen
46 x 36 cm

Collection of John and Elizabeth Gibbs

8 **Mark Cazalet**
Christ Meets his Mother, 1999
Oil on linen
46 x 36 cm

I was commissioned to paint a set of *Stations of the Cross* for the St Edmundsbury and Ipswich diocese millennium project, *Stations: The New Sacred Art*. My set was painted during the winter months of 1998 and spring 1999. Although it was destined for the mainly rural churches of East Anglia, I felt compelled to site the drama within a walking radius of my Ladbroke Grove home in West London. The combination of a personally familiar, and contemporary, urban setting gave the paintings the incarnational immediacy I wanted. Making this series has had the unexpected side effect of creating after-images in my mind. Sometimes cycling down a nearby street I will find myself thinking that this is the road in which they crucified him, or where he fell down. It can be a disturbing phenomenon, but it is essentially true to the Ignatian desire to see the Gospels as a participator or eyewitness would, rather than seeing them as a remote historical text.

9 William Hamper, aka Billy Childish
Crucifixion, 2003
Oil on wood
183 x183 cm

I have painted a very human Christ, who suffers agony and asks, 'Father, why have you forsaken me?' It is the same Jesus that Holbein painted in the tomb. The painting is oil on a wooden cross construction, which is as much the work as the painting is.

Photograph courtesy IAP Fine Art

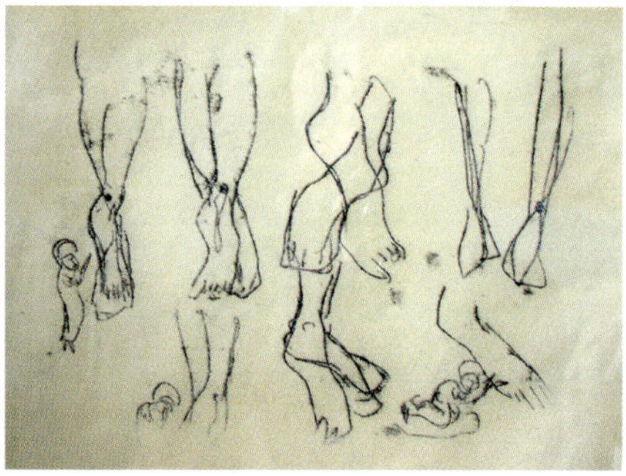

Collection of Stuart and Margaret Evans

10 Tracey Emin
Study of Feet and Mary Magdalene, 1989
30 x 40 cm
Monoprint on paper

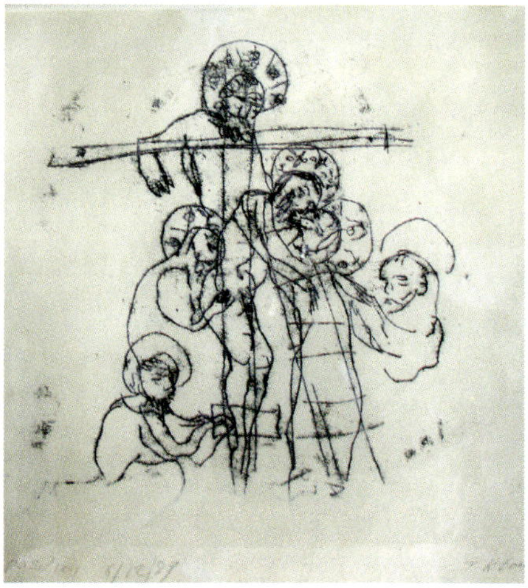

Collection of Stuart and Margaret Evans

11 Tracey Emin
The Disposition, 1989
30 x 40 cm
Monoprint on paper

12 Chris Gollon
Stations of the Cross IV: Jesus meets His Mother, 2003
Mixed media on canvas
102 x 76 cm

I am currently working on a commission for fourteen *Stations of the Cross* for a grade-one listed church in London. Having always considered *Station IV* to be very emotional, and of extreme interest with regard to the theme of this exhibition, it seemed appropriate to contribute something from the *Via Dolorosa.*

Photograph: Miki Slingsby

13 **Maggi Hambling OBE**
Good Friday, 2003
Oil on canvas
35 x 25.5 cm

Each Good Friday since 1986, I have produced paintings, drawings or sculptures on the theme of the crucifixion. This painting is the most recent in the series.

Collection of Andrew and Alison Rickard

15 **Paul Hobbs**
Head of Christ, 2000
Acrylic on paper
48 x 32 cm

Head of Christ is part of a collection of paintings entitled Body of Christ, made in 2000. They show him on the cross, with his skin lacerated from his earlier brutal flogging. The crown of thorns criss-crosses his brow, as he looks down at his tormentors and across at us through the centuries.

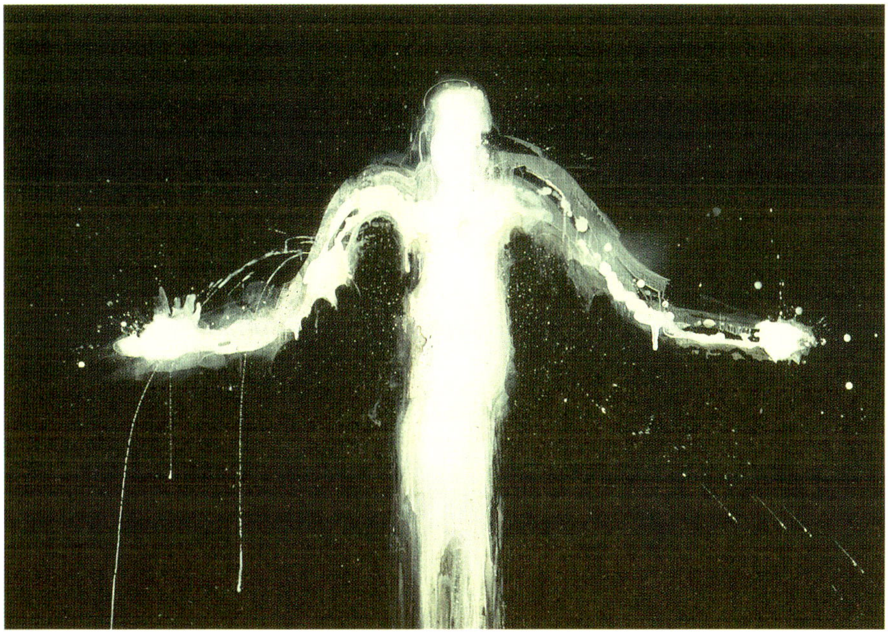

Photograph courtesy Paul Stolper

14 **Susie Hamilton**
Ecce Homo II, 2003
Acrylic on canvas
152 x 214 cm

This painting is part of an ongoing series of single figures begun in 1999 entitled *Mutilates* – a title suggesting both mutation and mutilation. Painted in many thin layers of watery white acrylic on varnished black backgrounds the figures are like outcasts and suggest states of fragility, decay and suffering. They are generally influenced by the racked and fragile poses of Northern Renaissance painting, but *Ecce Homo* refers directly to Christianity in its title and pose. The crucified figure is represented as a vulnerable, leaking body and seems perhaps to be in the process of disintegrating, dissolving and sinking down. Its flexible, twisting form can also appear to be rising upwards in a burst of light. Lit from within, it flashes out of the black void like a spirit, or an x-ray. On the one hand the painting represents the fragile, disintegrating, and decaying body and on the other, the semi-transparent, ghostly veils of paint evoke the notion of the spiritual. The painting sets up a tension between matter and spirit, materiality and the idea of the immaterial.

16 Robert Hardy
Journey of the crosses, 2003
Oil on board
26 x 30 cm

I wanted to assemble lots of Christian meanings and symbols in one picture, drawing directly on scenes from the *Stations of the Cross* (Pilate washing his hands, St. Veronica) and the Anastasis Icon of the Orthodox Church with its suggestion of Christ's descent into limbo transferred, in this painting, to the 'foul rag-and-bone shop' clutter found in the back of a builder's van. I wanted to emphasise movement passing across, through and beyond with theme of salvation; the s-shaped road/path; the builder's name on the van; the pilgrim on his way to the Holy City; the *Chi-Ro* symbol on the hubcap; the Salvation Army.

17 Albert Herbert
Jesus is stripped of his garments ii, 1987
Oil on board
14 x 11 inches

18 Albert Herbert
Simon of Cyrene carries the cross
1987
Oil on board
14 x 11 inches

19 Albert Herbert
Jesus falls under the cross 1987
Oil on board
14 x 11 inches

20 Albert Herbert
Jesus is laid in the sepulchre 1987
Oil on board
14 x 11 inches
© Albert Herbert. England & Co Gallery and Bridgeman Art Library

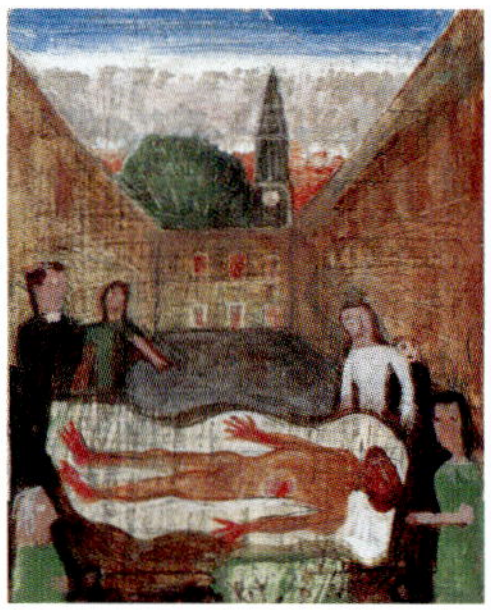

Since 1982, Albert Herbert has treated stories from the Bible as metaphors or universal symbols and archetypes. He does not start with a story and then illustrate it. He says, *'I usually start with some idea that could be put into words, but when I begin to paint I become entirely involved in the difficult process of making a painting … the original idea becomes lost in the paint and re-emerges as something quite different, and usually much more interesting.* Jane England

21 **Ghislaine Howard**
The Crucifixion, 1999
Oil on canvas
129 x 104cm

This work is the final study for the Crucifixion – part of a sequence of fourteen large monochrome paintings *The Stations of the Cross/The Captive Figure* – that were painted for Liverpool Anglican Cathedral in 2000. The sequence of paintings was the result of almost 10 years sustained exploration of the subject. They have been shown subsequently at Canterbury and Gloucester Cathedrals and are continuing to tour other religious and secular venues. The concentration upon the single, naked form highlights the fragility and vulnerability of the human condition – as history, recent and distant, has shown us time and time again, this suffering body, hanging on a cross to die, could be any one of us.

Photograph courtesy Flowers East, London

22 **Peter Howson**
Ecce Homo, 2003
Oil on canvas
183 x 112 cm
Private collection

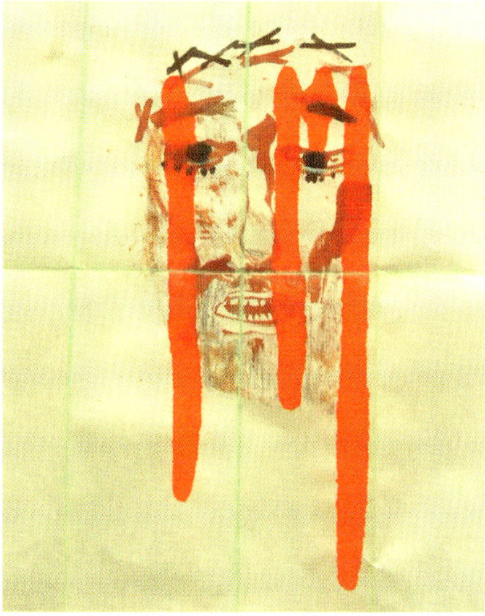

23 **Sonia Lawson RA**
The Sudarium of St. Veronica, 2003
Watercolour
54 x 44 cm

This subject has always intrigued me. It is said that Veronica wiped the face of Christ when he fell under the weight of the cross on his way to Calvary, and the image of his face was left upon the cloth she used. Some believe her name really means *vera icon* (true image). Her compassion awakens interest in the general devotional context of concern with the humanity of Christ himself, especially the Holy Face and the physical elements of his Passion.

Photograph courtesy Marlborough Fine Art

24 Christopher Le Brun RA
The Morning Watch, 2001-2002
Oil on canvas
160 x 180 cm

The Morning Watch is one of a series of paintings that followed a commission in 1996 for the choir of Liverpool Cathedral. Subsequent themes have included *Tobias and the Angel, The Pilgrim* and *Travellers in a Landscape*. The painting evokes a lyrical appreciation of nature that, despite it being profoundly characteristic of the native imagination, is comparatively rare in contemporary art. This atmosphere, or type of thoughtfulness, is conveyed through symbol and metaphor and sustained through links with poetry and music. It shows a feeling for the world that would not have been unfamiliar to William Blake, John Bunyan or Samuel Palmer. Although there is no image of Christ in this painting, it is arguable that post-medieval English art comes closest to a convincing depiction of the transcendent through the visionary imagination, and especially when it is inspired by nature and landscape.

25 Paul Martin
The Restorer, 1988-1989
Oil, wax
150 x 180 cm

The subject matter of the painting is fairly simple. A vaulted, frescoed space contains scaffolding and is illuminated by a dim light. Strong light enters from the left and lights up the end wall in sharp geometric configurations. The platform supports a single figure wearing an apron covered in paint and a covered, empty birdcage from which a bright, shining bird has escaped.

26 Louise McClary
And the Veil of the Temple was rent in the midst, 2001
Acrylic on linen
82 x 87 cm

I spent the summer of 2001 completing a series of paintings on *The Stations of the Cross*. I became very involved with the subject and particularly with the gospels in the King James version of the Bible.

The words 'the veil of the temple was rent in the midst' were the starting point for this painting; for me it conjures up the end. The green shoot coming from Christ's mouth is a sign of renewal, a hint of the resurrection to follow.

28 **Nicholas Mynheer**
Corpus, 1993/2002
Oil
16 x 11 cm

The painting was the result of listening to Bach's Cantata BWV 82, *Ich habe genug* (*For me, it is enough*). It was started in 1993 but then left until 2002 when it was finished.

27 **Iain McKillop**
The Reconciliation of Peter, 2002
Oil on board
30 x 22.5 cm

This painting is part of a cycle of 32 paintings that follow the Passion of Christ and on through his Resurrection to Pentecost. Each is accompanied by a short, poetic meditation. The paintings often emphasise the emotional content of the scenes, particularly through gesture. This enables the artist to reach beyond the narrative of the Biblical story to its spiritual and personal meanings. Here Christ's acceptance of Peter, despite the disciple's shame, is paralleled with our own experience. Christ's wounds open again with his yearning for reconciliation.

29 **Kate Rose**
The Entombment, 2003
Acrylic/gesso on board with gold leaf
118 x 83 cm

The structure surrounding Christ is stone coloured, representing the tomb. Carvings in the stone depict the presentation in the temple during his infancy. The words Earth, Man, God, and Heaven are inscribed in Greek. The figure plunges into the earth, watched over by the Holy Spirit in the form of a dove.

Private Collection, courtesy Anthony Mould Contemporary

30 Roger Wagner
Abraham and the Angels, 2002
Oil on board
92 x 122 cm

According to the mysterious story in the book of Genesis the LORD appeared to Abraham near the great trees of Mamre while he was sitting at the entrance to his tent in the heat of the day. Abraham looked up and saw three men standing nearby. He invited them to rest under the tree and prepared them a meal. Because the appearance of the LORD and the appearance of the three men are spoken of in one breath, Christian iconography – as in Andrei Rublev's great picture – has taken these three figures as a representation of the Trinity and their meal as a kind of communion.

What follows in the story, however, is the cataclysmic destruction of the cities of the plains. In an earlier painting I tried to evoke this sense of a picnic on the edge of doom, by setting Abraham's meal with the angels on the edge of a wheat field with the looming presence of the Sizewell nuclear reactor visible in the background. The same theme is present in this painting, where a cement factory in the Syrian desert stands in for Sodom and Gomorrah. The focus, however, is on the foreground, which is inspired by memories of the hospitality of the Syrian Bedouin.

The only place in which the New Testament refers to this Genesis story, it advises Christians not to forget to entertain strangers 'for by doing so some have entertained angels without knowing it'. The presence of strangers, it seems to suggest, can be a doorway into the presence of God.

31 Penny Warden
Phoenix No 19, 2003
Oil on muslin on wood
193 x 94 cm

Phoenix No 19 is one of a series of paintings in which I have tried to translate the traditional, familiar image of the crucifixion of Christ into a new arrangement of colour and form. I work almost life-size so that the viewer can enter into the painting and identify more fully with it. I apply paint with the maximum of spontaneity and work rapidly so that accidents can happen. The paint is flicked, splattered and destroyed again and again, producing a figure that disturbs the viewer, an uneasy figure, one that shows its suffering. Yet at the same time, because of the absence of the cross, I hope to convey that suffering is not only caused by external factors, or socially imposed by others, but is also an inner experience inseparable from life. I try to convey in paint the anguish of human existence and our feelings of abandonment and alienation. But the absence of the cross also expresses the survival of the human spirit, pointing to the hope of resurrection and immortality – like the phoenix, destroying itself only to rise again from the ashes.

32 Peter White
Figure and Bowl, 2001
Oil, acrylic and wax on board
182 x 153 cm

33 **Michael Gough and Barry Richardson**
Iconography, 2003
Performance

Artist Michael Gough and actor Barry Richardson first conceived *Iconography* in London in the summer of 1997. Richardson, robed as the archetypal robes of Christ, took to the streets of Soho, taking up the poses of classical Christian imagery. Gough photographed the ensuing interactions between the 'icon' and members of the general public.

On Shrove Tuesday and Ash Wednesday, Gough and Richardson will collaborate again for *Iconography*, bringing the timeless image of Christ to the City of London and the heart of the capital's financial district. The ensuing clashes and sympathies with the spectacle will again be documented and presented as a photographic exhibition.

Canterbury Cathedral

Canterbury Cathedral is the setting for Antony Gormley's sculpture, *Rise*. It lies in the Trinity Chapel, ultimate destination of mediaeval pilgrims. Here Thomas Becket's relics were housed in a magnificent shrine until it was destroyed at the Reformation.

Vigil, by Willie Williams is present after dusk from Palm Sunday. It will flood the Bell Harry tower, the altar and central crossing with deep purple light, changing to gold at midnight on Easter Sunday morning.

Photograph courtesy of the artist and Jay Jopling/White Cube (London)

34 Antony Gormley
Rise, 1983-4
Lead, fibreglass, plaster, air
30 x 58 x 190 cm

The crux of Gormley's sculptural strategy is the evocation of 'presence'. *Stephen Bann*

35 Willie Williams
Vigil, 2003
Installation

Vigil is a light installation occupying the vast central area of Canterbury Cathedral. It is a response both to the immensity of the building and to traditional elements of the Easter liturgy.

A column of light the width of the nave emanates from an unseen source in the roof of the central tower of the cathedral. An intense pool of light is centred on the stone floor surrounding the altar, with ambient reflections altering the perception of the building. In conjunction with the light itself, periodic use of incense and reflective elements intensify the space while leaving it physically unaltered.

St Mary's Episcopal Cathedral, Glasgow

The stated aim of St Mary's Cathedral is 'to be a spiritual home for the arts in Glasgow'. Two new works by Scottish painter Peter Howson, will be shown in the body of the cathedral, together with the drawings for his recently commissioned *Stations of the Cross*. The cathedral will also be host to installations and interventions by six young Glasgow artists, invited to respond to the theme of *Presence*.

36 Peter Howson
Jesus is taken down from the cross, 2003
Pencil on board
22 x 21 cm
Private collection. Image courtesy Flowers East, London

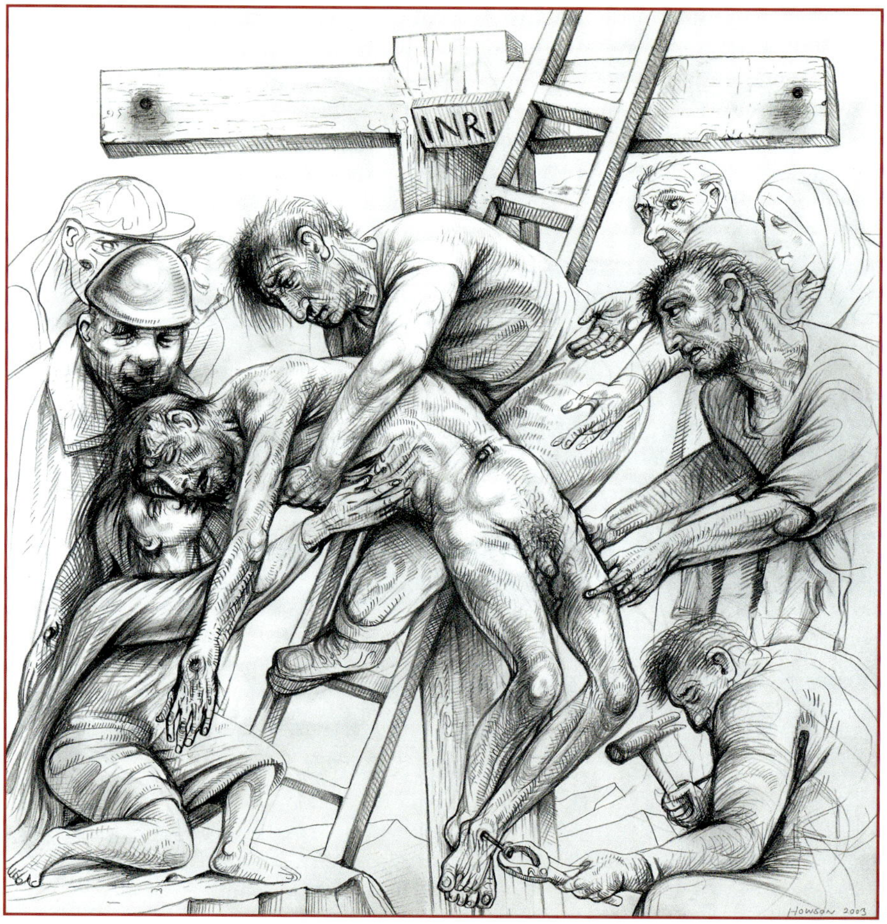

Photograph courtesy Flowers East, London

Peter Howson has revisited one of the great themes of Western art in this extraordinarily moving series of drawings made for a recently commissioned *Stations of the Cross*. Howson has drawn inspiration for these pieces primarily from the artists of the Northern Renaissance, creating a language that is both contemporary and timeless. This duality is especially obvious in the drawings, which combine the traditional image of Christ with figures, faces, weapons and dress that unquestionably come from present-day scorn and violence.
Adapted from the introduction by Angela Flowers to The Stations of the Cross.

Peter Howson
Crucifixion I, 2003
not shown
Oil on canvas

Peter Howson
Crucifixion II, 2003
not shown
Oil on canvas

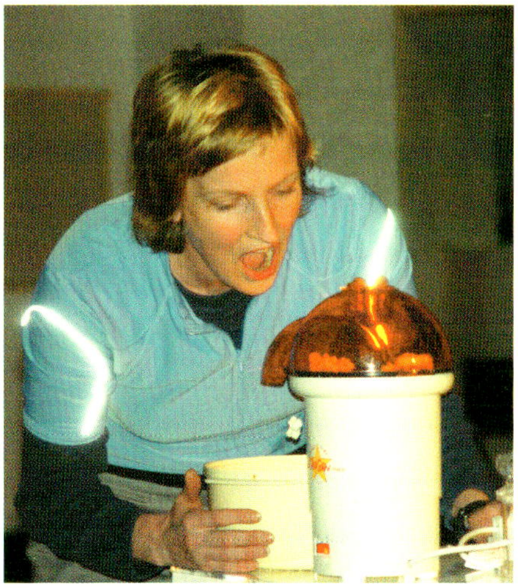

37 Aileen Campbell
I love my popcorn machine; it is so beautiful, 2003
Performance

My voice is part of an equation that includes the breath and presence of the body as a vessel for sound. I grew up in a busy household, full of noise. There was simply no quiet space for my singing practice, so I worked on a method of rehearsing where an object that had a reassuringly motorised sound could mask the voice as it developed. This habit of rehearsing with an object has never left me and the sound of the object has become a mask, an accompaniment and a duet, shaping the voice to its particular pitch.

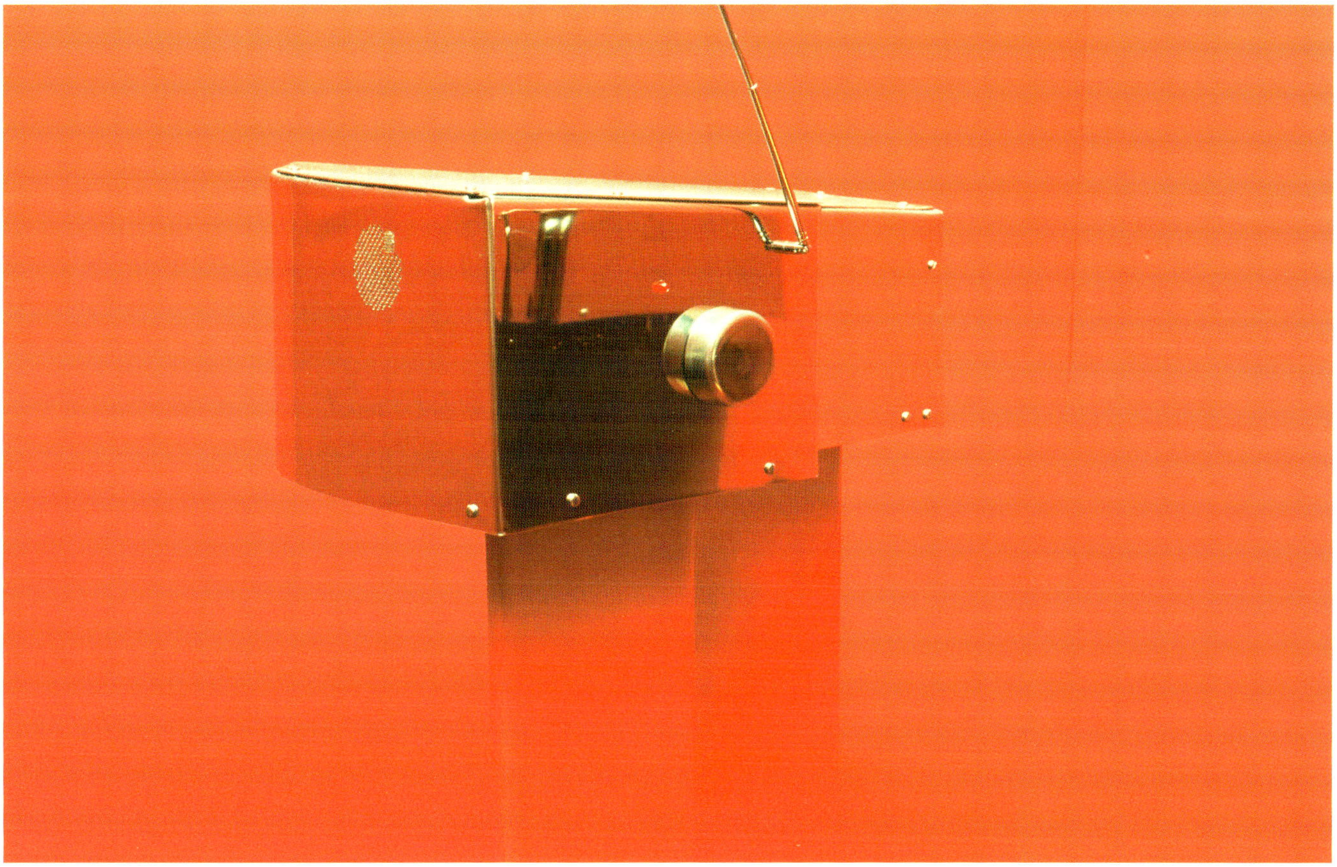

38 Alan Kean
The incorrigible survival of the religious impulse, 2002
Mixed media

Radio brings us an understanding of what goes on in the outside world. After the events of 9/11, BBC Radio 4's audience rocketed as people allowed themselves the comfort of a babbling radio's background sound. In the Cathedral, four radios, tuning up and down a frequency band, are discreetly placed in the pews in four corners of the building, their sounds reflecting the arched interior.

39 Cath Keay
Sssh, 2003
Installation
Glass test tubes

This work is composed of glass test tubes of differing heights laid out in pixillated snowflake forms. Snowflakes are metaphors for individuality, constructed here from standardised scientific apparatus.

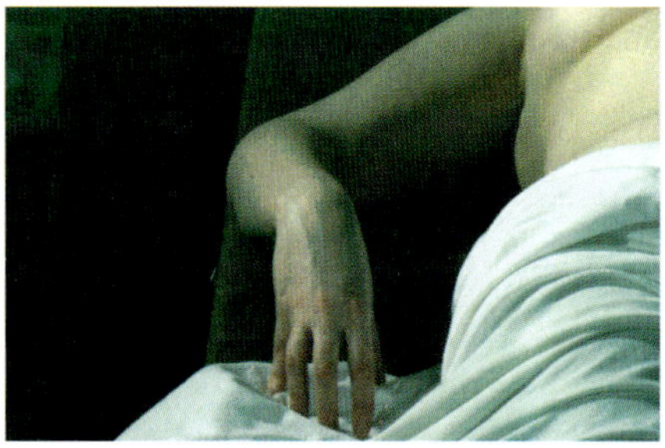

40 Mark Neville
The Dead Christ, 2003
6mm film on loop, 15 mins

Dead Christ, a 16mm film made with scientific stills and movie cameras, explores stereotypes in religious representation. It subjects religious artefacts to the kind of stress experiments normally used in industrial product testing, in an attempt to make concrete the immaterial.

41 Ciara Phillips
Eulogy Banner, 2003
not shown
Banner
4ft x 6ft

This work takes the form of a large, double-sided banner, celebrating the presence of the natural world in an absurdly extravagant gesture.

42 Michael Stumpf
Neverwhere, 2003
not shown
Mixed media
90 x 90 x 40 cm

This sculpture alludes to an unwritten narrative entitled *Beyond the Fragile Geometry of Space.*

Worcester Cathedral

Martin Rose's paintings – meditations on the seven last words spoken by Christ on the cross – will be shown in Worcester Cathedral during the two weeks before Easter day. The Lindsay Quartet will perform Haydn's *Seven Last Words* as part of a special service of meditation for Palm Sunday evening. On Easter Monday an exhibition of new work by four painters will explore the resurrection and ascension of Christ.

The Lindsay Quartet
Peter Cropper *violin*
Ronald Birks *violin*
Robin Ireland *viola*
Bernard Gregor-Smith *cello*

43 Martin Rose
The seven last words from the cross, 2003
Mixed media on gesso and panel
38 x 38 cm

I began these paintings for the first Arts Festival at Sheffield Cathedral, when the Lindsay Quartet performed Haydn's *Seven Last Words* – originally commissioned for Cadiz Cathedral in 1785. They are the first paintings with an overtly religious subject matter that I have undertaken.

Father, into thy hands I commit my spirit!

Father, forgive them, for they know not what they do.

Verily I say unto thee, today shalt thou be with me in paradise.

Woman, behold thy son! Behold thy mother!

Eloi, Eloi, lama sabachthani? My God, my God, why hast thou forsaken me?

I thirst.

It is finished.

Resurrection and Ascension:
an exhibition of paintings for the days after Easter

44 Iain McKillop
Resurrection, The Cry of Victory, 2000
Oil on canvas
128 x 91 cm

This was one of the first paintings to be completed in my series *Meditations on the Passion*. The pose of Christ is developed from the iconography of Grünewald's *Resurrection* in the Isenheim Altarpiece. Instead of springing up, Christ is seen as dynamically climbing the steps from death and pushing open the stone of the tomb. As the light of new life rushes in, he releases the spirits of the dead who are drawn up with him. This painting forms a triptych with *The Cry of Dereliction* and *Pentecost, The Cry of Release*. It is also a prototype for the Resurrection panel in the new triptych altarpiece for the Lady Chapel of Gloucester Cathedral.

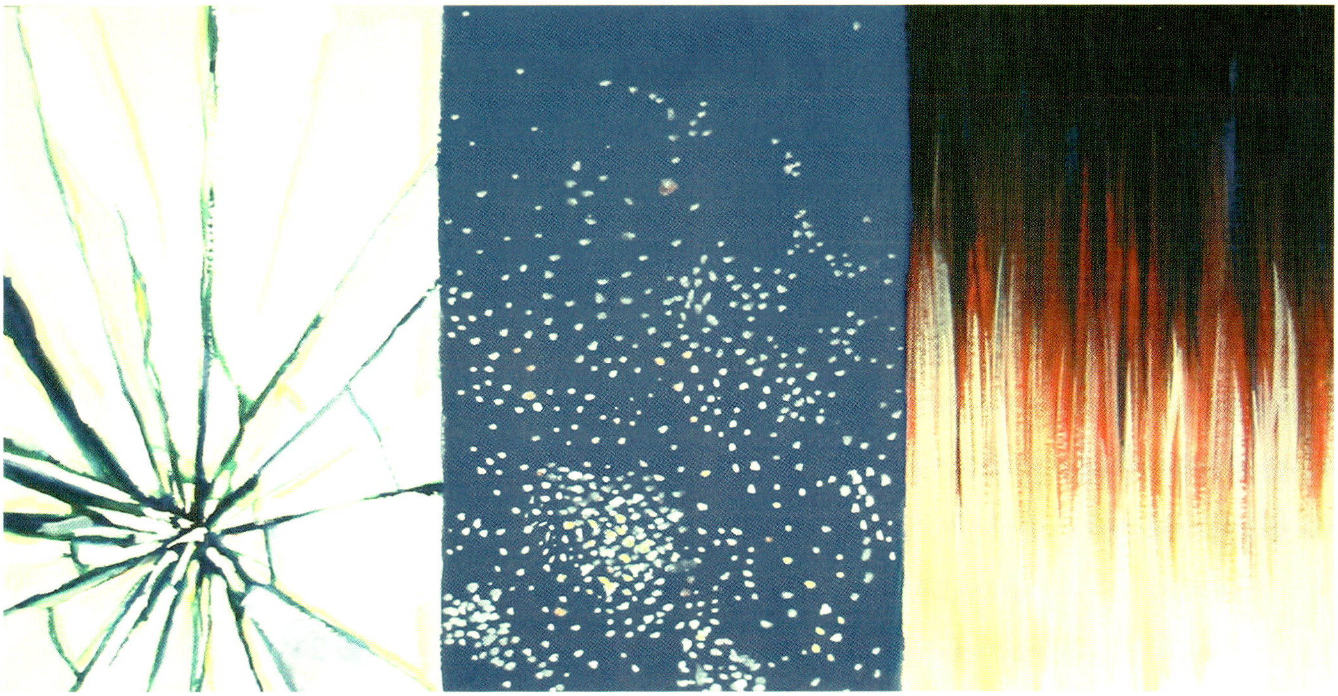

45 Adam Boulter
Triptych: The Resurrection that was; The Resurrection that is; The Resurrection that will be, 2003
Oil on canvas
152.5 x274.3 cm

---

46 Mark Cazalet
Ascension Day, 2001-2004
Oil on linen
182 x 122cm
not shown

Occasionally there is an hiatus in the studio, no obvious deadlines, commissions or projects pending. I started this large canvas on such an afternoon. I was thinking about Braque's late Atelier painting and the way in which a studio can be an ark or hermit's cell, a place of prayer, doubt and epiphany. As the evening drew in the sky performed one of those dusk miracles with the glow of the sun's last rays. The street's sodium lights described the ascendant slope of the road leading away from the studios and above it in the sky, there evolved a helix of marvellous golden, pinky-orange. On the radio the annual Ascension Day service was being broadcast.

There are three spaces in the image; the interior domestic realm of the studio, the view looking down into the world of the street, which in turn leads the eye up to the luminous lights of the heavens. It is also a picture about loss, and the comfort that came to the disciples after Christ's ascension, when the Holy Spirit became evident in the everyday surroundings of their lives. As the dates of the work show, it took years before I was able to find the insight and momentum to resolve what had started so spontaneously.

47 Louise McClary
Ascension, 2002
Acrylic on paper
66 x 102 cm

As something that has occurred, the resurrection of Jesus is a breakthrough, a shattering of assumptions. As something which is unfolding, it is millions of related lights. As something that is going to happen, it is a consuming transformation.

Lincoln Cathedral and The Usher Gallery

Lincoln Cathedral and the city's Usher Gallery have a history of imaginative collaboration on art projects. For *Presence*, the new sculpture, *Chowl*, by Nicola Hicks is shown at the eastern end of the cathedral and *Sorry, Sorry, Sarajevo* in the south transept. *Blue Christ*, by Jill Sim, stands outside the cathedral beside the West Door. The Usher Gallery are opening their new media facility with a continuous showing of Mark Wallinger's video installation, *Angel*.

48 Jill Sim
Blue Christ, 1999
bronze
height 183 cm

The Blue Christ's thorns were gathered on the Serbian/Kosovan border. This is Christ in inner conflict, a paradox, a mandorla, the overlap of heaven and earth. 'The fire and the rose are one', T.S.Eliot, *The Four Quartets*

49 Nicola Hicks
Chowl, 2002
Plaster
173 x 217 x 50 cm

50 Nicola Hicks
Sorry, Sorry, Sarajevo 1993-99
Limited edition Bronze
186 x 110 x 80 cm

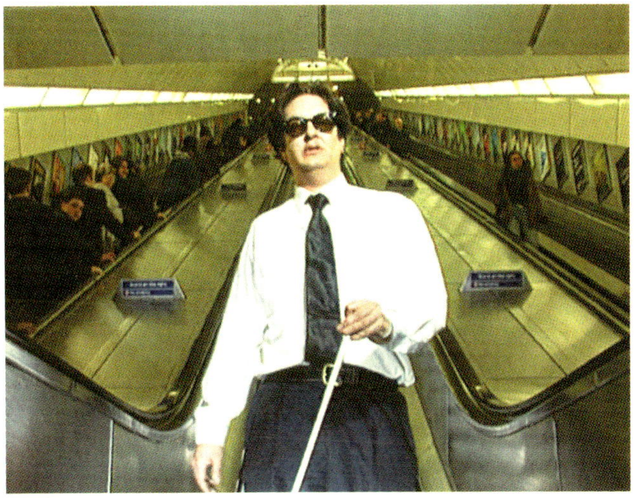

51 Mark Wallinger
Angel, 1997
Projected video installation
7'30" (loop)

Durham Cathedral

2004 marks the 900th anniversary of the translation of the relics of St Cuthbert into Durham Cathedral. To celebrate the year, the cathedral has commissioned a major retrospective exhibition of the work of Durham sculptor Fenwick Lawson. The exhibition will include four pieces relating to the person of Christ, which are also part of *Presence*.

52 Fenwick Lawson
The Risen Christ, 1974
Beech wood
height 450 cm

My reference for the formal content of this sculpture was Durham Cathedral, which epitomised my interest in the Romanesque. The sculpture was initially commissioned for Hexham Abbey and my intention was to add to the Abbey what I considered to be the visual dynamic of Durham Cathedral. The distinctive spiral motif in the Norman columns is echoed in the spiral movement of the form in the sculpture. This I saw as a formal device to give an upward movement for the eye, thereby conveying the idea of an ascending image.

53 Fenwick Lawson
Pieta, 1974-1983
Beech wood
height 270 cm

In this carving of the *Pieta* I have tried to embody a duality of meaning. Death is perceived through the brutalised, crucified body, the bruised bent knees showing the history of events. The dismembered, unformed arm adds to this discomfort. Resurrection and life are expressed through the lifting arm and the dynamic of the hand handing on to the mother, the chosen vehicle for life. The polished brass fragment, a metaphor for life, is meant to reinforce this. The mother also offers a duality of meaning. The break-up of the image through the tree splitting suggests the trauma of bereavement. At the same time, the carved form expresses calm and stillness and through the outward gesture of her hand, offers life through sacrificial death to the viewer. Perhaps this sculpture should be called *Behold your Mother.*

54 Fenwick Lawson
The Condemned, 1984
Elm wood
height 240 cm

The Condemned began with reference to the first Station of the Cross. The idea of the hair being pulled and the face distorted by a blow, occurred to me as an effective image of brutality. Hands tied behind his back; trapped in the tree; the bite of the chainsaw; split, fragmented wood; the formal content echoing the pain and cruelty of the subject. The condemned, everyman, Amnesty International, political prisoner – name it as you see it. It is important to see the universality of the image of Christ condemned.

55 Fenwick Lawson
Daughters of Jerusalem, 1986
Giant poplar
height 174 cm

'Don't weep for me, daughters of Jerusalem, weep for your children.' The theme of the sculpture is that of witness, the subject is the crucifixion – this is the starting point. My aim is to point to the evidence of cruelty, pain, and the horror of physical suffering wherever this may occur. The sculpture could equally be called *Bosnia, Vietnam, Iraq.* This image of weeping women has both historical and contemporary relevance.

About Bible*Lands*

Bible*Lands* has been at the very heart of Christian, compassionate ministry for 150 years, since its beginnings in 1854 at the height of the Crimean War.

Throughout the 20th Century, and now into the 21st, Bible*Lands* has maintained its crucial focus – bringing healing and the peaceful things of God to those most in need in the lands of the Bible – regardless of their faith or nationality.

Bible*Lands* continues to work with more than 50 Christian-led Partner Projects in Israel/Palestine, Lebanon and Egypt.

Without the prayerful and financial ministry and encouragement of its supporters and donors, the valuable work of helping so many in need, especially the children, could not continue. People in this strategic but unsettled region need our help as much as ever.

We hope that these pages will give you a broad insight into the work of Bible*Lands* and will encourage you to contact us for further information about how our Partners on the ground address those desperate needs.

We look forward to hearing from you and hope to welcome you into the Bible*Lands* supporting family in the very near future.

Medical Care

Bible*Lands* funds specialist surgery facilities, clinics and general hospitals, as well as local primary and secondary health care programmes, in those circumstances where travel to such specialised medical centres further afield is difficult.

Innocent victim

Following a rocket attack on the wrong car, this small boy lost two members of his family and his own left eye.

St John's Eye Hospital, Jerusalem, supported by a regular Bible*Lands*' monthly grant, has been restoring sight for over 100 years and treating those whose eyes have been threatened by disease or injury.

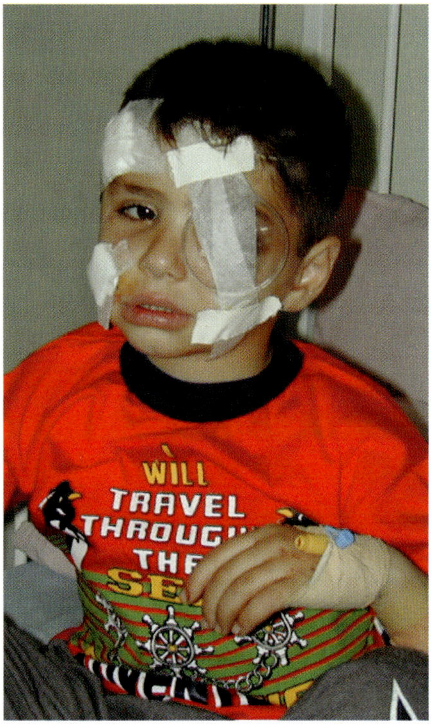

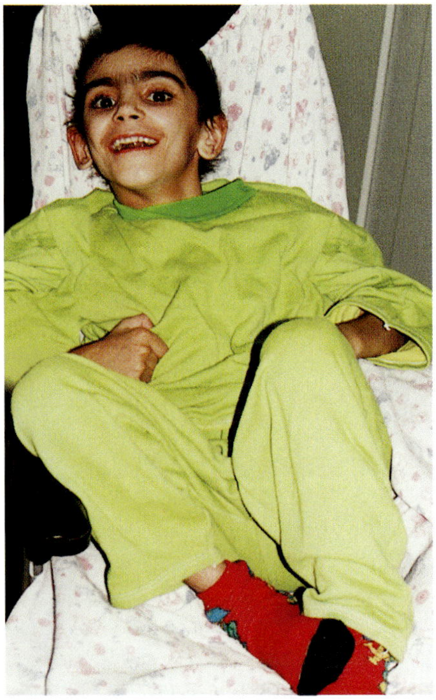

Dallal

Nine-year-old Dallal was admitted into the Bethlehem Arab Society for Rehabilitation (BASR) Hospital at Beit Jala, having been in a coma for seven weeks following a severe head injury. After receiving intensive care and rehabilitation over a long period, she has now returned home, but is still receiving treatment as an outpatient on a regular basis.

BASR provides medical treatment and rehabilitation services to children and young adults with serious head injuries and disabilities.

Social Care

Bible*Lands* works with those who have been orphaned and other people who live in particularly deprived circumstances across the region.

Children of the Nile

In the village of Beni Khalil on the Upper Nile, a comprehensive plan to relieve poverty includes plastering homes, providing clean running water, health and vocational training and revolving loans schemes.

Miryam

In Cairo, the Salaam Centre provides a variety of social and medical projects for the Zabaleen *'rubbish pickers'* community living in the most extreme poverty and squalor imaginable.

Education

Bible*Lands* supports schools and colleges that offer good quality Christian-based education for children whose families could not otherwise afford it.

The new girls

Bible*Lands* funds have recently enabled the JL Schneller Institute, Bekaa Valley, Lebanon to build a new Boarding Unit for girls who are orphaned or from poor families.

Ramzi and Ronza

Ramzi and Ronza are three and four years old. In October 2001, their mother Mary left the house in Bethlehem to buy milk for her children and was shot by a sniper, for no reason, from about 200 metres away. Only now are they beginning to open up and trust people but still remain very shy and frightened.

Support and Care of Refugees

Bible*Lands* works with those caring for refugees who are in immediate need of food, clothing or health care, particularly those from Sudan, Somalia and Ethiopia, who are now in Egypt.

Nyanut

A young refugee mother with her new-born baby at the Refuge Egypt clinic. Health and social care is provided to refugees at the All Saints' Cathedral clinic in Cairo. Families, pregnant women and the sick receive food, clothing and advice on a weekly basis.

Sonshine children

The Sonshine School in Alexandria provides basic education and a daily breakfast for 40 displaced refugee children and runs weekly evening language classes for adults.

Special Needs

Bible*Lands* and its Project Partners seek to provide education and specialist training to children and young people who are blind, deaf or who have other major physical or intellectual disabilities.

Friends

The Bible*Lands* supported project of Al Kafa'at, meaning 'Capabilities', in Beirut, caters for some 3,000 children and young adults with varying handicaps. The work of Al Kafa'at is carried out at six centres.

Blind courage

Twelve-year-old Sajeda has been at the Helen Keller Centre for the Visually Impaired, Jerusalem since she was $3^1/_2$. Since then, her already poor sight has virtually gone completely. The Centre cares for children aged from 3 to 13 years. They are taught the normal curriculum in Arabic Braille, as well as receiving mobility training and other skills.

Vocational and Adult Training

Bible*Lands* supports Project Partners involved in providing degree-level Nurse Training, as well as vocational training and rehabilitation facilities for young people.

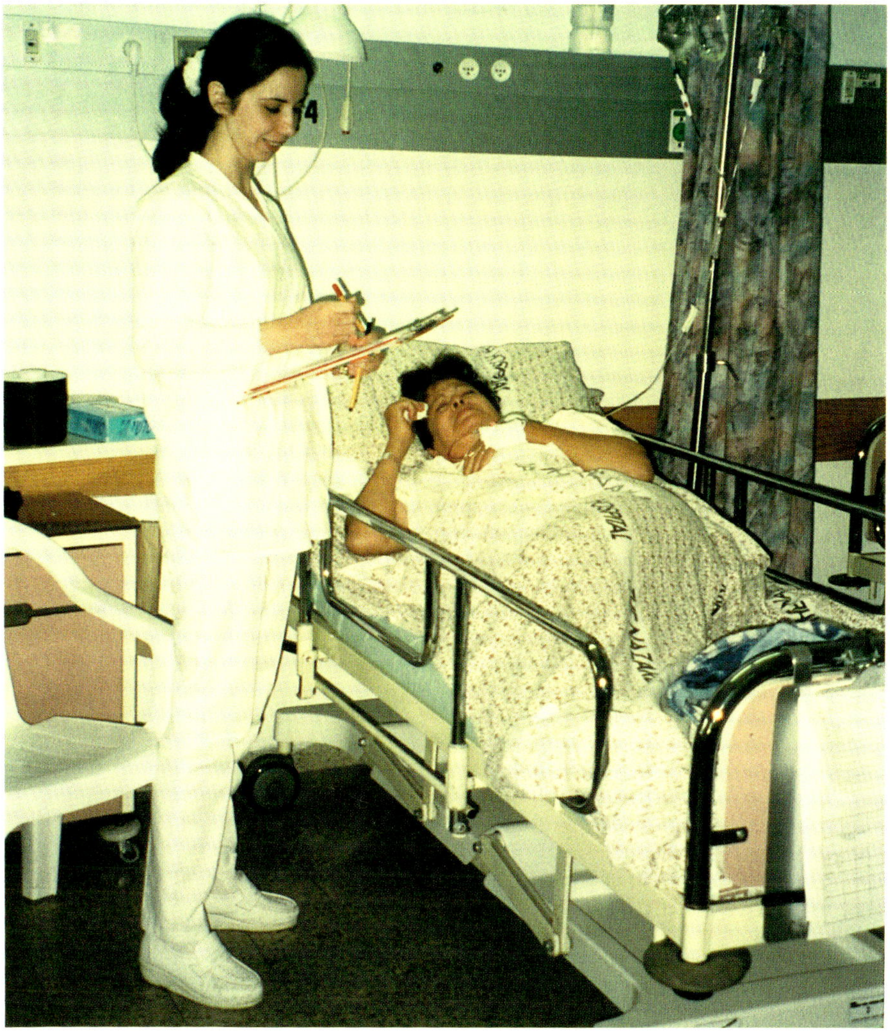

Learning to care

Nurses-in-training from the Nazareth School of Nursing, the particular focus for Bible*Lands'* 150th Anniversary Year, learn their caring skills on the wards of the adjoining Nazareth Hospital. Hundreds of them have brought healing and hope to the sick throughout the Galilean region, over the last 80 years.

The carpentry shop

The Vocational Training Centre of the Deaf Unit in Egypt offers a training programme that enables young adults to develop real skills and secure themselves a better future.

Bible*Lands* 150th Anniversary

As the 150th Anniversary of Bible*Lands'* work among the sick and the needy in the lands of the Bible, 2004 marks a very significant year for the charity and one in which many special events have been planned.

These include six pilgrimage tours to the Holy Land, an exhibition of paintings by artists accompanying Bible*Lands'* pilgrimage groups, a conference on Middle East issues in April and 'The Big Event' – a concluding celebration with special guest speakers and performers from the UK and overseas, on Saturday 9 October at Friends Meeting House, Euston Road, London.

We hope that you have enjoyed reading about *Presence* and the work of Bible*Lands* in this accompanying guide to the exhibition.

If you would like to support us, as we look forward to another 150 years of serving the needy in the lands of the Bible, we would be delighted to hear from you.

150 YEARS OF HEALING & HOPE
1854 2004
BibleLands
Christian love in action

For further information:

Bible*Lands*
PO Box 50, High Wycombe
Buckinghamshire HP15 7QU
Tel: 01494 897950
Fax: 01494 897951
email: info@biblelands.org.uk
www.biblelands.org.uk

Registered Charity Number: 1076329

Norman Adams RA
born Walthamstow 1927

1940-46 Harrow Art School
1948-51 Royal College of Art
1952 One man show, Gimpel Fils
1953 Designs for Ballet *Mirror for Witches* at Covent Garden
1954 Murals in Broad Lane Comprehensive School, Coventry
1962-70 Appointed Head of Painting, Manchester College of Art
1972-73 Murals in St. Anselm, Kennington
1975 *Stations of The Cross*, Our Lady of Lourdes RC Church, Milton Keynes
1994-5 *Stations of the Cross*, St. Mary's RC Church, Manchester

Recent solo exhibitions include:
Regular shows at Roland, Browse and Delbanco; Grosvenor Gallery; Christopher Hull Gallery; Beaux Arts; Third Eye, Glasgow; Abbott Hall, Kendall; City Art Gallery, Wakefield; Cartwright Hall, Bradford

Bibliography
Stations of The Cross in St. Mary's, Mulberry Street, Manchester 1995; *Angels of Soho,* (with A. Adams), R.A. Enterprises; *Island Chapters* (with A. Adams), 1991

Craigie Aitchison CBE RA
born Edinburgh 1926

1936-41 Loretto School, Musselburgh
1941 Basil Paterson & Ainslie, Tutors, Edinburgh
1970 Edwin Austin Abbey Premier Scholarship for Painting
1988 Member of Royal Academy of Arts

Recent solo exhibitions include:
Craigie Aitchison, Royal Academy; *Craigie Aitchison, Works on paper*, Royal Academy,London;*Craigie Aitchison,* The Ingleby Gallery, Edinburgh; *Craigie Aitchison*, The Museum of Modern Art, Powys; *Craigie Aitchison: Italian and other painting*, Timothy Taylor Gallery and Waddington Galleries, London; Galleria Barquet Ramis, New York, USA; Timothy Taylor Gallery and Waddington Galleries, London; Commissioned to paint *Calvary* for Liverpool Cathedral and Truro Cathedral; *Craigie: The Art of Craigie Aitchison*, Gallery of Modern Art, Glasgow; *Spirit of Lamlash: The Paintings of Craigie Aitchison 1954-1994*, Terrace Gallery, Harewood House, Leeds; *Crucifixion* on loan to King's College Chapel, Cambridge; *Craigie Aitchison, New Paintings*, Thomas Gibson Fine Art, London

Philip Archer
born Cardiff 1954

Sheffield Hallam University; Royal College of Art; Principal of the Leith School of Art; Judge for the Alistair Salvesen Travel Scholarship

Recent solo exhibitions include:
Bourne Fine Art, Edinburgh; The Gold Gallery, Edinburgh; *Towards Byzantium*, Leith School of Art, Edinburgh; The Open Eye Gallery, Edinburgh; The Muni Gallery, Pontypridd, South Wales

Adam Boulter
born Slough 1971

Central Saint. Martins College of Art, London
Bath College of Higher Education: BA (Hons.) Fine Art (Painting)
Kingston University: MA drawing as process

Recent solo exhibitions include:
St. Katherine Cree, Leadenhall St., London; Quaker Gallery, Upper St. Martins Lane, London;Clapham Art Gallery, London; Chelsea Methodist Church, London; Wolfson College, Oxford

John Bellany CBE
born Port Seton, Scotland 1942

1960-65 Edinburgh College of Art, studied painting under Sir Robin Philipson
1965-68 Royal College of Art, London, studied under Carel Weight and Peter de Francia
Official cultural visit to East Germany with Alan Bold and Alexander Moffat, visiting Dresden, Halle, Weimar, East Berlin and the concentration camp of Buchenwald
1968 Lecturer in Painting, Brighton College of Art
1969-73 Lecturer in Painting, Winchester College of Art
Visiting lecturer at Royal College of Art and Goldsmith's College of Art
1978-84 Lecturer in Painting, Goldsmith's College of Art
1983 Artist in Residence, Victoria College of the Arts, Melbourne, Australia
1988 Hon. Fellow Commoner of Trinity Hall, Cambridge
1994 Awarded CBE

Recent solo exhibitions include:
Raab Gallery, Berlin; Ruth Siegel Gallery, New York; Compass Gallery, Glasgow
Fitzwilliam Museum, Cambridge; Fischer Fine Art, London; *A Long Night's Journey into Day: A 50th Birthday Tribute*, Kelvingrove Art Gallery and Museum, Glasgow; *50th Birthday: A Celebration*, Beaux Arts Gallery, Bath; *Prints, Drawings and Watercolours 1970-1993*, Berkeley Square Gallery, London; *Recent Paintings*, Flowers East at London Fields, London; *Recent Paintings*, Terry Dintenfass Gallery, New York; *John Bellany: New Paintings, John Bellany; Print-Maker*, Talbot Rice Gallery, Edinburgh; *Monoprints*, Flowers East, London

Matthew Burrows
born Cheshire 1971

1999-2000 Artist's Residency, National Gallery, London; Royal Overseas League Travel Scholarship; Artist-in-Residence, Gloucester Cathedral
1993-97 Summers Studio Award, Connecticut, USA; Richard Ford Travel Award, Royal Academy, London; Basil Alkazzi Scholarship, RCA, London

Recent solo exhibitions include:
Anyone Here? Midlands Art Centre, Birmingham; *Flattering Overtures*, Eagle Gallery, London; *A Divine Comedy*, touring exhibition, Gloucester Cathedral, Gloucester City Art Gallery, Huddersfield City Art Gallery; *Comedy and Tragedy*, Lamont Gallery, London; *Inferno* Gloucester Cathedral; Midlands Art Centre, Birmingham; Mertz Contemporary Art, London; Barber Institute, Birmingham

---

Aileen Campbell

Recent solo performances include:
It's a wonderful lie, Wasps, Glasgow; *Bad Manners and Physical Violence*, Sculpture Court, Edinburgh; *Rock Candy*, Hoorn, Holland; *Interim Show*, Mackintosh Gallery, Glasgow School of Art; *Wood Group*, Aberdeen Royal Infirmary; RSA Edinburgh; *Salon Glasgow*, CCA Glasgow; *Metamorphosis*, Artworks Gallery, Greenock; *Swanston Art Studios*, Dalmamock, Glasgow; *Ascent to Nowhere* (Solo), St Mary's Cathedral, Glasgow; *Paperworks VI*, Seagate Gallery, Dundee; *SSA Annual Exhibition*, McLellan Galleries, Glasgow; *Christmas Show*, DeMarco EAF, Edinburgh; *Fuse 96*, McLellan Galleries, Glasgow; *A Sense of Place*, MacRobert Arts Centre, Stirling; *SSA Annual Show*, Edinburgh; *Fuse*, Loch Lomond

---

Mark Cazalet
born London 1964

Commonwealth Universities Scholarship: Baroda University, Gujarat State, India
French consul National Studentship award: awarded one year residency at L'ecole Nationale Superieure des Beaux-Arts, Paris
1983-86 Falmouth School of Art
1982-83 Chelsea School of Art

Recent solo exhibitions include:
The Sound of the Trees, Six Chapel Row Contemporary Art, Bath; *West London Stations of the Cross*, Carden Gallery, Dissenters Chapel, Kensal Green Cemetery, London; *The Four Quartets*, Lady Margaret Hall, Oxford University
Cathedrals of Industry, Museum of London; *City Margins*, Thornton Bevan Arts, London
Paradoxes and Paradigms, Lichfield Cathedral; *Intangible worlds*, East West Gallery, Blenheim Crescent, London; Royal Overseas House, Edinburgh and London; *The Path to Calvary*, Rocket Contemporary Art London, touring to: Lincoln (Cathedral, Usher Gallery, Lincoln Theological College); Winchester Cathedral; Lady Margaret Hall, Oxford; *Pictures out of India*, The Nehru Centre, London; *Indian Rhythms*, Wycombe Museum Gallery, High Wycombe, Buckinghamshire; Christopher Hull Gallery, London; Gallery 7, Bombay, India

---

Billy Childish
born Chatham, Kent, 1959

My father left home when I was 7. I was sexually abused by a friend of the family when I was 9. I left school at 16 with no qualifications and was turned down by Art School. I went to work in Chatham Dock as an apprentice stonemason. Got onto a painting course at Saint Martin's School of Art on what was called the Genius Clause. Expelled from St. Martins School of Art in 1981 for writing 'the worst type of toilet wall humour'. Diagnosed dyslexic at 28. I have won 2 commendations in the national poetry prize, published 30 collections of poetry and 2 novels, made 100 independent LP records and painted over 2000 paintings. My father has tried to kill himself several times. I believe that life is a spiritual journey.

Tracey Emin
born London 1963

1989 Royal College of Art
1986 Maidstone College of Art

Recent solo exhibitions include:
Tracey Emin, The Art Gallery New South Wales, Sydney; *Tracey Emin*, Lehman Maupin, New York; *Tracey Emin*, Haus der Kunst, Munich, Germany; *Tracey Emin*, Fort Lauderdale Museum of Art, Florida; *Tracey Emin*, MOMA, Oxford; *Tracey Emin*, White Cube2, London; *Love is a Strange Thing*, White Cube 2, Fig. 1, London; *What Do You Know About Love*, Galerie Gebauer, Berlin; *Every Part of Me's Bleeding*, Lehmann Maupin, New York; *Sobasex (My Cunt is Wet with Fear)*, Sagacho Exhibit Space, Tokyo; *Pandaemonium*, Electronic Arts Gallery, London; *Cunt Vernacular* Gebauer, Berlin; *I Need Art Like I Need God*, Gesellschaft für Aktuelle Kunst, Bremen; *Tracey Emin*, Phiippe Rizzo, Paris; *Solo Exhibition*, Moo Gallery, Helsinki; *I Need Art Like I Need God*, South London Gallery, London; *Istanbul Biennial*, Pera Palace Hotel, Turkey (performance); *It's not me that's crying, it's my soul*, Mot & Van den Boogaard, Brussels; *The Aggression of Beauty*, Arndt & Partner, Berlin; *Exorcism of the Last Painting I Ever Made*, Andreas Brändström, Stockholm; *Solo Exhibition*, Habitat, London; Tracey Emin Museum, 221 Waterloo Road, London SE1 (closed 1998); *My Major Retrospective*, Jay Jopling/White Cube, London; *Exploration of the Soul - Journey Across America*, Readings at the following USA locations: Rena Bransten, San Francisco; Regen Projects, Los Angeles; Museum of Contemporary Art, San Diego; David Klein Gallery, Detroit; Mattress Factory, Pittsburgh; Sandra Gering Gallery, New York; White Columns, New York; *Art Cologne* fair, sponsored artist, Jay Jopling/White Cube, Cologne; The Shop, 103 Bethnal Green Road, London (with Sarah Lucas); *From Army to Armani*, Analix Forever, Geneva (with Sarah Lucas)

Bibliography
Always Glad to See You,
Published by Tracey Emin 1997
Exploration of the Soul,
Published by Tracey Emin 1995

Chris Gollon
born London, 1953

1999-2000 Commissioned to paint *Stations of the Cross* for St. John, Bethnal Green
2001 *Big Fish Eat Little Fish* purchased by The River & Rowing Museum, Henley-on-Thames, with the aid of the Victoria & Albert Museum

Recent solo exhibitions include:
Berwin Leihgton Paisner Client Suite, London; IAP Fine Art @ Arndean Gallery, Cork Street, London; River & Rowing Museum, Henley-on-Thames; Huddersfield City Art Gallery; Simoncini, Luxembourg; Christiane Cloots, Brussels; Bretton Hall, W. Yorkshire; Ferens Museum Gallery, Hull

---

Antony Gormley
born London 1950

1968-71 Studied archaeology, anthropology and Art History, Trinity College, Cambridge
1974-75 Central School of Art
1975-77 Goldsmiths School of Art
1977-79 Slade School of Fine Art
1995 Awarded Turner Prize

Recent solo exhibitions include:
*Quantum Cloud (*Part Of North Meadow Sculpture Project), Millennium Dome, Greenwich, London; *Quantum Clouds And Other Work*, Galerie Thaddaeus Ropac, Paris; *Field*, Vieille Église, Caumont, Picardy, France; *Strange Insiders,* fig-1, London; DRAWN, White Cube^2, London; NEW WORKS, Galerie Nordenhake, Berlin; *Insiders,* New Art Centre and Sculpture Park, Roche Court, East Winterslow; *Insiders*, White Gallery, Brighton; *Antony Gormley,* Contemporary Sculpture Centre, Tokyo; *Some Of The Facts*, Tate St. Ives, Cornwall; *Dialogue: Antony Gormley Allotment,* Kockumshallen, Malmö*; Field For The British Isles*, Church of St. Mary the Virgin, Shrewsbury; Tullie House, Carlisle; *States And Conditions,* Orchard Gallery, Derry (touring to Model Arts and Niland Gallery, Sligo)*Antony Gormley: Sculpture*, Centro Galego de Arte Contemporanea, Santiago de Compostela*; Antony Gormley,* Galleria Scognamiglio, Naples; *Antony Gormley*, Galerie Xavier Hufkens, Brussels; *Tuscia Electa*, San Casciano, Italy; *Antony Gormley Drawing*, The British Museum, London; *Field For The British Isles*, The British Museum, London; *Inside Australia*, Lake Ballard, Menzies, Perth International Arts Festival, Western Australia; *Asian Field* Xinhuahuayuan Huajingxincheng, Guangzhou, and touring China; *Antony Gormley: Standing Matter,* Galerie Thaddaeus Ropac, Salzburg; *Antony Gormley*, Baltic, Gateshead

---

Michael Gough
born London 1973

1992-95 Norwich Art School
Finalist in the 2001 BHF Bank small painting competition
2000-02 Wimbledon School of Art, MA Painting

Recent exhibitions/performances include:
Contribution to *For Irma, Telephone Repeater Station*, by Dallas Seitz, Yorkshire; *Art and Business*, Butlers Wharf, London; *Art Futures 2003*, City School for Boys, London; *Blood Auction*, c/o Domo Baal, Contemporary Art, London; *Us and Them*, Great Eastern Hotel; *Discerning Eye*, ING Barings Bank, London; *Perspectives*, Lewisham Art House, London; *(IN)COMPLETE*, Assembly Gallery, Glasgow; *BHF Bank exhibition*, Queen Street, London; *On Desire*, Glass Gallery, London; *Kick Start,* Wimbledon School of Art (curated); *The Invisible City,* Wimbledon Library Gallery; *Document The Real*, Wimbledon School of Art; *Texas revisited,* Odessa USA

Maggi Hambling
born Sudbury, Suffolk, 1945

1964-67 Camberwell School of Art
1967-69 Slade School of fine art
1977 Arts Council Award
1980-81 First Artist in Residence, National Gallery, London
1995 Jerwood Painting Prize

Recent solo exhibitions include:
Henrietta Moraes by Maggi Hambling, Marlborough Fine Art, London; *Father - Drawings and Paintings*, Morley College Gallery, London*; Very Special Brew Series*, Sotheby's, London, exhibition and auction in aid of Depaul Trust for the homeless; North Sea paintings, Aldburgh Festival exhibition, Snape Maltings Suffolk; Scallop – a sculpture to celebrate Benjamin Britten, Aldburgh Beach Suffolk; *Jerwood Painting Prize*, Royal Academy of Scotland, Edinburgh; Royal Academy, London; Marlborough Fine Art, London; *A Statue for Oscar Wilde*, National Portrait Gallery, London; *A Conversation with Oscar Wilde*, Adelaide Street, London; *Den Haag Sculptuur*, The Hague*; Good Friday: Paintings, Drawings & Sculpture 1965-99*, Gainsborough's House, Sudbury, Suffolk, travelling to Lady Margaret Hall, Oxford

Bibliography:
Painting the Century, 101 Portrait Masterpieces 1900-2000, Robin Gibson & Norbert Lynton, National Gallery Publications, 2000; *Maggi Hambling – An Eye Through a Decade*, Mel Gooding & George Melly, Yale Center for British Art, 1991; *Life into Paint:, British Figurative Painting of the 20th Century*, James Hyman, Israel Museum, Jerusalem, 1992; *Maggi Hambling – Sculpture in Bronze*, Bryan Robertson, Marlborough Fine Art, 1996; *Maggi and Henrietta*, John Berger, Bloomsbury Publishing, 2001; *Maggi Hambling Sketchbook Facsimile*, Morley Gallery*, 2001*

Susie Hamilton
born London 1950

1970-72 St. Martin's School of Art; Dip AD Fine Art
1989-92 Byam Shaw School of Art.

Recent solo exhibitions include:
Church of Our Most Holy Redeemer, Exmouth Market, London**;** *Immense Dawn* Paul Stolper Gallery, London**;** *Paradise Alone*, Ferens Art Gallery, Hull; *Postmodernism and Spirituality*, University of Central Lancashire, Preston; *Mutilates*, St. Giles', Cripplegate, Barbican, London; *Works on paper*, Timothy Everest, London; *New Work*, *s*, A22 Projects, London; *White Light*, A22 Projects, London; *Paintings and works on Paper*, A22 Projects, London; *Stop Motion*, presented by Paul Stolper, at Cassian de Vere Cole Fine Art, London; *Paintings and Works on Paper*, The Coram Gallery, London

Bibliography:
Art Works: British & German Contemporary Art: 1960-2000, by Alistair Hicks, Merrell Publishing

---

Robert Hardy
born Salford, 1952

Since 1980 I have taught in secondary schools in London, for the past three years at the Swaminarayan Hindu School, Neasden

1971-74	North Staffs Polytechnic
1979-80	Lived and travelled in India and Nepal
1974-75	Chelsea School of Art

Recent solo exhibitions include:
Journey of the Magi, Reading Art Centre; *Robert Hardy: Recent Paintings*, England & Co. Gallery, London; *Visionary Landscapes*, Bury St. Edmund's Cathedral, Suffolk; *Robert Hardy: Recent Paintings*, England & Co. Gallery, London; *Visions of Gozo*, Malta; Ely Place Chambers, London

---

Albert Herbert
born London 1927

Recent solo exhibitions include:
Albert Herbert: Retrospective, England & Co, London; England & Co, London; Winchester Cathedral; England & Co, London; St Botolph, City of London (etchings)

Bibliography
Young Artists of Promise, Jack Beddington, Studio Publications, London & New York 1957; *From the Belly of the Whale, Biblical Imagery by Albert Herbert*, Robert Macdonald, Castlefield Gallery 1989; *Images or Idols: The Place of Sacred Art in Churches Today*, Keith Walker, Canterbury Press, 1996

Nicola Hicks
born London 1960

1978-82	Chelsea School of Art
1982-85	Royal College of Art

Recent solo exhibitions include:
Fire and Brimstone, Flowers East, London and Watermans Art Centre, Brentford; *Drawings*, Tegnerforbundet, Oslo, Norway; Flowers East, London; Peter Scott Gallery, Lancaster, Castlefield Gallery, Manchester; Flowers East at London Fields, London; *Nicola Hicks Sculpture and Drawings*, Djanogly Art Gallery, University of Nottingham; Flowers East, London; Kings Lynn Arts Centre; Aberystwyth Arts Centre; Flowers East at London Fields, London; *Furtive Imagination*, Whitworth Art Gallery, Manchester; Yorkshire Sculpture Park, Wakefield; Riverside Studios, London; Galerie de Bellefeuille, Quebec; *Art 28 '97*, Basel; *Outrageous Fortune*, Flowers East, London; Flowers West, Santa Monica, California; Galerie Rachlin Lemarié Beaubourg, Paris; *Outrageous Fortune*, Ferens Art Gallery, Hull

---

Paul Hobbs
born Nigeria 1964

1983-86	Pembroke College, Cambridge, M.A. Hons. Degree in Social & Political Science
1986-89	The Byam Shaw School of Art, London, Diploma in Fine Art
1989-91	Assistant Art Teacher at Canford School, Dorset

Recent solo exhibitions include:
St. Martin-in-the-Fields Gallery, London; Winchester Cathedral; L'Arc-en-Ciel Galerie, Poitiers, France; Holy Trinity, Cambridge; Christchurch, Abingdon; Bath Abbey; St. Stephen's, Westbourne Park, London; St. Michael's, Bath; Teddington Baptist Church; Gloucester Cathedral

Bibliography
Art and Soul, Brand & Chaplin, 1999; *The Art of God*, David Thistlethwaite 1999.

Peter Howson
born London 1958

1975-81	Glasgow School of Art
1985	Artist-in-Residence, University of St Andrews
1993	Appointed Official British War Artist for Bosnia
1995	Lord Provost's Medal, Glasgow
1996	Doctor of Letters *honoris causa*, University of Strathclyde
	Part-time Tutor, Glasgow School of Art

Recent solo exhibitions include:
New Paintings, Lannon Cole Gallery, Chicago; *The Blind Leading the Blind*, Flowers East, London; *Recent Paintings and Drawings*, The Maclaurin Gallery, Ayrshire; Galerie Estiarte, Madrid; *Peter Howson: A Retrospective*, McLellan Galleries, Glasgow; *Peter Howson: Bosnia*, Imperial War Museum London, and Flowers East, London; *The Rake's Progress and Other Paintings*, Flowers East, London; *Drawings*, Tegnerforbundet, The Drawing and Art Association of Norway; *Peter Howson*, Drumcoon, Wigan; *New Paintings*, Flowers East, London; Djanogly Gallery, University of Nottingham; Flowers West, Santa Monica, California; *New Paintings, Drawings and Prints*, Flowers East, London; Roger Billcliffe Fine Art, Glasgow; *The Third Step*, Rozelle Gallery, Ayr; *The Fifth Step*, Flowers Central, London; *Hand Coloured Etching from the Underground Series*, Flowers Graphics, London; *The Stations of the Cross*, Flowers East, London

---

Ghislaine Howard
born Eccles 1953

Recent solo exhibitions include:
Recent Work, Horizon Modern Art, Brussels; *The Body Electric*, Laurence Batley Theatre, Huddersfield; International Theatre in Prisons Conference, Manchester Victoria University; Wellcome Foundation, London; *Caught in The Act: a personal interpretation of Manchester's year as European City of Drama*, British Council, Manchester; *Inside Out*, a collaboration with inmates of Risley Prison, Warrington City Art Gallery; *A Shared Experience*, Manchester City Art Gallery.

Cath Keay
born Dundee 1969

1987-92	Glasgow School of Art
1997	Angus College Awards, Arbroath. 3D Award for *Reclining Wood* and *Bizarre Fry*
1998	J.D.Fergusson Travel Award to study woodworking techniques and contemporary sculpture in Japan Edinburgh College of Art, MFA (Sculpture)
2002	Scottish Arts Council, Small Assistance Grant
2002	John Kinross Travel Scholarship, Royal Scottish Academy
2002	Andrew Grant Travel Bequest, Edinburgh College of Art Laing Open, Solo show at Laing Art Gallery, Newcastle-upon-Tyne (in preparation)

Alan Kean

Sculpture Garden, House of an Art Lover; *RSA Show* (prize winner), McLellan Galleries, Glasgow; *Outdoor Furniture*, Smith Gallery, Stirling; *Glasgow's Hogmanay; Emerged*, vacant shop front project

2002	*Sawdust Project*, Group show, Civic Gallery, GSA
2001	*Group Show*, Newberry Gallery, GSA
2000	*Beltane Festival*, Stirling
1999	*£19.99 project*, Glasgow
1997	*STUC installation*, Tramway, Glasgow
1995	*Solo Show*, Crawford Arts Centre, St Andrews
1993	*Group Show*, Collins Gallery, Glasgow

Fenwick Lawson
born South Moor, Co Durham 1932

Royal College of Art, Sunderland College of Art

1958	Sir James Knott Travelling Scholarship (France, Italy and Greece)
1961-84	Lecturer and Head of Department, Sculpture, Newcastle-upon-Tyne Polytechnic
1970-95	Trustee of Durham City Trust Member of the Art and Architecture Department of the Bishops' Conference of England and Wales
1986	Hon. Member of Northumbria branch of RIBA
1987	Visiting Lecturer at Gordonstoun, Dundee
1987-89	Visiting Lecturer at The Royal Academy of Art
1991-94	Member of the Fabric Advisory Committee, St. Nicholas Cathedral, Newcastle-upon-Tyne
1995 –	Member of Advisory Committee for Historic Churches in the Diocese of Hexham and Newcastle

Sonia Lawson RA RWS
born Darlington 1934

1956-60	Graduate and postgraduate, Royal College of Art, London
1982	Elected Royal Academician
1984	Rowney Drawing Prize, Royal Academy
1984	Elected Royal Watercolour Society
1984	Eastern Arts Open Drawing, First Prize
1986-87	Lorne Award, Slade School of Fine Art
1989	*Augustine* (commissioned), presented by the Archbishop of Canterbury to Pope John Paul II, Vatican Collection, Rome
1990	Lady Evershed Drawing Prize, Eastern Arts Open, First Prize
1994	Travelling Scholarship to France; Commission, Imperial War Museum to record BAOR, Exercise Lionheart Westphalia Germany; Commissioned 2 works for University Centre Birmingham

Recent solo exhibitions include:
Vertigo Gallery, London; Carlow Arts Festival, Eire; Royal West of England Academy, Bristol; Shire Hall, Stafford; Dean Clough Gallery, Halifax; Retrospective Exhibition 1966 – 1996, Boundary Gallery, London; University of Birmingham

Christopher Le Brun RA
born Portsmouth 1951

Slade School of Fine Art, London; Chelsea School of Art, London

1987-88	D.A.A.D award, Berlin, Germany
1990-95	Trustee, Tate Gallery
1996	Commission for the Choir of Liverpool Cathedral; elected Royal Academician;
1996-2003	Trustee, National Gallery
2000	Professor of Drawing, Royal Academy; Trustee, Dulwich Picture Gallery and the Prince's Drawing School

Recent solo exhibitions include:
Art Center, Pasadena; LA Louver Gallery, California; Marlborough Fine Art, London; Fitzwilliam Museum, Cambridge; Astrup Fearnley Museum of Modern Art, Oslo; Marlborough Graphics, London; Fortlaan 17, Ghent, Belgium; Courtauld Prints and Drawings Gallery, London; Devin Borden Hiram Butler Gallery, Texas; Pollock Gallery, Texas; Christian Dam, Oslo and Copenhagen

Bibliography
Christopher Le Brun, Booth-Clibborn Editions 2001.
Christopher Le Brun: Fifty Etchings, Paragon Press 1991

Paul Martin
born Bournemouth 1948

Birmingham School of Art, The Royal Academy Schools
Head of Art, Rugby School; Lecturer, Leith School of Art, Edinburgh

Recent solo exhibitions include:
Flying Colours Gallery, Chelsea, London; Bourne Fine Arts, Edinburgh; St Luke's, Holloway, London; Longland and Ryle Gallery, London; Art Revisited Gallery, Groningen, The Netherlands; Evreux, France; Rugby; Burton Dassett Church, Warwickshire; De Weem Gallery, Westeremden, The Netherlands; Rugby School Exhibition, Warwickshire

Louise McClary
born Penzance 1958

1974-76 Penzance School of Art
1976-81 Head decorator, Troika Pottery
1993 Elected member of Newlyn Society of Artists

Recent exhibitions include:
New St. Gallery, Plymouth; *transition 4*, Newlyn Art Gallery; *Stations of the Cross*: Southwell Cathedral, Plymouth Arts Centre, Harbour House, Kingsbridge; New Street Gallery, Plymouth; Badcocks Gallery, Newlyn; Beaux Arts, Bath

Iain McKillop
born Gloucester 1954

1972-83 BA Hons, History of Art, Manchester University; PGCE, Art Education, Manchester Polytechnic; Advanced Certificate of Education; Combined Creative Arts in Education, St. Paul & St. Mary's College, Cheltenham; Biblical Studies, Moorlands Bible College
1977-1981 Art Department, Colwell Grammar School, Gloucester
1983-1986 Travelling Adviser to Art Students, Universities and Colleges Christian Fellowship
1986-2000 Head of Art and Design, Sir William Perkins's School, Chertsey, Surrey
1993-1995 M.A. Fine Art, Kingston University School of Art
1994-1997 Artist-in-Residence, Strawberry Hill House
1996 Fellow, University of Gloucestershire (Cheltenham College of Art)
2000 Lecturer in History of Art & Contextual Studies, Kingston College School of Art

Recent solo exhibitions include:
Meditations, Cirencester Parish Church; *Stations of the Cross & studies for Lady Chapel Altarpiece*, Gloucester Cathedral; *The Way of the Cross, Stations in a Suffering World*, Guildford Cathedral; *Meditations on the Passion and Resurrection*, Lichfield Cathedral, Gloucester Cathedral; *A Mediaeval Bestiary, The Painter in a Mediaeval Zoo*, Bede Centre, Jarrow; Retrospective Exhibition, St. Cuthbert's, Wells and St. Peter's, West Molesey; *A Mediaeval Bestiary*, Nature in Art Gallery, Walsworth Hall, Gloucestershire; *Meditations on the Passion*, Guildford Cathedral; *Strawberry Hill Paintings*, Brewhouse Gallery, Eton College; *Stones of Time* The Lace Market, Nottingham; *On the Morning of Christ's Nativity*, joint project with composer Paul Mitchell; *Cathedral Paintings*, Chertsey Museum; *So Great a Cloud of Witnesses*, ADT Gallery, Putney; Art Centre Group, London.

Nicholas Mynheer
born Oxford 1958

1977-81 Hornsey College of Art, London

Recent solo exhibition:
St. Asaph Cathedral, Wales 2003

Bibliography
Icons of the Present, Edward Robinson, SCM Press; *Cathedral Workshops on Religious Arts & Crafts*, the Vatican; *Stations: The New Sacred Art*, Bury St Edmunds Gallery 2000; *Light of the World*, City Art Centre, Edinburgh, 1999; *A Century of Art in Oxford*, Judith Salmon 1991.

Mark Neville

1994 Goldsmiths College of Art, London, MA Fine Art
1995 Rijksacademie, Amsterdam, postgraduate studies
1997-2002 Work purchased by Collection of Flemish Community, Antwerp
2003-04 Port Glasgow photo project
2004 *A Century of Artists' Film in Britain*, Tate Britain

Ciara Phillips
born Ottawa 1976

2000 Queen's University, Kingston, Ontario
2002 Glasgow School of Art

Kate Rose
born Nottingham 1948

Birmingham College of Art; Nottingham Foundation, Thomas Earpe scholarship for best student in year; Royal College of Art, London; work purchased for Arts Council Collection

Exhibitions include:
North Light Gallery, Huddersfield; British Art Show; John Moores, Liverpool; Ruskin Gallery, Sheffield; Mappin Gallery, Sheffield; Anna Mei Chadwick Gallery, London; Thumb Gallery, London; Hart Gallery, Nottingham; The Gallery, Ashbourne; The Royal Academy Summer Exhibition; Tolly Cobbold & Sainsbury's Touring Exhibition.

Martin Rose
born Preston1946

Manchester College of Art; Birmingham College of Art; Royal Academy, London
Portraits of the composer Sir Michael Tippett and the athlete Sebastian Coe commissioned by the National Portrait Gallery

Exhibitions include:
North Light Gallery, Huddersfield; Ruskin Gallery, Sheffield; Artists of Fame and Promise, London; Sheffield Cathedral; Free University, Amsterdam; Royal Academy Summer Exhibition; National Portrait Gallery; St Paul's Gallery, Leeds

Jill Sim

	Fine Art, Ruskin School, Oxford; St Martin's School of Art, London
1997-8	Resident Artist, Monastery Studenica, Serbia/Kosova

Recent solo exhibitions include:
St John's Church, Waterloo, London; Peter's Barn, Petworth

Michael Stumpf
born Mannheim, Germany 1969

State Academie of Fine Arts, Karlsruhe, Germany

2001	Co-founder of the independent exhibition space Kaiserpassage 21a
2002 –	Glasgow School of Art, MA

Recent exhibitions include:
Nacht der museen, Heimsteinwerk, Heidelberg; *Desiree,* freunde junger Kunst, Baden Baden; *Pralinen fuer des Meisters Tochter,* Taubenstr 13, Hamburg; *die Superzelle,* altes Kino Die Kamera, Karlsruhe; *Interim,* Mackintosh Gallery, Glasgow; *EAST-International,* Norwich Gallery

Roger Wagner
born London 1957

English, Lincoln College Oxford; Royal Academy School of Art, London

Recent solo exhibitions include:
The Ashmolean Museum, Oxford; The Bartlemas Chapel, Oxford; *Anthony Mould Contemporary, London; Bury St Edmunds Cathedral; Chester Cathedral; Ely Cathedral, Norwich Cathedral, Southwark Cathedral, Wells Cathedral, Worcester Cathedral; The Prince's Foundation*

Bibliography
Fire Sonnets, The Besalel Press; *In a Strange Land*, The Besalel Press; *The Book of Praises: A Translation of the Psalms*, The Besalel Press; *A Silent Voice*, The Besalel Press; *Out of the Whirlwind,* Solway

Penny Warden
born Epsom 1956

1980's	Graduated with Hons, Degree in Theology from Westminster College, Oxford; PGCE; Head of Religious Studies
1997	Studied for a degree in Fine Art at Buckinghamshire Chilterns University College
2001	Awarded a grant by the Christian Arts Trust, for six phoenix images

Recent solo exhibitions include:
Phoenix series: Bristol Cathedral; Coventry Cathedral; Ely Cathedral; Gloucester Cathedral; Lichfield Cathedral; Norwich Cathedral; Worcester Cathedral; St John's, Waterloo, London; Norden Farm Art Gallery, Maidenhead; Wellington College; St. Giles, Barbican, London; Wycombe Swan Theatre, High Wycombe; Holy Trinity, Guildford; Lancaster Arts Theatre; Wycombe Abbey School

Peter White
born Ayrshire 1959

Edinburgh College of Art
Royal Scottish Academy Latimer Prize; Square Gallery Small Painting Prize;
Marie Curie Foundation Open First Prize (joint); Scottish Arts Council Bursary
Scottish Academy Oppenheim Prize; RGI Royal College of Physicians and Surgeons of Glasgow Award

Recent solo exhibitions include:
Macaulay Gallery, Stenton; Square Gallery, London; Jill George Gallery, London; Scottish Gallery, Edinburgh; Browns Gallery, Tain; Leith School of Art, Edinburgh; Exhibition, after visiting aid projects in Malawi; Kilmorack Gallery, Inverness; Flying Colours Gallery, London; Tracey McNee Fine Art, Glasgow

Willie Williams
born Newcastle 1959

Willie Williams designs and directs multimedia events and installations. His work with live performance has included large-scale rock tours (*U2, R.E.M., David Bowie*), contemporary dance (*La La La Human Steps*) and permanent installations (*Skychurch, Experience Music Project, Seattle*). Current projects: *Sun Rings*, an audio-visual collaboration with Kronos Quartet, commissioned by NASA; stage production of *Barbarella*, based on the Jean-Claude Forest comic book; received EDDY award, New York, for excellence in entertainment design, 2001.